A NATIONAL CHALLENGE AT THE LOCAL LEVEL

A National Challenge at the Local Level
Citizens, Elites and Institutions in Reunified Germany

THOMAS R. CUSACK
Wissenschaftszentrum Berlin für Sozialforschung, Germany

LONDON AND NEW YORK

First published 2003 by Ashgate Publishing

Reissued 2018 by Routledge
2 Park Square, Milton Park, Abingdon, Oxon OX14 4RN
711 Third Avenue, New York, NY 10017, USA

Routledge is an imprint of the Taylor & Francis Group, an informa business

Copyright © Thomas R. Cusack 2003

Thomas R. Cusack has asserted his right under the Copyright, Designs and Patents Act, 1988, to be identified as author of this work.

All rights reserved. No part of this book may be reprinted or reproduced or utilised in any form or by any electronic, mechanical, or other means, now known or hereafter invented, including photocopying and recording, or in any information storage or retrieval system, without permission in writing from the publishers.

Notice:
Product or corporate names may be trademarks or registered trademarks, and are used only for identification and explanation without intent to infringe.

Publisher's Note
The publisher has gone to great lengths to ensure the quality of this reprint but points out that some imperfections in the original copies may be apparent.

Disclaimer
The publisher has made every effort to trace copyright holders and welcomes correspondence from those they have been unable to contact.

A Library of Congress record exists under LC control number: 2003048194

ISBN 13: 978-1-138-71209-6 (hbk)
ISBN 13: 978-1-138-71208-9 (pbk)
ISBN 13: 978-1-315-19930-6 (ebk)

Contents

List of Figures		*vii*
List of Tables		*ix*
Acknowledgments		*xiv*
1	Introduction	1
	Overview of the Book	1
2	Local Political and Administrative Elites: Roots and Roles	5
	Introduction	5
	Background	8
	Ties to the Community	32
	At Work	39
	Conclusion	57
3	Ideological Values of Elites and Citizens	59
	Introduction	59
	Differences in the Meaning of Democracy?	59
	Ideological Values: A First Cut	67
	Ideological Values: A More Refined View	73
	The Sources of Ideological Values	86
	Conclusion	108
4	Problem-Ridden and Conflict-Riven	111
	Introduction	111
	Problems Confronting the Local Communities	111
	Responsibilities and Power of Local Government	123
	Divisions and Conflicts within the Community	130
	Policy Action and Its Effectiveness	137
	Performance: Elites and Citizens	143
	Conclusion	147

5	Social Capital, Institutional Structures and Democratic Performance	149
	Introduction	149
	Explaining Democratic Governmental Performance	150
	Institutional Structures	154
	Analysis	173
	Conclusion	180
6	Conclusion	183

Appendix: The German Local Elite and Citizen Surveys	191
Introduction	191
Sampling Techniques Used in Previous Country Studies	192
Outline of the German Elite Samples	193
Selection of City Samples	199
Selection of Local Elites	202
Conduct of the Survey	218
An Overview of the Response Patterns	219
Information Related to International Comparisons	225
Citizen Survey	227
Bibliography	231
Index	245

List of Figures

Figure 2.1	Age and tenure in local government: differences between parties and regions	19
Figure 3.1	Elites' values: an international comparison	82
Figure 3.2a	Socialism-capitalism, citizens, East and West Germany	84
Figure 3.2b	Authoritarianism-libertarianism, citizens, East and West Germany	84
Figure 3.2c	Socialism-capitalism, elites, East and West Germany	85
Figure 3.2d	Authoritarianism-libertarianism, elites, East and West Germany	85
Figure 3.3a	Citizens and elites: socialism-capitalism and authoritarianism-libertarianism, East Germany	86
Figure 3.3b	Citizens and elites: socialism-capitalism and authoritarianism-libertarianism, West Germany	87
Figure 3.4	Regional economic development and net transfers to the East, 1989–1997 (gross domestic product per capita in 1991 DM)	96
Figure 3.5a	Education and expected position on socialism-capitalism scale	100
Figure 3.5b	Income and expected position on socialism-capitalism scale	100
Figure 3.5c	Age and expected position on socialism-capitalism scale	101
Figure 3.6	Effect of income level on expected gain from an egalitarian redistribution of income	106
Figure 4.1	Elites' views of the extent and severity of local problems: an international problem comparison	122
Figure 4.2	East German elites' views on the responsibility vs. power and autonomy of local government	125
Figure 4.3	West German elites' views on the responsibility vs. power and autonomy of local government	126
Figure 4.4	East German local elites' views on policy action and effectiveness	139
Figure 4.5	West German local elites' views on policy action and effectiveness	139
Figure 4.6	Elites' satisfaction with the way democracy works at the federal and local levels	143
Figure 4.7	Citizens' satisfaction with democracy in Germany	144
Figure 4.8	Citizens' interest in communal politics and politics in general	145
Figure 4.9	Citizens' trust in communal politicians and general trust	146
Figure 4.10	Citizens' satisfaction with local political and government institutions	147

Figure 5.1	Centralization of power in the chief executive's office	171
Figure 5.2	Joint power centralization index	172
Figure 5.3	Distribution of citizens' satisfaction with local government performance across the communities in East and West Germany	174
Figure 5.4	Simulated levels of citizens' satisfaction with local government performance in Germany based on low and high levels of institutionalized power centralization	180
Figure A.1	An overview of East and West German local government units (towns and cities) by population size	200
Figure A.2	Coverage of *Amt* functions in West and East Germany (number)	212
Figure A.3	Number of *Amt* functions and population size	213
Figure A.4	Relative coverage of *Amt* functions (per cent)	214
Figure A.5	An overview of response rates	220
Figure A.6	Number of respondents: frequency distribution for cities and towns in East and West Germany	221
Figure A.7a	Response rates by various categories, East and West Germany combined	222
Figure A.7b	Response rates by various categories, East Germany	222
Figure A.7c	Response rates by various categories, West Germany	223
Figure A.8a	Council member party affiliation: sample and respondents, East and West Germany combined	224
Figure A.8b	Council member party affiliation: sample and respondents, East Germany	224
Figure A.8c	Council member party affiliation: sample and respondents, West Germany	225

List of Tables

Table 2.1	Local political/administrative elites holding office in town of birth: an international comparison (per cent)	10
Table 2.2	Average age of local political/administrative elites: an international comparison	13
Table 2.3	Age characteristics of all elites, council members and adult citizens (per cent)	13
Table 2.4	Percentage shares of German town/city council seats held by women, 1996	14
Table 2.5	Women in local government: political/administrative elites positions (per cent)	15
Table 2.6	Length of tenure in politics/administration: an international comparison	17
Table 2.7	Average number of years in present position: an international comparison	18
Table 2.8	Local political and administrative elites with either or both parents in politics/government: an international comparison (per cent)	21
Table 2.9	Elite class background based on father's occupational status (per cent)	22
Table 2.10	Local political and administrative elites with university education: an international comparison (per cent)	24
Table 2.11	Training background by office (per cent)	26
Table 2.12	Training background by party, East Germany (per cent)	28
Table 2.13	Training background by party, West Germany (per cent)	29
Table 2.14	Occupational status by office (per cent)	30
Table 2.15	Main occupation by party, East Germany (per cent)	30
Table 2.16	Main occupation by party, West Germany (per cent)	31
Table 2.17	Patterns of associational membership amongst elites and citizens by region	33
Table 2.18	Elites' associational membership by office and party affiliation in East and West Germany	34
Table 2.19	Similarities and differences in associational membership patterns between elites and electors (correlation matrices)	36
Table 2.20	Patterns of reliance by department heads and other officials (per cent indicating they rely on specific groups or individuals in their political and/or administrative functions when making decisions)	38

Table 2.21	Elites' patterns of reliance by party affiliation (per cent indicating they rely on specific groups or individuals in their political and/or administrative functions when making decisions)	40
Table 2.22	Evaluations of top-level administrators in intermediate zone of politics and administration by office (per cent)	42
Table 2.23	Role identification by office (average values)	44
Table 2.24	Role identification by party (council members only, average values)	45
Table 2.25	Principal component analysis of role orientations (based on orthogonal rotation)	48
Table 2.26	Role orientation as a function of political/administrative position, party affiliation and other characteristics: regression analyses (t-statistics in parentheses)	51
Table 2.27	Self-evaluated scope of influence on public affairs (per cent indicating significant influence on one or more of 12 areas of policy/politics)	55
Table 2.28	International comparison: local elites' self-evaluated scope of influence on public affairs (average number of policy/politics areas where significant influence claimed; 12 possible areas)	56
Table 2.29	Perceived influence and dissatisfaction with the way local democracy functions (per cent)	57
Table 3.1	Categories and coding schemes for respondents' conceptions of democracy	61
Table 3.2	Conceptions of democracy: regional and generational differences – a comparison between Rohrschneider's Berlin local elites and local elites included in this study (per cent expressing view)	66
Table 3.3	Democracy and Local Governance Project's ideological dimensions	68
Table 3.4	An international comparison of local elites' ideological values: international project scales (average positions)	70
Table 3.5	Germany: party-regional differences on international project scales (average scale positions)	72
Table 3.6	Basic political values: results from principal component analysis	74
Table 3.7a	Principal component analyses of elites' values	78
Table 3.7b	Principal component analyses of citizens' values	79
Table 3.8a	Principal component analyses of Central European local elites' values	80
Table 3.8b	Principal component analyses of Western local elites' values	81
Table 3.9	An international comparison of partisans' attitudes towards government's role in the economy based on data from the 1990 and 1996 ISSP surveys on the role of government (per cent)	88
Table 3.10	Cross-regional comparison of partisans' attitudes towards government's role in the economy based on data from the 1990 and 1996 ISSP surveys on the role of government (per cent)	89

Table 3.11	Opinion about the Federal Republic's economic and political systems in East and West Germany (per cent)	92
Table 3.12	Socio-economic characteristics and average position on socialism-capitalism scale	94
Table 3.13a	Regression analyses: socialism-capitalism	98
Table 3.13b	Regression analysis: socialism-capitalism from ISSP, 1996	99
Table 3.14	Logit analysis: expectations about changes to one's income as a consequence of an egalitarian redistribution	105
Table 4.1	Salience of problems in the eyes of the elites (percentage identifying area as one of the three most important facing the community)	113
Table 4.2	Salience of problems in the eyes of the citizens and the elites compared (percentage identifying area as one of the three most important facing the community, based on sub-sample of 30 cities)	116
Table 4.3	Broad overview of types of problems confronting elites (per cent)	118
Table 4.4	Percentage of cities where at least 50 per cent of elites consider the area a major problem	119
Table 4.5a	Broad overview of types of problems confronting elites in East Germany and four Central European countries	120
Table 4.5b	Broad overview of types of problems confronting elites in West Germany and six Western countries	121
Table 4.6	Responsibility vs. power and autonomy of local government: inter-German comparisons	124
Table 4.7a	Responsibility vs. power and autonomy of local government: comparison between East Germany and four Central European countries	128
Table 4.7b	Responsibility vs. power and autonomy of local government: comparison between West Germany and six Western countries	129
Table 4.8	Conflicts interfering with the solution to problems and the development of community: inter-German comparison (per cent)	130
Table 4.9	An international comparison of conflicts interfering with the solution to problems and the development of community (per cent)	131
Table 4.10	Types of conflicts hindering problem-solving in the communities as specified by the elites: inter-German comparison	133
Table 4.11	Degrees to which different types of conflict and divisions exist within local community: inter-German comparison (regional percentages)	134

Table 4.12a	Degrees to which different types of conflict and divisions exist within local community: comparison between East Germany and four Central European countries (national percentages)	135
Table 4.12b	Degrees to which different types of conflict and divisions exist within local community: comparison between West Germany and six Western countries (national percentages)	136
Table 4.13	Overview of elites' reports on policy action and effectiveness: inter-German comparison	138
Table 4.14a	International comparison of elites' reports on policy action and effectiveness: comparison between East Germany and four Central European countries	141
Table 4.14b	International comparison of elites' reports on policy action and effectiveness: comparison between West Germany and three Western countries	142
Table 5.1	Standard classification of local government forms generally found in the literature	157
Table 5.2	Institutional characteristics of the office of the chief executive (CEO)	163
Table 5.3	Institutional characteristics and the centralization in the office of the chief executive	169
Table 5.4	Determinants of citizens' satisfaction with local government performance: regression results	178
Table A.1	Sample selection procedures in previous Democracy and Local Governance studies	194
Table A.2	Sample frames of communities in West and East Germany	201
Table A.3	Information on the sample frames and samples of communities in West and East Germany	203
Table A.4	Respondent sample frame based on data from 77 communities in Germany	205
Table A.5	Overview of samples by potential respondents' positions	209
Table A.6	Characteristics of higher political/administrative officials in samples	211
Table A.7	Frequencies of different types of department heads in samples	216
Table A.8	Sample frames and samples for party chairpersons (per cent)	217
Table A.9	Sample frames and samples for council party caucus chairpersons (per cent)	217
Table A.10	Local council members' sample frames and sample distribution by party affiliation (per cent)	218
Table A.11	Comparative information on the German and other surveys from the International Project on Democracy and Local Governance used in this study	226

Table A.12	Percentage breakdowns of age distribution for the regional samples of citizen surveys (population figures in parentheses are from the 1997 Mikrozensus)	229
Table A.13	Percentage breakdowns by positions in the labor markets for the regional samples of citizen surveys (population figures in parentheses are from the 1997 Mikrozensus)	229
Table A.14	Percentage distribution by net household monthly income for the regional samples of the citizen surveys (population figures in parentheses are from the 1997 Mikrozensus)	230

Acknowledgments

A large number of people contributed to the successful completion of the survey projects that are described in this book. I express my appreciation for their efforts. There are a few people whose assistance and help merit explicit mention. Included here are Bernhard Weßels, who provided an extensive amount of useful advice on carrying out such projects. Ruth Nabholz provided helpful guidance based on her experience in carrying out an elite survey in Switzerland. I am particularly grateful to Susanne Fuchs, Britta Heinrich and Christoph Klose for their careful work in the preparation of the large data bank on potential respondents in the elite survey. Equally helpful and appreciated are the efforts of Angelika Costa and Holgar Straßheim, who undertook the coding of the responses to the open-ended questions included in the elite questionnaire as well collecting and organizing some of the other data used in this volume.

My thanks to Hans-Dieter Klingemann, David Soskice and Hellmut Wollmann, who provided significant parts of the financial resources needed to carry out the survey projects. The efforts of Konstanza Prinzessin zu Löwenstein in dealing with the mass of organizational and administrative details associated with carrying out any large-scale project from within a public institution once again proved invaluable.

Many cross-national comparisons of local elites are made within this volume. A lot of these are based on material drawn from the International Project on Democracy and Local Governance's copyrighted multinational databank. My thanks to the DLG Consortium members who were responsible for producing these data, including Antal Bohm, Michiel de Vries, Samuel J. Eldersveld, Soledad Garcia, Wolf Linder, Werner Pleschberger, Jan Rehak, Lars Stromberg and Jerzy J. Wiatr, as well as Krzysztof Ostrowski and Henry Teune, the international coordinators, and Tatiana Iskra, the database manager.

Ken Newton and Hans-Dieter Klingemann read an earlier draft of the manuscript and provided numerous helpful suggestions to improve the quality of the presentation. Their efforts are gratefully appreciated. My thanks as well to Lutz Engelhardt for his work on converting a large part of the manuscript from one text processing system to another, Angelika Zierer-Kuhnle, who labored long and hard to correct and lay out the final version of the manuscript, and Tim Eisert for producing the final versions of the graphics.

Berlin, 25 February 2003

Chapter 1

Introduction

This book grew out of a study conducted in cooperation with an international network of scholars working on the problems of Democracy and Local Governance (DLG). The international group has conducted over twenty national studies of local government and political elites. The emphasis of these various national studies has been on identifying the backgrounds of local government and political elites, their values and opinions on a variety of subjects. In particular, attention has been paid to the degree to which these elite values conform to democratic principles.

This study of local government and politics in Germany was motivated by this concern as well as a broader set of questions. Not only are elites seen as important, but so too are the citizens in the communities governed by these elites. To what extent do elite and citizen values coincide? In the context of a reunified Germany, this concern as well as the differences in political values, at both the elite and citizen levels, between the two parts of Germany have a special importance. While there are appreciable differences in the economic vitality of East and West Germany, there are also, as many commentators and analysts have pointed out, a significant gap in the political and economic values held by the populations of these two regions reigns. The inter-regional economic disparities make integration of these two areas difficult; the value gaps could ultimately undermine the creation of a real political community within Germany.

In addition, the publication in 1993 of *Making Democracy Work* by Robert Putnam drew a great deal of attention to the basis of successful democratic government performance. The thesis presented by Putnam in this work is that political culture, particularly in the form of social capital, is the determining factor in shaping government performance in a democracy. While admiring this work, I was skeptical about a number of issues, in particular, the short shrift actually given to the role of institutions in Putnam's work. The German local government setting provided an ideal opportunity to examine this question. Unlike Italian regional governments, municipalities across the federal states of Germany are characterized by radically different political structures. If institutions do matter, then one should find systematic differences in performance outcomes across such a diversity of settings.

Overview of the Book

The core of the data used in this book flows from two large scale surveys conducted in mid- and late-1995. One of these surveys focused on a broad range of political and administrative elites in local government in a large number of towns and cities in the two parts of Germany. The second concentrated on citizens within a sub-sample of the municipalities selected for the elite survey. The appendix documents the way in which two surveys were conducted. It first describes the broader international project and how other national groups went about conducting their studies. It then goes on to outline the sampling procedures used in selecting 77 cities (40 in West Germany and 37 in East Germany) and elites (mayors, city managers, senior executives, department heads, council caucus leaders and other council members, local party chairpersons) within these cities (number of respondents equals 1,231). An account of the way in which the survey was conducted follows and then an overview of the response patterns is provided. In addition, a description of the survey of citizens conducted within a sub-sample (a total of 30 with 15 in each region) of the communities is provided (total sample size of 2,400, an average of 80 respondents in each community). This includes an explanation of the way in which the sub-sample was selected; a process designed to maximize variation on the two principal factors in the model on local government performance presented in chapter 5, a municipality's social capital (amongst the elites) and the institutional form of the local government. In addition, response rates and basic demographic characteristics of the sample are provided.

Chapter 2 provides an extensive overview of the political and administrative elites in local government within both East and West Germany. It sets out the patterns of origin, the age profiles and the gender composition of these elites. In addition, it traces their class origins and educational backgrounds. Since many of the members of these elites dedicate only part of their working days to politics, it also examines their principal occupational characteristics. Space is also given over to their careers in public service.

The chapter then examines the ties that these elites hold to their communities. Emphasis is given to the kinds of organizations to which they belong and the groups and individuals on whom they rely in dealing with the issues associated with their public offices. Finally, it turns to the question of how these elites define their roles in public affairs and the extent to which they assess their efforts as being successful in influencing public policy at the local level.

Chapter 3 moves on to examine the ideological values of local elites in the two parts of Germany and contrasts these with the values of citizens within their communities as well as the values of local elites in other democracies. It shows, contrary to a widely accepted image, that East German and West German local elites actually possess quite common views about the meaning of democracy. In examining the reputed scales of ideological values that have been employed in many of the Democracy and Local Governance studies, it was discovered that these scales really do not provide a very reliable picture of the ideological predispositions of these elites. It turns out that a combination of selected items in the DLG's large battery of questions on ideology and values actually form a more reliable portrait of the main ideological dimensions of German (and other nations') local elite political culture. These two dimensions are also reflected in the way in which citizens themselves define their ideological preferences.

When local elites and citizens are placed along these two ideological dimensions, socialism-capitalism and authoritarianism-libertarianism, it turns out that there are some significant differences, both across regions and between elites and citizens. While the modal tendency of citizens in both regions is toward a more authoritarian position than that of the elites in both regions, the really distinguishing characteristic of elite and citizen political culture is along the socialism-capitalism scale. East German citizens, in particular, are far and away more supportive of socialist principles than are their fellow citizens in the West. While there is a gap on this dimension as well, between the elites of the two regions, it is nowhere near as great.

It has become almost conventional wisdom to attribute the preferences that East Germans express for more socialist principles as arising out of their socialization experiences. A direct implication of this view is that the gap between the political cultures of the two regions will remain large for a long time, at least until the generations socialized under the GDR system die out. In this chapter I lay out an alternate explanation for this gap, one based on rational self-interest and examine the empirical validity of this model. This model does very well in accounting for the variation in socialist-capitalist values, among both citizens and elites. I am able to demonstrate that the attributes of an individual that would prompt a rational being to support either socialism or capitalism have the effects ascribed to them by the model. The implications of this model for closing the gap in ideological values that exists between East and West are far more sanguine than those that follow from the conventional view. In other words, the present-day population of East Germany is not permanently wedded to the non-market ideological preferences that sharply distinguish them from the far more pro-market values of the West. A greater effort at equalizing living standards between the two regions would help reduce appreciably this gap in values between the two regions.

Chapter 4 presents a picture of what the elites see as the political situation within their communities. It systematically describes the scope and extent of problems that the elites say they are confronted with and also compares this problem agenda with what the citizens in these communities say are the major problems. It also points out the partial discrepancy in these two different collective views. While elites and citizens alike emphasize general economic problems confronting their communities, elites are much more prone to emphasize the various tasks of maintaining the capacities of local government while citizens are far more exercised by more mundane concerns. Elites in both regions acknowledge an extensive array of problems confronting their communities, particularly in the East and, indeed, by international standards, the local elites of the two German regions seem to possess some of the most crowded and severe problem agendas.

The elites of the two German regions view local governments as being responsible for a broad swath of activities. At the same time they sense that local governments are not provided with sufficient autonomy and power to handle these responsibilities. In addition, these elites are more prone than other nations' local elites to see their communities as marked by a lot of conflict that hinders problem-solving by local government. Despite this, they generally believe that effective policy actions have been implemented although they simultaneously emphasize the difficulty of coping with economic problems in their communities and being effective in getting a handle on the financial situation of local government.

While local elites are generally very optimistic about the way in which the democratic system works at both the local and national levels, these sentiments are not fully shared by the citizens who live in the communities governed by these elites.

This leads naturally to the question posed in chapter 5: What conditions facilitate or hinder good performance by local governments at least as seen by the citizens whose lives are directly affected by these governments? In order to answer this question I lay out in this chapter a model of citizen satisfaction with local government performance. This model brings together some of the important characteristics of the city elites and the cities themselves in the attempt to understand the bases for differences in the performance of local governments. Particular emphasis is given to the roles that social capital, institutional structures and partisan and other conflicts play in enhancing or hampering the problem-solving capacities of city governments.

Based on data drawn from the survey of citizens, a measure of satisfaction with local government performance is presented and an effort is made to determine the extent to which the cultural and institutional theses help in explaining variation across cities on this democratic performance measure. The results produced here point to the following two conclusions. First, a form of social capital (one less extensive than that described by Putnam) does indeed seem to facilitate superior government performance. Second, institutions matter importantly in terms of government performance. Contrary to the Putnam thesis, institutional engineering, a process East Germans engaged in when setting up their local governments after reunification, has helped to foster far better performance as assessed by their citizens, than would have been expected given the economic and social problems they confront.

Chapter 2

Local Political and Administrative Elites: Roots and Roles

Introduction

This chapter examines the backgrounds, community ties and roles of German local political and administrative elites. It gives particular emphasis to the question of whether significant differences exist, both between the two parts of Germany and between different types of elites, as well as differences that occur along partisan lines. Additionally, where possible it contrasts the two German regions' local elites with those of other countries in both the transitional democracies of Central Europe and the more established democracies of the West.[1]

There are different theoretical perspectives on the origins and characteristics of democratic elites. Controversy has prevailed for a long time on which of these perspectives most accurately portrays the dynamics of elite recruitment and reproduction. Studies of local elites have mirrored this controversy and reached their peak in studies of local political decision-making in the United States during the 1950s and 1960s. Today it would be difficult to say that a consensus opinion on the issues surrounding this controversy has developed. In this chapter I hope to shed some light on the questions raised in these debates by examining the backgrounds of local government elites within Germany.

Three visions or theoretical images of political elites within democracies are prominent in modern discussions. One rests upon the classical image of elites being dominated by the traditional leading classes of their communities. Access to the elite is restricted. The restrictions to access are class-based and there is a strong tendency for elite members to be drawn from classes within the community that have higher socio-economic status (Bachrach, 1967; Putnam, 1976). This corresponds to Lasswell's 'agglutination' model where stratification in the political system is nearly or perfectly correlated with stratification in the socio-economic system. In its more extreme version, the restrictions are keyed to origins that reflect the involvement of family members in political/administrative activities. In other words, political/

---

[1] To the extent that data are available, comparisons are made with local elites in ten other countries. These countries include the Czech Republic, Hungary, Poland, Slovakia, Austria, the Netherlands, Spain, Sweden, Switzerland, and the United States. In addition some comparisons are also made between the elites and the citizens they govern in their local communities.

administrative elite membership is heavily dependent upon one's parents' membership in such elites (Aberbach et al., 1981).

A second general view sees restrictions to membership within the elites as based on the acquisition of skills which themselves require extensive training and education (Aberbach et al., 1981). In other words, those who achieve elite status, for example, within local government, are individuals who, through their native abilities and capacities acquired through efforts in educational institutions, most qualify to fill these functions. This is a vision of meritocracy. There are two variants to this view. One is the elitist version which suggests that the acquisition of these skills through education is biased toward the children of the upper classes; their families are in the position to afford them extensive education, an experience relatively rare amongst the lower classes, and through this bias the tendency is for the offspring of existing elites to dominate political/administrative positions within communities.

An alternative and more democratic version of the meritocratic vision suggests that modern society, with its emphasis on equal opportunity, permits all those with the basic native abilities to acquire extensive education and training and through this process enhance their abilities to enter various elites. In this vision, while elites have educational backgrounds that are more extensive than the average citizen, the elite members have social class backgrounds that are typical of the communities in which they serve in political/administrative office.

The third general vision is a participatory-democratic view. Here, access to elite membership is not restricted by the workings of traditions, social, economic, or political hegemony; nor do the biases that accrue through meritocratic forces work such an effect (Putnam, 1976). Leaders and representatives of the people come from all the people. Their position within the political/administrative elites of their community is independent of their social origins or acquired skills. The members of these elites are interested and concerned citizens motivated to participate in their communities' civic affairs; they are neither blocked nor hindered from such participation by extraneous constraints. Neither birth nor education plays an appreciable role in the filtering process by which people enter the elite.

An ancillary controversy related to elite background has marked the contemporary German scene. This is the debate surrounding the manner in which the population and territory of the former GDR have been integrated within the existing structures of the Federal Republic. 'Colonization' is a term that one often hears being used to describe the way in which the East and West have been joined together. The latter region is not only seen as imposing its values and institutions without regard to the desires and wishes of the population in the East, but also as engaging in a process of implanting its own personnel in important political and administrative positions at all levels of government. Certainly there is something to be said for this description when it comes to state government (see, e.g., Derlien, 1998; Wollmann, 1998); is this image of carpet-bagging also valid for local government elites?

As Putnam (1993) has demonstrated, the character of civic life and the ability to cooperate with others in a community, both on the part of politicians and non-politicians alike, reflect the level of social capital within a community. He also has shown that the latter facilitates successful political (and economic) performance. With this in mind I will attempt to assess the extent and character of ties with their communities that prevail within these elites. To do so I will focus on a number of questions that deal with the patterns of associational membership maintained by these elites, the degree to which these correspond with their supporters in the local electorates, and the profiles of groups and individuals on whom these elites rely.

How well integrated are these elites within their communities? In particular, what sorts of organization/associational ties do they have? Are these ties extensive or narrow? Do they reflect the basic socio-economic character of the supporters of the parties to which the elite members belong or are they more broadly representative of the entire community? To whom do these elites turn when making decisions? Are they likely to seek advice, support and help from those within the community or from outside? Do they rely on other politicians/administrators, or do they go to organized interests, the media, or less established participants in the political process? Both of these general issues, the nature of associational affiliation and the patterns of reliance, reflect a concern with the degree and manner in which these elites are tied into political, social and economic networks of their communities and they should also shed light on the capacity of these elites to both reflect the concerns of their fellow citizens as well as to engage in the cooperative behavior needed to create a well-functioning governmental system within their communities.

It is often the case that political/administrative elites approach their jobs in dramatically different ways (Aberbach et al., 1981). The roles that politicians and administrators take on are likely to reflect their partisan affiliations, the constraints of the positions they hold and the context within which they operate, as well as a host of factors that characterize their backgrounds. On the one hand, there is the traditional divide between administration and politics. How wide or narrow is this gap among local government elites within Germany? Do administrators overstep the bounds of their traditional duties and engage in activity of a clearly political character or do they confine themselves to purely administrative roles? For politicians there is a corresponding division that often comes to the fore. Do they see themselves as representatives of special and partisan interests or are they prone to see themselves as the representatives of the broad community interests and those with little resources and power?

By concentrating especially on the backgrounds of these elites and then turning to the question of the kinds of roles they play in their local political systems, I am attempting to focus on one aspect of the 'so what?' question Putnam (1976) has raised about elite-origin studies. Elites may originate out of the dominant classes of society or their origins may faithfully reflect the socio-economic structure of their communities, but do these origins have an impact on the way in which they go about fulfilling their official functions and, as I address in the next chapter, the values and ideology that guide their decisions?

The three themes of origins, ties and roles are explored in the sections that follow. First, the socio-economic backgrounds of these elites are examined. The questions addressed here allow one to evaluate contending models of democratic elite origins. Do German local government elites fit into the image classic elite theory suggests, i.e., are their origins and life experiences skewed in the direction of the dominant classes of society? Or do these elites fit into either a more meritocratic image or one that more faithfully reflects the social structure of the society in which they live? To address these questions I examine the types of backgrounds of these elites (viz., familial, educational, training, occupational and the residential ties with the cities in which they serve, as well as the length of time they have been involved in politics and administration). In addition, I also focus on the intensity of involvement in their political-administrative work: are these professionals or simply very active citizens?

Second, I deepen the exploration of their connections with their communities by scrutinizing the intensity of their connections with others in the community (organizational/associational memberships) and the identity of those to whom they turn in trying to deal with their political/administrative decision-making tasks.

Third, I probe the way in which they see themselves. Here I place particular emphasis on the way in which they describe their political/administrative roles. In addition, an effort is made to account for differences in the political-administrative roles that the elite members see themselves as playing. Stress is given here to the influence of their official positions, their partisan affiliations, the ties they have to their communities and a number of background factors.

Background

Origins and Time in Residence

Following the major movements of population connected with World War II and its aftermath, neither part of Germany was noted for exceptionally high, at least by international standards, residential mobility on the part of the population. If residences changed, more often than not the new residence was within the same town or city. Still, there has been a fair amount of mobility. For example, in the old federal states between 1970 and 1991, each year an average of 4.9 per cent of the total population moved from one town to another.[2] The members of the local government elites within the samples would appear to have been somewhat similar to their fellow-citizens in this regard. In both East and West, a little more than a third of the entire samples perform their political/administrative functions within the towns or cities in

---

2   This figure is based on calculations made on data for population movements drawn from the Statistisches Bundesamt's Datenreport 1994: Zahlen und Fakten über die Bundesrepublik Deutschland.

which they were born.³ Nevertheless, quite large proportions come from the nearby regions of the towns or the federal states within which the towns are located. Adding these three categories (viz., same town, region and state) together, over 61 per cent of the sample in the East and 71 per cent of the sample in the West were born in the same states where the towns that they now carry out their political/administrative jobs are situated.⁴

By international standards, the elites of both regions seem unexceptional in this regard. Among four Central European transitional democracies, the proportion of elected and appointed local elites that hold office in the town or city of birth ranges from 34 to 42 per cent (see Table 2.1). The comparable figure for East German elites is 35 per cent. And the West German figure of 37 per cent is well within the range observed among local elites in other Western countries.

There are some significant differences across the categories of offices as well as parties with regard to this background characteristic. Council members in both East and West have a slightly higher average tendency to be carrying out their jobs in their hometowns.⁵ Caucus leaders in the West stand out as the group most likely to have their origins in the cities in which they carry out this function with nearly 49 per cent), although in the East this group, with 33 per cent, is below the sample average on this

---

3   Classification by office held is based on information collected prior to the survey fieldwork. This classification scheme is generally used throughout this chapter. One should keep in mind that a fair number of individuals hold more than one office. Their characteristics are incorporated in the values reported for each of the offices held.

    Five categories of office or function within local political and administrative elites are used. Council members are elected officials holding a seat in the town or city council. Caucus leaders are members of the council who simultaneously function as the leaders of the party caucuses within the council. Party leaders head up the local party organizations. Department heads are the executives responsible for the operation of the basic administrative units of the town or city government. The category of higher office includes a variety of official positions (elected or appointed) at the levels of local government administrative responsibility and power. Included are mayors (various types), city managers, members of executive collegial bodies, and directors of services (that is, executives responsible for more than one administrative department).

4   The range in the East extends from 50 per cent of the holders of higher office up to 66 per cent of council members. The other three categories of office holders in the region stand closely together with about 60 per cent. In the West nearly 70 per cent of four of the five categories of office holders originate from within the same state as the community in which they carry out their political administrative functions. Only 58 per cent of the higher office holders fall into this broader definition of native origin.

5   In the East natives constitute 39 per cent of the council members. The corresponding figure in the West is 43 per cent. Note that these region-wide averages are far higher than those in the results reported in Redlingerhöfer and Hoffmann-Lange's (1998, p. 71) case study of the members of the first two post-'Wende' city councils of Jena. They report that less than 25 per cent of the members were born in the city.

Table 2.1 Local political/administrative elites holding office in town of birth: an international comparison (per cent)

Country	Percentage	Country	Percentage
East Germany	35	West Germany	37
Czech Republic	34	Austria	45
Hungary	34	Netherlands	n/a
Poland	36	Spain	47
Slovakia	42	Sweden	n/a
		Switzerland	29
		United States	27

n/a not available.

Source: Democracy and Local Government International Data Base.

dimension. Party leaders in both East and West are below the entire sample averages, as are department heads and individuals holding higher office.[6] Indeed, those holding higher office in the West have the lowest propensity to serve in the towns in which they were born (approximately 21 per cent).

It should be noted that there are no office groupings in the East in which people born in the West constitute a very large proportion of the whole.[7] Within the entire Eastern sample transplants from the West constitute only seven per cent of the total; most of these, i.e., 6 per cent, were people who came East after the 'Wende' or fall of the Communist regime in the GDR. The office category with the largest share of West transplants to the East is that of the department heads, with 15 per cent being from the West, all of whom appear to have come after the 'Wende'. The category with the second largest group on this dimension is that of higher office holders. About eleven per cent of these have come from the West and nearly all (i.e., ten) arrived after the 'Wende'. Among council members the share is four per cent for all members and slightly less than nine per cent for caucus leaders. About half of the transplants from the West among council members came after the 'Wende' and slightly more than a third of the caucus leaders who have come from the West arrived after that. Among local party leaders this share is extraordinarily low, at one per cent, none of whom claim to have migrated after the 'Wende'.

---

6 Natives constitute only 25 per cent of the party leaders in the East and 34 per cent in the West. The corresponding figures for department heads are 30 and 26 per cent in East and West. For holders of higher offices, these numbers are 33 and 21 per cent.

7 Glaeßner (1996, p. 192) reports that in two of the new federal states, Brandenburg and Saxony, the senior civil service was composed of a majority of West imports, most of whom had held similar positions in the West.

Only one party stands out for its exceptionally low level of natives amongst its elites; this is the Greens.[8] This is particularly the case in the West where less than 20 per cent of the party members were born in the towns in which they hold political or administrative office. In the East the figure for this party is less than 29 per cent, which, again, is the lowest in the region. Still, when one looks at where most of these individuals came from, it is clear that there is a strong tendency on the part of this party's members to stem at least from the same regions or states wherein the towns they now serve in public office are located. In the West, the Union members have the strongest tendency to be from the same town – a pattern mirrored in the East as well.[9] In the East there are no parties with a very large share of post-'Wende' transplants. The party with the largest share, the Social Democrats, is composed of only about eight per cent of people from this category. Non-partisans constitute the group with the largest share of post-'Wende' transplants (nearly 12 per cent). About 5 per cent of the elites from the Greens, the Union and the Liberal Democrats are transplants. None of the PDS and minor party elites moved from the West to the East after the 'Wende'.

Despite the relatively low number of natives, the average length of residence in these communities for the members of both samples of local elites is still quite high: in the East the typical elite member has spent 64 per cent of her/his life in the place where the office is held, while in the West this figure is 69 per cent.[10] There are no major differences in this regard with respect to the kind of office held, although department heads in the East do have a lower figure, i.e., 55 per cent, while caucus leaders in the East score with a relatively high figure of 76 per cent. Differences across the parties do exist, but only in a few cases are there appreciable deviations. The lowest figure is for the Greens in the West (56 per cent), while the highest figure is also to be found in the West where Union members score with 78 per cent.

---

8 A note on the terms used when referring to the names of the parties. The Bündnis 90/Die Grünen is the union of the Green (environmentalist) party of the West and various environmental and dissident electoral groupings that arose at the end of the GDR regime in the East. In the text I generally refer to the party as the Greens or the Green Party. The Christlich-Demokratische Union/Christlich-Soziale Union (Christian Democratic Union/Christian Social Union) are generally referred to as the Christian Democrats or the CDU. The CDU operates in 15 of the federal states and generally acts in unison with its sister party in Bavaria, the CSU. The FDP, the Freie Demokratische Partei (Free Democratic Party), is generally referred to as the Liberal Party, the Liberals, or the FDP. The PDS, the Partei des Demokratischen Sozialismus (Party of Democratic Socialism), is the successor party to the Communist Party (SED) of the German Democratic Republic. In the text it is usually referred to by its acronym. The SPD, the Sozialdemokratische Partei Deutschlands (Social Democratic Party) is referred to as the Social Democrats or by the party's acronym.

9 Over 44 per cent of the CDU/CSU members in the West are native to the town in which they hold office. The corresponding figure for the CDU in the East is 40 per cent.

10 Similarly high levels of long-term residence on the part of non-native born local elites have been reported in Redlingshöfer's and Hoffmann-Lange's (1998, p. 71) study of the Jena city council.

The non-natives among the elites in these communities, while constituting a large share of both samples, are still not strangers to these places. Most have spent a large part of their adult lives in the towns/cities that they serve in public office. Few important differences hold between East and West in this matter; indeed, non-natives in the East have spent, on average, 72 per cent of their adult lives in these communities and non-natives in the West have lived for 76 per cent of their adult lives in these places.

In sum, while the local political/administrative elites are not notable for having relatively large numbers of native-born, they seem to have fairly strong connections to the cities in which they carry out their official functions given the proportions of their adult lives that they have spent within these communities. There are also few signs, at least at the local government level, that colonization, in the form of the presence of large numbers of post-'Wende' transplants from the West, has occurred in the region of the former GDR. Few officials have migrated from West to East to serve in local government, particularly in elective office capacities. Where there are sizable groups of transplants, i.e., among department heads and holders of higher office, the shares are still surprisingly low, 15 and 10 per cent, respectively. And while many may have migrated to these towns, the typical migrant has still spent a relatively long period of her or his adult life in these communities. If the amount of time spent in a community can be seen as the basis for establishing roots there, then these elites are well rooted in their towns/cities.

Age and Gender

While slightly younger on average in the East, the typical member of these elites is in her or his late 40s to early 50s. Few differences also hold with respect to the average ages of the various elite categories. In both regions, the elites from the Green Party are the youngest on average (45 in the East and 42 in the West). Liberal Democrat elites are generally the oldest (49 in the East and 54 in the West). Of course, there are much younger and much older people active in local political and administrative offices, indeed the range extends from the age of 18 to well past the usual retirement age, membership in this elite is typically held by people with significant life experience. Indeed, in the West two-thirds of the elites are over the age of 40. In the East, the percentage over 40 is nearly 56 per cent.

In this regard, both regions of Germany are quite typical by international standards (see Table 2.2). In four Central European countries, the average age of local political and administrative elites ranges from 45 to 50, while in five Western countries the averages range from around 45 to 52. And in comparison with the adult populations they govern, the average ages of the local elites in both East and West Germany are representative. However, the age distributions are markedly different with the elites possessing comparatively few younger people as well as few people past the traditional retirement age of 65 (see Table 2.3).

Table 2.2 Average age of local political/administrative elites: an international comparison

Country	Average age	Country	Average age
East Germany	47	West Germany	50
Czech Republic	48	Austria	48
Hungary	49	Netherlands	49
Poland	45	Spain	45
Slovakia	50	Sweden	52
		Switzerland	n/a
		United States	49

n/a not available.

Source: Democracy and Local Government International Data Base.

Table 2.3 Age characteristics of all elites, council members and adult citizens (per cent)

	East Germany			West Germany		
Age category	All elites	Council members	Citizens	All elites	Council members	Citizens
18–24	1.3	2.2	4.7	0.6	1.1	8.1
25–34	11.5	11.1	18.7	7.1	8.2	20.6
35–44	27.2	24.3	20.6	22.9	21.4	19.8
45–54	35.5	33.8	18.5	34.5	30.9	16.4
55–64	21.4	24.0	17.1	28.0	29.8	15.8
65 + older	3.1	4.6	20.3	6.9	8.7	19.2
Average age	46.9	47.4	48.6	49.7	50.0	46.9

Note that age categories are shown as percentages of total.

Source: Democracy and Local Government in Germany, Elite and Citizen Surveys.

Despite the fact that women are under-proportionately represented within the political elites of the industrialized democracies, recent times have seen some progress in reducing this gap. This is evidenced by women's greater success in achieving political office. An example here can be seen in the number of women gaining seats in national parliaments (see Table 2.4). Thus, in Sweden, women now hold nearly 43 per cent of all seats. Nevertheless, there is a good deal of variation across the

Table 2.4 Percentage shares of German town/city council seats held by women, 1996

Population size	East Germany	West Germany
1,000,000 +	–	38.1
500,000 – 1,000,000	–	33.8
200,000 – 500,000	27.2	31.4
100,000 – 200,000	27.4	31.6
50,000 – 100,000	25.2	26.5
20,000 – 50,000	25.2	22.6
10,000 – 20,000	21.9	20.1
Total	24.1	22.8

Source: Statistisches Jahrbuch Deutscher Gemeinden (1996), Deutscher Städtetag, Köln.

industrialized countries on this score. While an average of 24 per cent of all seats in the lower house of national parliaments are now held by women (note that the German figure is slightly higher), their success has been lacking in a number of countries, such as France and the United States, with 11 and 13 per cent, respectively.[11] In Central Europe, the average for four countries (the Czech Republic, Hungary, Poland and Slovakia) is only 12 per cent.[12]

In Germany, one can see progress in women's achievement in holding political office at the local level. Thus, while women held only 8 per cent of all seats in city councils throughout the Federal Republic in 1976, the share has steadily increased. By 1996, women held 24 per cent of all city council seats in the new federal states, and 23 per cent were held by women in the Western States.[13] A pattern that has held over the last twenty years is for women's relative presence to be significantly greater in larger towns and cities than in smaller communities, as demonstrated in Table 2.4 with data from 1996.

The overall averages for women's control of seats in town and city councils are consistent with the figures one sees at the national and state level. In the mid-90s women held 26 per cent of the seats in the *Bundestag*, as well as 29 and 24 per cent of the seats in the East and West German state parliaments.[14] These figures line up con-

---

11 This average is for 20 Western industrialized democracies. The source for this data is the Inter-Parliamentary Union's web page: <www.ipu.org/wmn-e/classif.htm>.
12 The source is the same as that cited in footnote 11.
13 Sources: Statistisches Jahrbuch Deutscher Gemeinden (1976, 1996), Deutscher Städtetag, Köln. Note that in our survey results, women constitute slightly more than 22 per cent of the Council members in the East and nearly 20 per cent in the West.
14 Data on the *Bundestag* were kindly provided by Achim Kielhorn. Data on state parliaments are drawn from Beate Hocker (1996, p. 31).

Table 2.5 Women in local government: political/administrative elites positions (per cent)

Country	Overall	Political	Administrative	Mixed*
East Germany	21.3	20.8	21.8	–
Czech Republic	21.6	–	–	–
Hungary	31.9	–	–	–
Poland	23.2	17.3	29.3	–
Slovakia	22.5	–	–	–
West Germany	15.8	18.8	6.4	–
Austria	17.6	20.5	2.9	–
Netherlands	16.4	26.7	5.4	–
Spain	17.3	17.3	20.8	8.5
Sweden	24.1	26.3	18.3	–
Switzerland	15.1	17.3	9.6	19.9
United States	24.6	30.3	20.1	–

* Not possible to classify in only one type of position.

Source: Democracy and Local Government International Data Base.

sistently as well with female membership in political parties, which accounts for about 27 per cent of the total across both regions in Germany.[15]

In terms of other offices in German local government and politics, however, women frequently do less well, particularly in the Western towns and cities (see Table 2.5). In both regions, women are far more under-represented in positions of higher office, for example, mayoral positions. In the East only one in nine such positions are held by women and only one in eleven in the West. While in the East, women hold a quarter of the caucus leadership positions in the councils, they account for only 13 per cent of these positions in the West. Female occupation of party leadership roles is also lower in both regions, with women constituting only 17 per cent in the East and 14 per cent in the West. Particularly marked differences exist between the two regions in terms of women's occupation of positions at the head of administrative departments. While women in the East hold slightly more than a quarter of all such positions, women in the West hold only 6 per cent of these positions.

In comparison with some other countries, the success of German women in acquiring positions of importance in local government and politics has not been that

---

15 Party membership figures are based on data drawn from a paper by Beate Hocker (1996, p. 28).

great (see Table 2.5). Comparing data on towns and cities in the Western states with information on local government in six other Western nations one can see that the position of West German women lags behind most, and this is particularly the case in administrative positions. And, while in East Germany women have done better than their peers in the West, they do not appear to be exceptionally better-off than their colleagues in four Central European transitional democracies.

Involvement in Politics/Administration and Political Parties

One place where significant differences in experience between the two sets of elites exist is to be found in the length of involvement in politics and administration. Here, perhaps not surprisingly, the average length of involvement is markedly shorter in the East than in the West. On average, the typical member of the local elite in the East has spent approximately eight and one half years in politics/administration; it should be pointed out that 76 per cent of these people entered politics/administration only after the 'Wende'. In other words, the members of the political/administrative elite in the East are overwhelmingly people who had no official connection to the SED regime. In contrast, the typical elite member in the West has spent nearly 19 years in politics/administration. Few significant differences are to be found across the different types of office-holders, although in the West it can be seen that party leaders have relatively shorter tenures in public affairs (average is 15 years); in contrast, department heads and holders of higher office have relatively longer tenures (averages of 23 and 21 years, respectively).

By international standards, the average tenure of West German local political and administrative elites is quite high (see Table 2.6). Indeed, among the Western countries for which data are available, West German elites have the longest average tenure observable, slightly greater than that found in Sweden which is noted for having local elites with lengthy political/administrative careers (Eldersveld, et al., 1995). The East German average tenure, by contrast, stands midway in the range observed among the Central European transitional democracies.

In Germany, the length of political experience varies significantly across the different parties. In the East, the PDS members have typically spent a greater amount of time in politics/administration in comparison with the members of other parties in this region. The average tenure for members of this party is nearly 15 years. Indeed, more than 50 per cent of the members of the party were involved in politics/administration prior to the transformation of the SED into the PDS. The two former block parties (CDU and FDP) also have a fair number of holdovers from the previous regime. In the case of the FDP 36 per cent were in public affairs before the 'Wende', and in the case of the Christian Democrats 29 per cent were so involved when it still had its block status. In contrast, only twelve per cent of the Greens and six per cent of the Social Democrats claim to have had involvement in politics/administration prior to the 'Wende'. Interestingly, none of the members of the miscellaneous electoral groups and parties claim to have had political/administrative involvement before to

Table 2.6 Length of tenure in politics/administration: an international comparison

Country	Years*	Country	Years*
East Germany	8.6 (24)	West Germany	18.6 (80)
Czech Republic	5.3 (16)	Austria	13.0 (62)
Hungary	14.4 (64)	Netherlands	16.0 (70)
Poland	10.0 (55)	Spain	7.1 (26)
Slovakia	3.7 (4)	Sweden	17.6 (82)
		Switzerland	13.8 (61)
		United States	13.9 (64)

* For each country the first figure is the average number of years in politics/administration. The figures in parentheses for East Germany and the Central European countries represent the percentage of the elites who where in politics or administration prior to 1989. For West Germany and the Western countries, the parenthesized numbers represent the percentage of the elites who have been in politics/administration longer than ten years.

Source: Democracy and Local Government International Data Base.

the 'Wende'. In the West only one party stands out for its difference in this regard. This party, the Greens, has a low average level of about 11 years of involvement in politics/administration for its typical member.[16] All of the larger parties' elites are far and away more experienced in politics and administration, with the average number of years in public life being close to 20 years for all of these parties' elites.

Pronounced East-West differences are also manifest in the number of years in the present office. Across office categories, the individuals with the smallest percentage of their careers in the present office in both East and West are caucus leaders. For Eastern caucus leaders the figure is 52 per cent while that in the West is 37 per cent. In the East department heads have spent the greatest proportion of their careers in their present positions.[17] In the West, though, it is council members who hold this distinction (55 per cent).

By international standards, the West German elites stand out on this dimension as well. They have the lengthiest tenure in their present offices of all the Western local

---

16 This pattern of active involvement in politics under the previous regime accords with the findings of Derlien and Lock's (1994, pp. 71–2), Glaeßner's (1996, p. 191) and Welsh's (1996, pp. 509–510) studies of the backgrounds of state legislators in the Eastern states. It is also consistent with Redlingshöfer and Hoffmann-Lange's (1998, pp. 713–7) findings from their case study of the Jena city council members.

17 The figure for department heads in this region is 66 per cent as compared to the level of 45 per cent for the corresponding office holders in the West.

Table 2.7 Average number of years in present position: an international comparison

Country	Years	Country	Years
East Germany	3.3	West Germany	8.9
Czech Republic	3.1	Austria	6.7
Hungary	5.4	Netherlands	6.6
Poland	3.3	Spain	4.4
Slovakia	2.9	Sweden	n/a
		Switzerland	8.1
		United States	5.9

n/a not available.

Source: Democracy and Local Government International Data Base.

elites for which data are available (see Table 2.7). By contrast, the East German elites have held positions for lengths of time comparable to quite a number of local elites in the Central European transitional democracies.

Let me restrict attention to council members for a moment in further examining this facet of the elites' careers. In the West, the Greens have the shortest average number of years in office (about three) and these years also constitute the smallest share of their careers in politics (less than 50 per cent). For council members of all the other party groupings in the West, the average amount of time this office has been held ranges from nearly eight years to more than eleven years. In the East the average tenure in the office of council member is about three years and the most noticeable grouping in this region is once again the PDS. For members of this party the time they have held this office constitutes a markedly shorter proportion of their careers in public office (43 per cent) when compared to the range for the other parties' members in the regions that extends from 59 to 85 per cent.

The length of time in politics/administration thus varies markedly across the different parties. Given some of the age differences that exist across a number of the parties, it is interesting to ask what was the typical age of entry into politics? Figure 2.1 provides some information on this question. Here one can see that while the non-partisan grouping in the West has a significant amount of political/administrative experience, its members also entered at relatively early age, i.e., approximately 27. The Greens in the West, though marked by the least experience, are also one of the groups whose members entered at a relatively early age, approximately 30. This is similar to the members of the Union and the SPD in the West, as well as to the PDS in the East. Most of the party members of the East, though, both have little experience and entered politics/administration at a much later age – as can be seen by their concentration in the upper right hand quadrant of Figure 2.1.

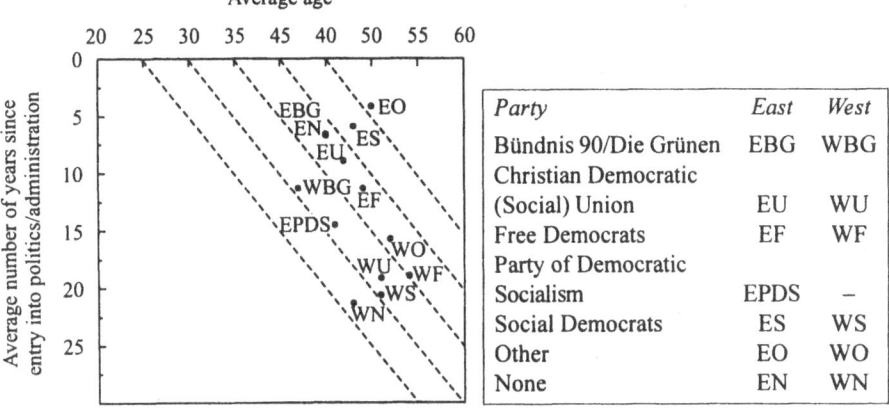

Figure 2.1 Age and tenure in local government: differences between parties and regions

Of course, the average length of tenure in local politics/administration may be influenced by whether one grew up in the town/city where one is serving in office. This seems to be the case only in the West. Here, non-natives have spent slightly less than 60 per cent of their adult lives in politics/administration, while the figure for natives is closer to 70 per cent. These differences hold across the several office categories to varying degrees and is only contradicted in the case of the different parties when one sees that non-natives have spent longer parts of their adult lives in this area only amongst the Greens and the members of the smaller parties and elector groups. Interestingly, in the East the PDS members have spent far and away greater parts of their adult lives (on average over half) in politics/administration than the members of all the other parties in the region.

The length of membership in political parties also differs markedly. In the West, the typical member of a political party joined in 1976, while in the East the typical member entered her/his party in 1985. Indeed, in the East, nearly 70 per cent of the party members joined after the 'Wende'. In the West, the two groupings that stand out are the Greens and those members of the smaller parties and electoral groupings. In both cases the typical member joined in the mid-1980s while in all the other parties the typical member joined in the early to mid-1970s. In the East, the picture is similar. The typical member of the Greens and the smaller parties and electoral groupings joined in 1991. In the case of the former, 95 per cent joined after the 'Wende'. Members with late entry also mark the Social Democrats. The average year of entry was 1989 but fully 94 per cent joined after the 'Wende'. On the other hand, the PDS and the former block parties, the CDU and the FDP, are characterized by members with long-term membership dating back to the late 1970s and early 1980s. Approximately half or less of their members joined after the 'Wende'.

In sum, particularly in the West, these elites can be characterized as having quite extensive experience in politics/administration. The typical politician/administrator in local government in this region has close to 20 years experience in this field. In the East, the picture is starkly different. Most are relative newcomers to politics and administration. Only in the case of parties connected to the old regime does one find a large number of people with more lengthy tenure in politics/administration.

Parents in Politics

Research on the background of political/administrative elites in the federal government in Germany (Aberbach et al., 1981) has demonstrated that there is a very pronounced tendency for people in such positions to come from families whose members have held political or public administration jobs. In other words, there is in Germany, and indeed elsewhere, a 'political class' which tends to reproduce itself, at least at the central government level. This is not to say that political/administrative office is inherited or that people coming from non-political familial backgrounds have no chance to enter and succeed in politics/administration. Rather it is meant to suggest that there is a very high likelihood that one's involvement in public affairs is often associated with members of one's family having been likewise engaged.

At the local government level it would appear that this tendency, while not absent, is quite attenuated. In both regions of Germany nearly one in five of the local elites had at least one parent involved in such activity – a much lower rate than found in the study of federal officials, but still a relatively high level. There are no major differences between East and West in this regard, particularly with respect to the different types of office-holders. However, across the parties there are some moderate differences. In particular, the PDS in the East (with over 27 per cent), and the smaller party/electoral groupings in both regions (27 and 23 per cent in East and West, respectively), have higher than average rates of parental involvement in politics/official life. Remarkably, in the West one-third of the party members of the smaller parties and electoral groups had one or both parents that were engaged in politics/official life.

In terms of international standards, the local elites in both German regions do not appear to be atypical with respect to their likelihood of having had one or both parents involved in politics or government (see Table 2.8). The Swedish elites clearly outrank the West Germans in this regard and the Polish elites have a slightly greater likelihood to have had parents involved in political or governmental affairs than the East German elites.

Family Class Background

What are the class origins of these elites? Are they, as traditional elite theory would have it, from the upper reaches of society or are they drawn from backgrounds that more faithfully mirror the social structure of their communities? In order to answer this question I have relied on the individual's reply to a question as to what was the

Table 2.8 Local political and administrative elites with either or both parents in politics/government: an international comparison (per cent)

Country	Percentage	Country	Percentage
East Germany	19.2	West Germany	20.4
Czech Republic	15.6	Austria	13.0
Hungary	14.5	Netherlands	16.7
Poland	23.8	Spain	12.9
Slovakia	16.4	Sweden	31.8
		Switzerland	15.7
		United States	14.7

Source: Democracy and Local Government International Data Base.

last principal occupation of the respondent's father. More frequently than with most questions asked of the respondents, no answer was given to this question or the answers provided proved impossible to code reliably. Thus, nearly 25 per cent of the respondents in the East cannot be categorized with respect to their fathers' occupation; in the West the figure is around 19 per cent. The basic categorical scheme used here allows one to classify the father's last occupation in the following ways: (1) a politician or representative or executive in government; employed in the public sector with professional jobs in (2) education and science or (3) in the traditional civil service, in (4) non-professional civil service jobs, or (5) not classifiable as to professional/ non-professional character; employed in the private sector as (6) a manager or self-employed, (7) a professional, (8) a skilled worker, or a (9) non-skilled worker. Two other categories are also provided. These are for those described as (10) unemployed (or retired) and those for which (11) no answer was given or for which the answer provided did not allow for classification.

Let me summarize the information presented based on this detailed breakdown by focusing on the question of the percentage of the elites having clear working class origins. This is presented in Table 2.9. In constructing this table, I excluded from the total those for which an unclear, non-specific answer or no answer was provided as well as those who reported that the person was not working (5, 10 and 11). Counted as working class or lower occupational status are three of the remaining eight categories; these include (4) non-professional workers in the traditional public service, (8) skilled and (9) unskilled workers in the private sector. In the middle class or higher occupational status I include categories 1, 2, 3, 6 and 7.

On this basis it is clear that a significant proportion of the elites, both in the East and in the West, has working class origins. Close to 66 per cent of the total sample in the East fit into these three categories and nearly 70 per cent of those in the West also have such origins. Across the different office categories there are only two groupings

Table 2.9 Elite class background based on father's occupational status (per cent)

Panel A: By office

	Entire sample	Council members	Caucus leaders	Party leaders	Depart. heads	Higher office
East:						
Higher	34.2	28.2	28.8	43.8	26.2	38.3
Lower	65.8	71.8	71.2	56.2	73.8	61.7
West:						
Higher	30.4	33.3	43.6	32.7	25.0	32.5
Lower	69.6	66.7	56.4	67.3	75.0	67.5

Panel B: By party

	Greens	CDU/CSU	FDP	PDS	SPD	Other	None
East:							
Higher	47.1	29.6	45.0	26.2	35.1	50.0	33.3
Lower	52.9	70.4	55.0	73.6	64.9	50.0	66.7
West:							
Higher	48.9	28.2	34.8	–	27.6	36.0	23.4
Lower	51.1	71.8	65.2	–	72.4	64.0	76.6

Source: Democracy and Local Government in Germany, Elite Surveys.

where clear East-West differences manifest themselves. Party leaders in the East are far less likely to have working class origins than are such office holders in the West. Indeed, this category stands out in the East for having far and away fewer members with working class origins. Similarly in the West, caucus leaders are much less likely than their colleagues in the East to come from a working class background and stand out in the West on this dimension as well.

Table 2.9 also provides further information on class background with breakdowns by party groupings for the samples in East and West. A number of significant features emerge from this table. First, in both East and West, members of the Greens are generally among the least likely to have working class family backgrounds. The figure is about 53 per cent in the East and 51 per cent in the West. Second, members of the

Union parties and the SPD in both regions very heavily tend to have working class backgrounds (on average, about two out of every three). This is also the case for the members of the PDS. Third, for the remaining partisan groupings the picture varies. Members of the FDP and minor parties in the East are less likely than most other groupings to have working class origins.

Education

Within Germany, high officials in the federal bureaucracy overwhelmingly tend to have had a university education. And while certainly not a prerequisite for membership in the *Bundestag*, nevertheless at least two thirds of the parliamentarians interviewed in the Aberbach et al. (1981) study also had university degrees. Does a similar pattern prevail at the local government level? While not quite as widespread, there is still a markedly high percentage of local government political/administrative elites who possess university degrees). In addition, there are significant differences here between East and West. Note that in the East, in communities of approximately similar size to those included in this study, 17 per cent of the general population have university degrees; the figure in the West is lower, i.e., 12 per cent.[18] The corresponding figures for the elites in the two regional samples are appreciably higher. In the East it is nearly 60 per cent while in the West it is 44 per cent.[19] Amongst the Eastern elite, approximately 69 per cent of holders of higher office and department heads hold degrees. It is slightly less for party leaders (65 per cent) and caucus leaders (62 per cent). About 52 per cent of the council members in the region possess degrees – a figure higher than all but one office category in the West. In the West caucus leaders are the most prone to have a university education, 55 per cent. Following this group are holders of higher office (50 per cent), department heads (47 per cent) and council members and party leaders (both with 41 per cent.)

Inter-party differences are quite large on this dimension. Members of the Greens lead the list with 76 per cent in the East and 73 per cent in the West. Only one grouping in the East, the mix of smaller parties and electoral groups, has less than 50 per cent with a university degree. In the West, the members of the Union have a lower than sample average percentage of party members with university degrees (37 per cent), but one that is slightly higher than found among the members of smaller parties and electoral groups (33 per cent). Approximately 41 per cent of the Social Democrats hold university degrees. Aside from the Greens, the only two partisan groupings in the West where a majority have university degrees are the Liberal Democrats (56 per cent) and those professing no partisan affiliation (51 per cent).

---

18 These figures based on analysis of data from the 1994 ALLBUS Survey Data Set, ZA-N₁. 2400. Information relates to German citizens living within towns or cities with a population size between 20,000 and 500,000.

19 This level of university education among the Eastern local elites is even more remarkable given that 47 per cent of the state legislators in the region report holding a university degree (Welsh, 1996, p. 510).

Table 2.10 Local political and administrative elites with university education: an international comparison (per cent)

Country	Elites	Citizens*	Country	Elites	Citizens*
East Germany	59.3	17.3	West Germany	44.0	12.2
Czech Republic	52.2	7.3**	Austria	24.3	4.8
Hungary	72.8	9.7	Netherlands	–	9.1
Poland	72.3	6.8	Spain	66.8	5.6
Slovakia	64.6	7.3**	Sweden	57.5	10.4
			Switzerland	37.9	7.3
			United States	87.5	27.3

*   Share of population (age 25 or older) with university education.
** Based on the 1990 Czechoslovakian figure.

Sources: Elites – Democracy and Local Government International Data Base; citizens – based on estimates from the 1994 ALLBUS survey in Germany and Barro and Lee's data on the other countries. These latter figures are for the year 1990.

In sum, many of the members of the local elites in both regions have extensive formal educational experience. This is particularly the case in the East. In both regions, though, these elites have educational experiences that, on average, are considerably greater than those of the general populations within their communities.

As Table 2.10 shows, the figures for West Germany are not out of line with patterns that prevail among local elites in other Western countries, and the same holds with respect to East Germany when compared with transitional democracies in Central Europe. While West German local elites have a far smaller proportion of university graduates than the United States, Sweden and Spain, they nevertheless surpass both the Austrian and Swiss local elites on this dimension, The East German pattern appears to be typical of the transitional democracies, all of which have local political/administrative elites wherein appreciable majorities hold university degrees.

There is also evidence that suggests the possession of a university degree will become more widespread within the West German local elites. The younger cohorts appear to be far more educated than their older colleagues.[20] However, in the East there is no pattern to suggest any connection between age and educational attainment among the local elites.

---

20 In the West, at least, the share of the cohorts with university education generally grows progressively smaller with age: 59 and 56 per cent of the cohorts between 25 and 34 and that between 35 and 44. Forty-five per cent of the next cohort, ages between 45 and 54, have a university education. 33 per cent and 40 per cent of the two oldest cohorts, those between 55 and 64 and those 65 and older, have a university degree.

Class Background and University Education

Data on the educational backgrounds of these elites can be broken down by their class origins. These data provide some evidence that is supportive of the elitist version of the meritocratic image of the origins of these elites. Thus, those coming out of professional and managerial family backgrounds have a significantly higher likelihood of having obtained a university degree. While for the overall sample the figure in the East is 59 per cent, for those with higher-class backgrounds in this region the figure is 70 per cent. Similarly in the West one sees that, while 44 per cent of the entire sample have university degrees, those coming out of professional and managerial class backgrounds have a much higher rate of university education, viz., 66 per cent. For those with working class backgrounds, the figures are reversed. 51 per cent in the East and 35 per cent in the West with this background have university degrees.

Still, when one recalls the much lower percentages of the non-elite populations with university degrees, these figures for elite members from the working class point in an interesting direction. They are supportive of the democratic image of meritocracy. Elites in both East and West with working class origins have nearly three times the likelihood of having a university degree relative to the general population. Such figures fit comfortably with an image of an elite that has both skills beyond the average citizen and yet comes from humble origins. This is consistent with the notion of a situation of equal opportunity: there is a state of affairs that has afforded those with the abilities and willingness to advance themselves and to succeed in entering the elites within their communities.

Qualifications and Skills

Related to the question of education is the issue of the sorts of qualifications and skills these elites bring to their political and administrative work. Tables 2.11 through 2.13 provide information on this issue. The data contained there represent the results from coding of an open-ended question where the respondents were queried as to the kind of occupational training that they had received. Ten general categories are used. The first set contains four categories where the training clearly took place at university.[21] A parallel set of four categories is used for non-university training. In each set of four, one category contains responses where it is not possible to provide a precise description of the training that was received. Outside of these eight categories there are two others. One is for those still in education or training programs and one is for those who did not answer the question.

---

21 Note that the figures here do not correspond to the values provided on German local elites in Table 2.10. The data in that table are based on answers to a close-ended question dealing with educational background. Here the data are based on responses to an open-ended question where the respondents were queried as to the type of occupational training that they have undergone. Often more than one response was given. The data presented in the tables of this section are based on the codings for the first occupational training response provided.

Table 2.11 Training background by office* (per cent)

Training category	Entire sample East	West	Council members East	West	Caucus leaders East	West	Party leaders East	West	Depart. heads East	West	Higher office East	West
University training:													
– Law, administration, economics, social sciences	7.2	18.9	3.7	11.8	2.2	20.2	6.7	12.5	16.1	34.8	15.5	38.7
– Technical, mathematical, natural sciences, medical	27.3	10.9	25.8	9.2	32.6	10.7	30.7	12.5	30.1	16.5	31.0	14.5
– Education, humanities, social work, library science	14.3	15.5	13.2	20.7	19.6	26.2	14.7	15.0	17.2	5.2	11.3	11.3
– Other, not specified	0.6	0.2	0.9	0.0	1.1	0.0	1.3	0.0	0.0	0.9	0.0	0.0
Non-university training:													
– Banking, public administration, legal	8.1	28.2	7.1	26.4	3.3	26.2	4.0	31.3	12.9	33.9	9.9	19.4
– Technical, medical, engineering	37.1	19.8	42.9	25.1	39.1	10.7	41.3	23.8	20.4	4.3	26.8	12.9
– Social, educational	1.5	1.4	1.5	1.8	1.1	2.4	0.0	0.0	0.0	0.9	4.2	0.0
– Other, not specified	2.0	2.1	3.1	2.1	0.0	0.0	0.0	0.0	0.0	1.7	1.4	0.0
Still in training, education	0.2	0.6	0.3	0.8	0.0	0.0	0.0	0.0	0.0	0.0	0.0	0.0
Unclear, no answer	1.8	2.4	1.5	2.1	1.1	3.6	0.0	0.0	3.2	1.7	1.4	0.0

* Note that some respondents reported training in two fields. The data here refer to the first training field supplied by the respondents.

Source: Democracy and Local Government in Germany, Elite Surveys.

Perhaps the most salient difference between the Eastern and Western elites here (and this holds across all office categories) is the fact that a technical occupational training background is the dominant trait in the East while a background in such fields as law, administration and the humanities marks the Western elites (see Table 2.11). To a significant extent this difference reflects the educational and economic priorities and structures of the two earlier regimes. In the former DDR, as in other socialist countries, there was a very heavy emphasis on skills related to physical production. Indeed, Wolter (1990) notes that by the mid-1980s the former GDR led all other nations in the number of engineers per employed persons within the economy. The tertiary sectors in the communist systems were very underdeveloped and despite the real growth that occurred in these economies throughout the post-World War II period, there was no marked shift toward service or information-related sectors. This stands very much in contrast to the widespread expansion of the services sectors in the capitalist economies during this period.

The excessively high proportion of elite members with technical training in the East (and the correspondingly low numbers of individuals with training in such fields as law and administration) may also reflect a weeding out process that accompanied German Unification. If people with the latter backgrounds were serving in political/administrative functions under the old regime, then their chances of holding similar positions under the new regime were diminished.

This finding accords with Welsh's (1996) results from an examination of the biographies of East German state-level parliamentary members after the first elections in October 1990. She notes that a preponderance of these legislators came from technical occupations and the natural sciences and posits that this resulted in part from 'the complete discrediting of the social sciences and the legal profession' in the area of the former GDR. She also argues that the occupational structure of the GDR, with its large share of technical and engineering positions, provided a 'parking place' for many individuals with latent political aspirations (Welsh, 1996, p. 511).[22]

Tables 2.12 and 2.13 provide breakdowns on training background by party for the entire samples in the East and the West. In the East the dominance of technical training background holds across all of the party groupings. In the West, the non-technical training background is common to all party groupings but there is variation across these grouping in terms of the character of this non-technical training. Particularly distinct here is the Green Party. Among this party's members nearly a third have university training in such fields as education and the humanities. This represents the largest grouping within the party. On the other hand, non-university training in such fields as banking and administration represent the largest contingent of people in all of the other party groupings in the West.

---

22 For a similar line of argument, see Yoder (1997).

Table 2.12 Training background by party, East Germany* (per cent)

Training category	Greens	CDU/CSU	FDP	PDS	SPD	Other	None
University training:							
– Law, administration, economics, social sciences	9.5	9.3	3.6	2.1	5.7	0.0	15.9
– Technical, mathematical, natural sciences, medical	35.7	27.1	39.3	20.0	27.0	40.0	26.1
– Education, humanities, social work, library science	11.9	8.5	17.9	22.1	14.2	8.0	15.9
– Other, not specified	2.4	0.0	0.0	2.1	0.0	0.0	0.0
Non-university training:							
– Banking, public administration, legal	0.0	10.9	10.7	4.2	7.8	4.0	11.6
– Technical, medical, engineering	40.5	37.2	21.4	41.1	41.1	44.0	26.1
– Social, educational	0.0	2.3	0.0	3.2	0.7	4.0	0.0
– Other, not specified	0.0	3.1	3.6	3.2	2.1	0.0	0.0
Still in training, education	0.0	0.0	0.0	0.0	0.7	0.0	0.0
Unclear, no answer	0.0	1.6	3.6	2.1	0.7	0.0	4.3

* Note that some respondents reported training in two fields. The data here refer to the first training field supplied by the respondents.

Source: Democracy and Local Government in Germany, Elite Surveys.

Main Occupation

Table 2.14 provides information on the occupational classes of some of the elite office categories. I have employed the same set of occupational categories that were used to describe the last principal jobs of the respondents' fathers. The table provides the occupational class breakdowns by the type of political/administrative office held. I focus exclusively here on three offices (council member, caucus leader and party leader).[23] One can see across the three office categories that a rather large share of the elites, in both East and West, describe themselves as principally employed in professional or managerial positions. Overwhelmingly from working class family back-

---

23 By definition, department heads and holder of higher office fit into the higher status occupational class scheme.

Table 2.13 Training background by party, West Germany* (per cent)

Training category	Greens	CDU/CSU	FDP	PDS	SPD	Other	None
University training:							
– Law, administration, economics, social sciences	21.2	15.9	26.5	–	17.7	13.9	30.8
– Technical, mathematical, natural sciences, medical	16.7	10.4	14.7	–	6.5	8.3	20.0
– Education, humanities, social work, library science	33.3	10.0	11.8	–	18.6	22.2	6.2
– Other, not specified	0.0	0.0	0.0	–	0.0	0.0	1.5
Non-university training:							
– Banking, public administration, legal	7.6	34.8	29.4	–	25.1	27.8	35.4
– Technical, medical, engineering	13.6	22.4	17.6	–	23.7	22.2	4.6
– Social, educational	4.5	0.5	0.0	–	2.3	0.0	0.0
– Other, not specified	0.0	4.0	0.0	–	1.9	2.8	0.0
Still in training, education	0.0	2.0	0.0	–	0.9	0.0	0.0
Unclear, no answer	3.0	1.0	0.0	–	3.3	2.8	1.5

* Note that some respondents reported training in two fields. The data here refer to the first training field supplied by the respondents.

Source: Democracy and Local Government in Germany, Elite Surveys.

grounds, relatively few of these elites have not been upwardly mobile.[24] With the exception of department heads and holders of higher office, the majorities in both East and West have their principal occupations outside of the public sector.[25]

---

24 Recall that large proportions of the elites claim a working class background given their fathers' occupations. Approximately 73 per cent of the elites in both regions with such a background have achieved a higher occupational status. Less than 10 per cent of the Easterners with a higher-class background have been downwardly mobile and only 13 per cent of the Westerners with such a class background have wound up in the lower occupational status group. In sum, among the elites of both regions, there has been a lot of class mobility and nearly all of this mobility has been upward.

25 In the East, less than 30 per cent of council members hold jobs in the public sector. The corresponding figure for the West is about 40 per cent; indeed the figures for caucus and party leaders in the West are quite close to this figure. Thirty-five per cent of caucus leaders and 41 per cent of party leaders in the East have employment in the public sector.

Table 2.14 Occupational status by office (per cent)

Occupational status	Council members East	Council members West	Caucus leaders East	Caucus leaders West	Party leaders East	Party leaders West
Higher	71.1	67.5	80.0	87.0	76.7	69.4
Lower	28.9	32.5	20.0	13.0	23.3	30.6

* Note that some respondents reported more than one occupation. The data here refer to the first occupation supplied by the respondents.

Source: Democracy and Local Government in Germany, Elite Surveys.

Table 2.15 Main occupation by party, East Germany* (per cent)

Occupational category	Greens	CDU/CSU	FDP	PDS	SPD	Other	None
Representative, executive in government, politician	0.0	7.0	7.1	3.2	5.0	4.0	1.4
Public service:							
– Education and science, professional	11.9	6.2	3.6	20.0	6.4	4.0	1.4
– Traditional public service, professional	28.6	31.0	35.7	6.3	24.8	16.0	69.6
– Traditional public service, non-professional	4.8	6.2	0.0	1.1	5.7	4.0	11.6
– Other, not specified	4.8	1.6	3.6	1.1	2.8	0.0	1.4
Private sector:							
– Self-employed and managers	14.3	13.2	21.4	6.3	17.0	12.0	2.9
– Professionals	19.0	7.0	14.3	13.7	7.1	16.0	4.3
– Skilled workers	9.5	15.5	7.1	9.5	13.5	8.0	1.4
– Non-skilled workers	0.0	0.8	0.0	0.0	0.0	0.0	0.0
Not employed	7.1	9.3	3.6	31.6	14.2	28.0	1.4
Unclear, no answer	0.0	2.3	3.6	7.4	3.5	8.0	4.3

* Note that some respondents reported more than one main occupation. The data here refer to the first occupation supplied by the respondents.

Source: Democracy and Local Government in Germany, Elite Surveys.

Table 2.16 Main occupation by party, West Germany* (per cent)

Occupational category	Greens	CDU/CSU	FDP	PDS	SPD	Other	None
Representative, executive in government, politician	6.1	5.5	5.9	–	7.0	5.6	4.6
Public service:							
– Education and science, professional	21.2	7.5	11.8	–	10.2	13.9	1.5
– Traditional public service, professional	19.7	18.5	17.6	–	22.3	13.9	60.0
– Traditional public service, non-professional	1.5	1.0	0.0	–	3.7	2.8	3.1
– Other, not specified	1.5	9.5	5.9	–	9.3	2.8	18.5
Private sector:							
– Self-employed and managers	7.6	14.9	17.6	–	8.4	16.7	3.1
– Professionals	19.7	6.5	14.7	–	4.7	5.6	3.1
– Skilled workers	4.5	19.4	5.9	–	12.1	25.0	3.1
– Non-skilled workers	1.5	1.0	0.0	–	0.0	0.0	0.0
Not employed	16.7	13.4	14.7	–	17.7	11.1	1.5
Unclear, no answer	0.0	3.0	5.9	–	4.7	2.8	1.5

* Note that some respondents reported more than one main occupation. The data here refer to the first occupation supplied by the respondents.

Source: Democracy and Local Government in Germany, Elite Surveys.

Tables 2.15 and 2.16 provide detailed occupational breakdowns based on party affiliation for the entire samples of the elites in the East and the West. In the East the parties are relatively similar on this dimension although there is a stronger tendency for PDS members to be either employed in the public sector within the fields of education or science or not to be employed at all. A large share of those affiliated with smaller parties or local electoral groups also have a much higher rate of non-employment (either unemployed, retired or still studying). Greater variation in the occupational patterns is to be seen across the parties in the West. Members of the Greens are overwhelmingly in professional occupations and they also have the largest share of professionals employed in the public sector while engaged in educational and scientific occupations (this is particularly pronounced among town/city council members representing this party). The Union parties in the West have the highest share of non-professional workers (mainly employed in the private sector) and, once again, this is particularly pronounced amongst the council members with this partisan affiliation.

In sum, most of these elites are presently employed in professional or managerial occupations. While quite a few are employed in the public sector, outside of department heads and holders of higher office, these jobs are clearly un-associated with the political positions these elites hold. Overwhelmingly from working class backgrounds, the typical elite member has clearly achieved a fair degree of upward class mobility.

Ties to the Community

Organizational Involvement

Strong ties to their community help politicians and administrators understand the nature of their communities' problems as well as the attitudes and preferences of their fellow citizens. One particularly important form of connection to the community can be found in involvement in the organizational/associational life of the community (cf. Parry et al., 1992; Putnam, 1993). In this regard, the local government political/ administrative elites of the two regions appear to be intensively linked to their fellow citizens (see Table 2.17). In the East, 89 per cent of the sample has one or more associational membership. In the West, the corresponding figure is an extremely high 96 per cent. Note that the figures for ordinary citizens in a sub-sample of 30 towns and cities are 46 per cent in the East and 53 per cent in the West.[26]

While the two regional elites are rather similar in that nearly all belong to at least one association, they do differ in the scope of their associational affiliations. In the East, the typical elite member belongs to at least two types of associations. In the West, the figure is higher, slightly more than three. The most marked difference across office types is to be found between administrative department heads, on the one hand, and all the other office groupings. For the former grouping in the East the average figure is about 1.5 while in the West it is 2.3. All of the other groupings in the East have averages above two with the largest average being registered by holders of higher office (2.3). In the West, the only other office grouping with a figure of less than three is that of party leaders (2.6). All of the others have well above three on average, with both council members and caucus leaders registering 3.4 and holders of higher office again having the largest figure (3.5).

In what kinds of associations do these elites hold membership? In the East there are five types of associations that are the most common. These include unions (30 per cent), sports as well as religious or church associations (27 per cent), cultural associations (27 per cent) and welfare associations (26 per cent). Environmental (8 per cent)

---

26 Information on East and West German citizens living within towns or cities with a population size between 20,000 and 500,000 provide a comparable picture of associational membership. This is based on analysis of data from the ALLBUS Survey Data Set (1992).

Table 2.17 Patterns of associational membership amongst elites and citizens by region

	East Elites	East Citizens	West Elites	West Citizens
Average number of memberships	2.0	0.7	3.2	1.0
Per cent belonging to:				
– Occupational associations	22	8	37	12
– Unions	31	26	32	21
– Educational associations	12	4	26	11
– Cultural associations	27	6	46	13
– Sport associations	27	21	57	35
– Religious or church associations	27	12	39	17
– Environmental associations	8	1	23	8
– Economic associations	7	2	10	2
– Welfare associations	26	10	38	10
– Other	14	16	8	24
– Any	89	46	96	53

Note that total membership is the sum of the number of types of organizations to which membership is claimed.

Source: Democracy and Local Government in Germany, Elite and Citizen Surveys.

and economic (7 per cent) associations trail well behind all of the other kinds of associations in terms of their popularity as measured by elite membership in the East. While unions are the locus of membership for an even larger percentage of the Western elites (37), they trail behind in popularity to sports (57 per cent), cultural (46 per cent) religious or church associations (39 per cent) and welfare associations (38 per cent). Environmental associations also have a much wider membership basis in the West with 23 per cent of the elite having a membership with one or another of the associations in this category.

In terms of differences in this matter across the political parties one finds variation in the degree to which party members have at least one associational tie (see Table 2.18). In the East, members of smaller parties and electoral groups have the lowest rate of membership, 80 per cent, while elites within the Green Party have the highest, 93 per cent. In the West, elites without party affiliation have the lowest rate, 92 per cent, and members of the Union parties enjoy the highest rate, 98 per cent. The breadth of membership in different associational types varies. In the East, non-party members have the lowest average rate, 1.6, while the Greens have the highest, 2.5. Interestingly in the West it is the Green Party that has the lowest rate, 2.6, while the SPD has the highest, 3.7.

Table 2.18 Elites' associational membership by office and party affiliation in East and West Germany

Panel A: By office

	Entire sample	Council members	Caucus leaders	Party leaders	Depart. heads	Higher office
East:						
Average numbers of organizations	2.0	2.0	2.2	2.1	1.5	2.3
Per cent belonging to any organization	89	90	90	92	84	90
West:						
Average numbers of organizations	3.2	3.4	3.4	2.6	2.3	3.5
Per cent belonging to any organization	96	97	95	96	93	98

Panel B: By party

	Greens	CDU/CSU	FDP	PDS	SPD	Other	None
East:							
Average numbers of organizations	2.5	2.1	1.7	1.8	2.3	1.8	1.6
Per cent belonging to any organization	93	92	82	90	90	80	86
West:							
Average numbers of organizations	2.6	3.1	3.2	–	3.7	2.7	2.6
Per cent belonging to any organization	96	98	97	–	97	92	92

Note that total membership is the sum of the number of types of organizations in membership is claimed.

Source: Democracy and Local Government in Germany, Elite Surveys.

Are there differences in the kinds of associations that the different parties' members maintain ties with? This is very much the case. In both East and West, the members of the Greens are most likely to be members of environmental associations, with 40 per cent in the East and 56 per cent in the West holding such an affiliation. No other party in the East has as much as 10 per cent of its membership holding such affiliations. The situation is somewhat similar in the West, although it should be noted that nearly 29 per cent of the Western Social Democratic elites have membership in environmental organizations. There is a concentration of membership in religious or church associations on the part of the Union parties in both East and West (51 per cent). In the West, as well, the Union has even higher percentages of its membership connected to sports associations (59 per cent) and occupational associations (55 per cent). The Liberal Democrats are very similar to the Christian Democrats in this region in terms of associational ties, with sport and occupational associations being the most frequent places of membership (68 and 56 per cent, respectively). However, widespread ties to church or religious organizations on the part of these elites are absent. In the East, however, only one kind of organizational affiliation stands out for the FDP party members; this is with cultural associations where the membership rate is 43 per cent. For the PDS, far and away the most popular associational affiliation is with labor unions (58 per cent). This predilection is also evident amongst Social Democrats in both East and West. However, in the West other types of associations enjoy nearly the same level of popularity with the local elites of the SPD. Thus, 61 per cent belong to sports associations, 59 per cent are members of welfare associations, and 55 per cent belong to cultural associations.

Elite members having no political party affiliation or who belong to small parties and electoral groups tend to have lower overall rates of organizational membership. In the East there seem to be no particular types of associations that attract the membership of these elites to any wide extent. In the West, sports associations seem to be highly favored, particularly among elites from the smaller parties and electoral groups (72 per cent).

In sum, the typical local government elite member appears to have relatively strong ties to her/his community through associational memberships. Associational life in Germany is rather vibrant and reputedly more so in the West than in the East. Nevertheless, these elite members can be characterized as being far more likely to have such ties than their fellow citizens. Variation holds across the different types of office holders in this regard, and it is clear that political office holders are far more active in their communities associational life than are administrative office holders.

Partisan differences are also evident in terms of associational ties. And while there is a modest degree of variation in the extent to which members of the different parties belong to at least one association, and even more significant variation in the number of types of associational affiliation, the most striking differences hold with respect to the kinds of associations with which the members of the various parties retain ties. The patterns of these ties appear to be very much in keeping with the political principles and concerns of the different party elites.

Table 2.19 Similarities and differences in associational membership patterns between elites and electors (correlation matrices)

East			Elites:			
	Greens	CDU/CSU	FDP	PDS	SPD	Other
Voters:						
Greens	.22	.31	−.08	.72	.60	.12
CDU/CSU	.15	56	−.18	.59	.65	.21
FDP	.26	.43	.03	.72	.96	.48
PDS	.13	.07	−.18	.88	.88	.08
SPD	.14	.29	−.13	.84	.84	.15
Other	.25	.62	−.23	.47	.56	.28

West			Elites:			
	Greens	CDU/CSU	FDP	PDS	SPD	Other
Voters:						
Greens	.69	.18	.17	–	.54	.40
CDU/CSU	.07	.73	.52	–	.53	.79
FDP	−.43	.67	.84	–	.21	.71
SPD	.34	.33	.27	–	.77	.56
Other	.05	.69	.69	–	.50	.93

Source: Democracy and Local Government in Germany, Elite and Citizen Surveys.

But do these patterns of ties coincide with those of the citizens in their community, and in particular, supporters of the elites' political parties? In the survey of citizens within a sub-sample of 30 towns and cities information was collected on citizen associational membership. The extent of organizational membership differs between the two regions with Western citizens, like the elites in this region, having a greater likelihood of being a member of one or another association. What is really of interest here is the extent to which the patterns of elite and citizen membership intensities match up across the political parties, that is: do elites and citizens of the same party share memberships in the same organizations? Table 2.19 provides a relatively straightforward way of summarizing the situation.

This table presents the correlations between the associational membership patterns of the party elites (horizontal dimension) and the patterns of associational membership among the voters of all these parties (vertical dimension). One would expect the strongest correlations to be between the associational membership patterns of the elites of a party and those of the citizen supporters of that party. These are the numbers along the main diagonal.

In the East, there appears to be limited correspondence. Note that the elites and citizen-electors of the Liberal Democrats and the Greens show almost no correpondence in associational membership patterns. And while Union elites and electors have relatively similar patterns of organizational ties, the Union elites appear to be even closer to those voters who support the smaller, non-mainstream parties. The PDS and Social Democratic elites share very similar associational patterns with their respective voters, but then they also have similar patterns to those of nearly every other electoral group as well as non-voters.

In the West, however, the overall pattern is far and away different. Here one can observe very strong similarities between associational ties of each party elite and those of its electoral supporters. In the case of each and every partisan grouping, the elite of that grouping has associational membership patterns that match most closely those of its electoral supporters.

In sum, perhaps because of the situation of flux prevailing in East German society after Unification, there are some severe gaps between partisan elites and their electoral supporters in terms of associational membership. Conversely, in West Germany one sees a fairly tight fit in the way in which partisan elites and their electoral supporters align themselves in associational life. The greater similarity in membership profiles that holds in the West is most likely a function of the greater longevity of the political, economic and social systems in this region. One would expect that as time passes a similar alignment between elites' and supporters' associational membership patterns will emerge in the East. In the meantime, however, this disjunction can only add to the difficulties of democratic governance in this region.

Patterns of Reliance

In order to get a more refined sense of the ties that these elites have to their community and the influence these ties have on how they go about their business the following question was posed to them: 'to whom do they turn for support when making a political/administrative decision'. A lengthy list of groups/individuals that they might rely upon was provided, and they were requested to simply check off those to whom they often turn for such support. In the West there were 21 such categories of groups and individuals. In the East the same list was used but another category, 'colleagues in West German partner cities', was added, thus making 22 categories. Tables 2.20 and 2.21 provided detailed breakdowns of the responses to these questions across the two regions both by political/administrative office and by political party affiliation. Obviously, an extensive amount of information is being provided here and to facilitate the interpretation of these results I have organized the many categories of potential targets of reliance into 9 broader groupings. The first deals with party politicians at both the communal and higher levels of government. The second includes elected officials inside the city government. The third deals with administrators at both local and higher levels of government. The fourth includes activist groupings inside the community. The fifth incorporates economic associations and institutions. The sixth is a miscellaneous grouping containing various categories of what could be referred to as the general public. The seventh deals only with the local media in the form of

Table 2.20 Patterns of reliance by department heads and other officials*
(per cent indicating they rely on specific groups or individuals
in their political and/or administrative functions when making
decisions)

	Other elites		Department heads	
	East	West	East	West
1 Local party politicians	59	72	35	21
Party politicians, higher level	52	65	23	13
Groups in local party organization	34	39	9	9
2 Members of city council	57	49	48	48
Mayor/chief mayor	55	58	86	74
3 Leading city administrators	54	63	73	80
Administrative colleagues	21	19	75	82
Higher administrative officials	14	23	51	46
4 Local representatives of political movements	31	28	10	15
Local civic and occup. groups involved in city politics	41	40	10	5
5 Regional economic groups	30	30	22	23
Unions	23	24	9	16
6 General public	49	51	16	19
Local ethnic groups	0	1	1	2
Local church groups	11	15	4	10
Neighborhood groups	1	1	2	5
Poorer people	14	1	2	2
Wealthy people	0	0	1	1
7 Local newspapers	29	42	15	21
8 Colleagues in neighboring cities	14	23	35	46
Colleagues, WG partner cities**	29	–	63	–
9 Close friends and sympathizers	58	53	16	22

*   Includes council members, caucus leaders, party leaders and holders of higher office.
** Asked only in the Eastern federal states.

Source: Democracy and Local Government in Germany, Elite Surveys.

local newspapers. The eighth contains colleagues in other cities. The ninth includes the single category of 'close friends and sympathizers'.

In terms of the different office categories of elites, the most striking contrast is between administrative officers, i.e., department heads, and all of other categories of office holders. In Table 2.20, then, the presentation of the breakdowns of patterns of reliance is restricted to department heads and all the other elite groups combined. Department heads are less likely to call on politicians (outside of the mayor) and are dependent on higher executive and administrative officials. They are clearly much less reliant on non-governmental actors and are also more likely to depend on administrative officials at higher levels of government as well as colleagues in other cities. This patterns holds across both regions of Germany. For the other categories of office holders, there seems to be strong reliance on local and higher level party politicians. These groups of elites are far more reliant on local organizations, the general public and the news media than are the administrative officers.

Table 2.21 provides the breakdown of reliance patterns in East and West by party affiliation. The most striking differences here are to be seen between the more established parties, the Union, the Liberal Democrats and the Social Democrats, on the one hand, and the other groupings, such as the Greens (in both East and West) and the PDS (in the East), on the other. The latter are far more likely to cite non-establishment groupings and individuals, such as those in category 4, as well as the general public, local newspapers and 'close friends and sympathizers', as sources of support. On the economic side, parties of the left, particularly the SPD and the PDS, are more likely to cite unions as sources of support while the center and right parties (at least in the West) are more likely to seek support from regional economic groupings such as the local chamber of commerce. As with associational affiliations, general political orientations of the parties correspond with patterns one sees in terms of who their members rely upon.

At Work

Amount of Time Involved in Carrying out Official Duties

Using the information provided by the respondents in answer to the question '[w]hat is your most important political or public position?', I classified the elites into the five functional categories that have been used throughout this chapter. This classification served as the basis for then ascertaining how intensively involved (in terms of time spent) these individuals are in carrying out their political and/or administrative jobs. Since a fair proportion of the elites hold more than one official function, the values provided here will tend to understate the intensity of their involvement in politics and public life. Nevertheless, the amount of time spent by these elites in carrying out political and/or administrative tasks is quite significant. Simultaneously, the time demands vary dramatically across offices or functions.

Table 2.21 Elites' patterns of reliance by party affiliation (per cent indicating they rely upon specific groups or individuals in their political and/or administrative functions when making decisions)

	Greens		CDU/CSU		FDP		PDS	SPD		Other		None	
	East	West	East	West	East	West	East	East	West	East	West	East	West
1 Local party politicians	55	67	58	68	50	79	67	65	65	28	61	33	18
Party politicians, higher level	45	47	48	63	46	56	60	55	62	20	28	23	15
Groups in local party organization	21	36	29	32	21	24	57	35	42	4	19	4	2
2 Members of city council	52	47	56	42	54	50	66	57	56	52	53	49	43
Mayor/chief mayor	50	41	65	63	75	74	40	60	59	40	61	78	80
3 Leading city administrators	50	61	60	71	43	56	46	59	67	52	61	68	80
Administrative colleagues	21	24	33	24	39	26	6	30	28	20	25	67	78
Higher administrative officials	14	26	23	27	25	9	6	17	27	16	14	48	48
4 Local represent. of pol. movements	40	52	22	18	29	12	46	25	27	12	36	12	14
Local civic and occupational groups involved in city politics	67	80	25	24	14	21	58	29	39	48	53	19	15
5 Regional economic groups	21	11	33	36	29	53	24	28	25	40	47	25	22
Unions	21	24	7	9	0	6	38	29	39	4	6	7	9
6 General public	55	58	36	37	29	44	67	44	44	48	69	20	34
Local ethnic groups	0	14	3	1	0	3	2	3	7	4	6	1	2
Local church groups	19	20	19	18	0	12	2	5	10	16	14	4	11
Neighborhood groups	2	12	5	5	0	3	12	1	9	4	14	4	8
Poorer people	12	17	6	2	4	6	25	11	10	12	3	4	5
Wealthy people	0	6	2	3	0	3	3	3	5	0	0	3	3
7 Local newspapers	57	67	21	30	18	50	39	19	37	48	47	14	26
8 Colleagues in neighboring cities	17	33	16	26	18	26	9	18	20	12	28	32	49
Colleagues, WG partner cities*	26	–	43	–	36	–	6	41	–	20	–	58	–
9 Close friends and sympathizers	64	70	43	41	36	56	75	51	50	64	44	19	26

* Asked only in the Eastern federal states.

Source: Democracy and Local Government in Germany, Elite Surveys.

Thus, council members in the East spend about 11 hours a week on average in carrying out the tasks related to this official function. The time spent by their colleagues in the West is slightly greater, around 13 hours per week on average.[27] Caucus leaders spend more time than other council members on average. In the East the mean figure is 13 and one half hours. It is appreciably higher for caucus leaders in the West where the average is 19 hours per week. Local party chairpersons spend, on average, about one third of the normal working week carrying out the tasks related to this office. In the East, the average is about 13 hours while in the West it is about 14 hours. Clearly, while the elites holding these three functions are not engaged full time in carrying out the work associated with their offices, they still spend an appreciable amount of time attending to the tasks involved. As pointed out earlier in this chapter, most of these elites state that their main occupation is some position outside of politics. Devoting a third or more of a normal work week to carrying out these political tasks, mostly with little or no remuneration (see Borchert and Golsh, 1999, p. 122), represents a major measure of commitment on their parts.

Department heads and holders of higher office are, on average, far more engaged in their political and administrative jobs. In general, they devote more than a normal number of working hours to carrying out their jobs. This is especially so in the new federal states where department heads average 48 hours a week on the job (the comparable figure in the West is slightly lower at about 46 hours per week). Holders of higher office average 58 hours per week in the East on the job and 48 hours per week in the West. These differences between East and West are clearly associated with the immensity of the tasks confronting the Eastern leaders.

Political/Administrative Roles

Often the border between politics and administration is nebulous. Indeed, many argue that there is a large gray zone wherein leading administrators take on activities that appear to be very political in their character. The respondents in the study share this view. When asked whether they believed that 'top-level administrators operate in an intermediate zone – where matters not purely administrative but also political are dealt with', the overwhelming majority of the local elites in both East and West said that this was often or always the case. In the West, about 88 per cent characterized the situation in this way, while, in the East, nearly 80 per cent responded similarly. In the West, only about 7 per cent said this is never or hardly ever the situation, while about 6 per cent indicated that they did not know. In the East, only 7 per cent disagreed, while about 13 per cent said they could not answer this question.

It may indeed be the case that the reality of modern day communal government requires such a departure from the traditional conception that there should be a strict

---

27 These figures on the time given over to official activity connected with carrying out one's mandate are comparable to those reported by Range (1994) in his time budget study of council members in Wuppertal and Hamburg.

Table 2.22 Evaluations of top-level administrators in intermediate zone between politics and administration by office (per cent)

	East			West		
	Very bad or bad	Mixed	Good or very good	Very bad or bad	Mixed	Good or very good
Entire sample	21	54	25	20	51	28
Council members	21	59	20	24	50	27
Caucus leaders	30	53	18	22	54	24
Party leaders	29	49	21	24	64	12
Department heads	16	50	33	12	54	34
Higher office	11	42	46	21	36	43

Source: Democracy and Local Government in Germany, Elite Surveys.

separation of politics from administration. Ultimately, the question is how well the two are mixed. Does this mixture produce satisfactory or unsatisfactory outcomes? In both regions the answer to this question is to be seen in the fact that the majority of the respondents saw the results as mixed and approximately 20 per cent in both regions saw the practice as bad or very bad (see Table 2.22). On the other side, 25 per cent in the East and 28 per cent in the West evaluate the situation positively. There are clear differences in these evaluations across the various office categories. Those with exclusively political offices, i.e., council members and caucus and party leaders are much less likely to view this practice positively than are department heads and holders of higher office.[28]

Among the political parties, two clearly stand out for their tendency to see this practice in a less than positive light. These are the Greens (in both East and West) and the PDS. Among the Green Party members only about 12 per cent in the East and slightly less than 17 per cent in the West say that the situation is good or very good. Indeed, among the members of this party in the East, approximately 40 per cent see it as bad or very bad. Only 13 per cent in the PDS see it positively. One might also note that the members of the smaller parties and elector groups in the West are also less than positive in their evaluations of this practice.

---

[28] In the two regions the following patterns hold. Among council members 20 per cent in the East and 27 per cent in the West view the situation positively. Only 18 per cent of the caucus leaders in the East and 24 per cent of those in the West hold a positive perspective on such involvement. By contrast, about a third of all department heads in both regions and around 45 per cent of higher office holders in the two regions view this situation in a favorable light.

Role Orientations

How do politicians and administrators view the roles that they themselves perform? This has long been a controversial issue. In particular, the question of the degree to which administrators conform to the classical non-political style of behavior is often a matter of debate, both in practice and in scholarly discussion. Further, the role of politicians is a classic concern. In particular, the extent to which politicians act for the common good or alternatively orient their behavior toward satisfying particularistic or partisan interests is a matter of disagreement.

Since the data on which I rely are drawn from survey questionnaires, they clearly cannot give one a full and complete picture in this regard. Rather, one must depend on the self-reporting of the respondents. In this case, the respondents were directly asked about the extent to which they agree or disagree that their conception of their role accords with a variety of characterizations. Obviously this is not an ideal way to come at this important question. However, the approach has been used successfully in other studies (e.g., Aberbach, et al., 1981; Gunlicks, 1969; Newton, 1972), both cross-nationally and within Germany, at both the federal and local government levels. Indeed, I have drawn on the Aberbach et al. study in constructing the battery of possible role conceptions used in the questionnaire.

There are nine role characterizations within the Aberbach et al. battery. With one exception, all of these were relatively easy to adapt to the present context. The eight that were not difficult to adopt included the following role descriptions: (1) technician, i.e., an expert with the specialized knowledge needed to solve problems; (2) advocate, i.e., a spokesperson for broad social groups and general societal interests; (3) facilitator, i.e., a representative of organized groups working to protect their interests; (4) broker, i.e., an intermediary between conflicting interests, or one who attempts to mediate or resolve political and interest conflicts; (5) partisan politician, i.e., one who sees herself or himself carrying out a specific partisan program; (6) trustee, i.e., one who sees her or his role as representing the town/city that one is active in; (7) legalist, i.e., one who accepts the role definition of a legal technician; (8) ombudsman, i.e., a citizen advocate who is concerned with and takes care of citizens' problems. Another is described as a (9) policy-maker in the Aberbach et al. study. This proves difficult to bring over clearly into the German language. Indeed, the awkward phrase of 'one who translates what is politically allowed' was employed. For present purposes I will refer to this role characterization as one of being an 'implementer'. Finally, one other role characterization was added to the battery of nine drawn from the earlier study. This is the role of an (10) initiator of new projects and problem-solver, which for shorthand purposes below is referred to as initiator.

Tables 2.23 and 2.24 provide descriptive statistics on how the various elites define their roles in politics and in administration. The values given in these tables represent averages for the group categories. The scaling of these variables ranges from 1 to 5. A value of 1 implies complete rejection of the notion that the elite members see themselves fulfilling such a role. A value of 3 implies neutrality toward the description,

Table 2.23 Role identification by office (average values)

		Technician	Advocate	Facilitator	Broker	Implementer	Partisan politician	Trustee	Legalist	Ombudsman	Initiator
Council member	East	3.15	3.86	2.81	3.00	2.78	2.88	3.01	2.26	3.59	3.40
	West	3.17	3.72	2.38	3.16	2.99	2.92	3.17	2.10	3.86	3.84
Caucus leader	East	3.28	3.94	3.11	3.10	2.97	3.02	3.12	2.22	3.67	3.57
	West	3.26	3.68	2.40	3.17	2.94	2.90	3.13	2.37	3.73	4.04
Party leader	East	3.45	3.87	2.90	3.14	2.88	3.31	2.91	2.18	3.49	3.67
	West	3.12	3.65	2.38	3.08	2.92	3.14	2.76	2.15	3.81	3.98
Department heads	East	3.87	2.71	2.10	3.03	3.40	1.52	3.43	3.10	2.67	3.58
	West	4.16	2.88	1.85	3.52	3.63	1.34	2.96	3.29	2.81	3.70
Higher office	East	3.63	3.61	2.49	3.59	3.44	2.21	3.90	2.66	4.41	4.08
	West	3.62	3.81	2.22	3.63	3.29	2.19	4.25	2.45	3.71	4.12

Role variable scoring: 1 to 5 with 1 = low identification and 5 = high identification.

Source: Democracy and Local Government in Germany, Elite Surveys.

Table 2.24 Role identification by party (council members only, average values)

		Tech-nician	Advo-cate	Facili-tator	Broker	Imple-menter	Partisan politician	Trustee	Legalist	Ombuds-man	Initiator
Greens	East	2.77	3.91	3.00	2.77	2.41	2.54	2.46	2.09	3.73	3.22
	West	3.00	3.56	2.61	2.49	2.34	3.03	2.10	1.70	3.69	4.08
CDU/	East	3.05	3.56	2.71	3.11	3.00	3.18	3.46	2.57	3.44	3.38
CSU	West	3.23	3.75	2.29	3.30	3.09	2.97	3.37	2.17	3.76	3.74
FDP	East	4.08	3.83	2.27	3.54	2.27	2.46	3.17	1.91	3.36	3.17
	West	2.62	3.38	2.24	3.43	2.95	3.19	3.43	2.43	3.81	3.95
PDS	East	3.13	4.05	3.07	2.64	2.51	2.68	2.46	2.16	3.64	3.26
	West	–	–	–	–	–	–	–	–	–	–
SPD	East	3.15	4.02	2.62	3.14	3.01	3.22	3.10	2.09	3.60	3.52
	West	3.30	3.80	2.46	3.22	3.23	3.04	3.18	2.02	3.99	3.78
Other	East	3.60	3.67	3.35	2.76	2.71	2.38	2.95	2.30	4.14	3.81
	West	3.50	3.45	2.65	3.25	2.30	1.60	3.55	2.45	3.85	4.50
None	East	3.11	3.89	3.22	3.89	2.11	1.11	3.50	2.78	3.44	3.56
	West	3.40	3.60	1.40	3.40	1.80	1.00	3.83	2.40	4.33	4.17

Role variable scoring: 1 to 5 with 1 = low identification and 5 = high identification.

Source: Democracy and Local Government in Germany, Elite Surveys.

while a value of 5 entails complete acceptance of the characterization of how they see themselves.

Let me turn first to the differences and similarities that obtain across the various types of office holders in the two regions (see Table 2.23). Council members, caucus leaders and party leaders look rather similar in both regions. There are three roles that all lean toward in an appreciably positive direction in terms of self-definition. These are the roles of advocate, ombudsman and initiator. In addition, party leaders in the East also tend toward accepting the role of technician in their self-definition. Interestingly, all three of these classes of office holders appear to be relatively neutral toward the acceptance of the role of partisan politician. The only case here that contradicts this point, and only mildly so, is that of party leaders in the East; they seem more willing to characterize themselves in this way. The role of legalist is one that all three of these groups of office holders clearly reject. One interesting regional difference is that in the West the three groups seem to reject the characterization of facilitator while the same groups in the East are relatively neutral toward this self-definition. Across both regions the typical council members, caucus leaders and party leaders are relatively neutral toward the role self-definitions of broker, implementer and trustee.

The picture is markedly different for administrative department heads. The most accepted self-definition in terms of roles is that of technician. There is also a strong propensity to see oneself as an initiator and implementer. Some interesting inter-regional differences also exist. Thus, while in the West department heads take, on average, a somewhat positive stance with respect to the role of broker, those in the East are neutral toward this role. At the same time, those in the East view positively the self-description as trustee while those in the West are neutral toward this self-characterization. Something approximating neutrality holds in both regions with respect to the self-definition as legalist, ombudsman and advocate. In both regions, there is a relatively strong rejection of the roles of facilitator and partisan politician on the part of department heads.

Holders of higher office have the largest inventory of roles that they are willing to accept in their self-definition. In the East, while there is extraordinarily high acceptance of the description as ombudsman, it is not as widely shared in the West but it still meets with positive resonance. For both Eastern and Western higher officials, the self-description as initiator meets with very strong acceptance. Other role definitions that find acceptance in both regions include trustee (the role with the strongest acceptance in the West for this category of office holders), broker, advocate and technician. In addition, particularly in the East, there is some acceptance of the self-definition of implementer. As with department heads, holders of higher office in both regions appear, on average, to reject the role descriptions of facilitator, partisan politician and legalist.

In terms of inter-party differences, the focus here is exclusively on council members (see Table 2.24). Although there are some interesting inter-regional differences, most of the major variation that obtains here is to be seen across the parties. Council members, regardless of political persuasion, uniformly identify with two roles; these include the role of advocate and that of ombudsman. This holds in both the East and the West. One role that members of all political parties identify strongly within in the West is that of an initiator. This is a role that meets with positive, though weaker resonance among the parties in the East. Close to neutrality on this are the members of the Greens, the Liberal Democrats and the PDS. The role of technician meets with strong resonance in both regions only among members of the smaller parties and electoral groups. In addition, non-party council members in the West and Liberal Democratic members in the East (this latter group to a very high degree) identify with the self-description of technician.

The role of facilitator finds little resonance in the West, particularly among the council members not affiliated with any political party; in the East, there is a very mixed picture with respect to this role. Some are quite neutral, i.e., the Greens and the PDS, some reject it, the Union, Liberal Democrats and Social Democrats, and the remaining groups are strongly attracted to this role description. The role of broker is one that finds some positive acceptance among the parties in the West, although the members of the Green Party tend to reject it. In the East the broker role finds acceptance, and indeed relatively strong acceptance, only among the Liberal Democrats and those not affiliated with any political party of electoral group. Interestingly, there is a mixture of rejection and neutrality with respect to both the roles of partisan politician and implementer. The role of trustee finds generally widespread acceptance among the parties in the West but is clearly rejected by the members of the Greens. In the East this role finds strong acceptance only among the members of the Union and those not affiliated with political parties or electoral groups. Otherwise it is met with at best neutrality or rejection as in the case of both the Green Party and the PDS. Finally, there is uniform rejection in both regions for the role of legalist amongst council members of all political hues.

Accounting for Role Orientations

One of the major objectives of this chapter is to account for the differences in role orientations that exist among the local political elites. Obviously, the large number of role definitions and the variations therein that have just been described make this difficult to do. In order to resolve this problem I employed the following strategy. First, I attempted to ascertain whether (1) there exists a smaller number of underlying dimensions that capture the major variation in the role definition variables and (2) whether these dimensions could be given a meaningful interpretation. Second, having succeeded in identifying these dimension, I went on to determine the extent to which the nature of one's public office, one's political party affiliation and a variety of personal characteristics contribute to systematic variation in these general role definitions.

Table 2.25 describes the results of the principal components analysis of the ten specific role definition variables. The results, seen from a statistical perspective, are satisfactory. Approximately 50 per cent of the variation is captured by the three

Table 2.25 Principal component analysis of role orientations (based on orthogonal rotation)

Variables	Factors		
	I	II	III
Technician	.68	−.12	−.09
Legalist	.67	−.20	.11
Broker	.55	.37	.01
Trustee	.50	.17	.43
Advocate	−.16	.74	.05
Ombudsman	.04	.72	−.06
Initiator	.47	.50	−.06
Facilitator	−.03	.47	.31
Implementer	.29	−.09	.76
Partisan politician	−.36	.16	.73
Variance explained:	20.9	17.5	12.8
Eigenvalues:	2.1	1.8	1.3

Source: Democracy and Local Government in Germany, Elite Surveys.

components with eigenvalues greater than 1.0. In addition, there is generally clear delineation between the components in that most individual variables load very heavily on only one of the factors.

Substantively, the three dimensions that emerge allow for a plausible and intuitive interpretation. The first dimension has four variables that load principally on it. The two leading elements, the role of technician and that of legalist, clearly suggest a traditional administrative orientation. The other two terms, broker and trustee, do not contradict this interpretation. Indeed, both role descriptions neatly fit the kinds of orientations that one would expect of an individual carrying out public administrative duties and functions.

The second dimension appears to reflect mainly the characteristics of an individual committed to representing and serving the broad and non-partisan interests of the community in which she/he holds public office. The two dominant variables, in terms of their loadings on this component, are those of an advocate, or one who acts as a spokesperson for the general social interests and broad social groupings, and that of ombudsman, one who works to deal with the problems and interests of the average citizen. The two other terms that load principally on this dimension, initiator and facilitator, also have relatively strong connections to one or another of the other principal dimensions. Thus, the initiator role, a role of one who starts new projects and acts as a problem-solver, is also strongly connected to the general administrative dimension described above. The fourth term, facilitator, a role which suggests that the individual sees her/himself as serving the interests or organized groups (a more particularistic orientation) is also strongly linked to the third principal dimension, which will be described below. On the whole, though, this second dimension essentially appears to tap into a general role orientation that is political but at the same time non-partisan.

The third dimension reflects principally two terms. The one, which I have described as the role of implementer, refers to the role of an individual who implements what is politically allowed. The second is the partisan politician role. As noted previously, the implementer role is difficult to interpret. On the whole, though, this dimension does seem to reflect the orientation of one engaged in partisan political activity.

In a preliminary effort at determining the forces that shape the elite members' role orientations, I have used three sets of explanatory variables that may have an influence on self-definition. First, of course, I include a set of binary variables representing the type of political and/or administrative office that the elite member holds. Clearly, one can expect that purely political offices will lead individuals toward rejecting the administrative role orientation while those holding administrative offices will be more prone to having such an orientation. On the other hand, one would expect that administrative office holders would shy away from identifying with either political role orientation (non-partisan and partisan) while those with political/electoral offices would, to varying degrees, feel more comfortable with such descriptions of their roles in local governance.

A second set of factors has been introduced to reveal the extent to which partisan affiliation influences the acceptance of different types of roles. Again, binary variables capturing whether or not the individual is a member of one or another political party have been employed. No variable has been introduced for individuals without party affiliation. This means that the coefficient on any party variable captures the distance between an elite member of that party and an elite member without party membership. The influence that non-membership in any political party has is captured in the constant term of the equation.

Finally, a set of background variables that might influence role orientation has been introduced into the regression equation. Two groupings within this set reflect the family-class background of the individuals and the kind of occupational training that the elite member has had. Both groupings are composed of binary variables. In the first grouping, I include two variables. One reflects whether the individual comes from a family where the father's occupation was in the managerial or professional class ('upper'). The other reflects whether the father was a worker ('lower'). The second grouping is composed of six binary variables. Three of these six training variables specify that the training was at university, while the other three specify that the training was outside of the university. For each type of training locus, there are three binary categories: 'administrative' (e.g., law, administration, etc.), 'technical', and 'social' (including, for example, the humanities, social work, etc.).

A binary variable registering whether the individual is from the West or the East is included here as is another binary variable for gender. In addition, the age of the individual is included. Lastly, I have introduced a term meant to capture the degree to which the individual is linked to her/his community. This is a variable that represents the count of the number of types of associations in which the individual is a member.

The same specification was used for all three role orientation variables and takes the following general form:

$$Role_{i,j} = \lambda_{1,i} + \lambda_{2,i} O_{i,j} + \lambda_{3,i} P_{i,j} + \lambda_{4,i} B_{i,j} + e_{i,j}$$

where:

$Role_{i,j}$ = specific role i for individual j;
$\lambda_{1,i}, \lambda_{2,i}, \lambda_{3,i}, \lambda_{4,i}$ = regression coefficients for role i;
$O_{i,j}$ = vector of office variables for role i and individual j;
$P_{i,j}$ = vector of party affiliation variables for role i and individual j;
$B_{i,j}$ = vector of background variables (family class, training, region, gender, age, associational ties) for role i and individual j;
$e_{i,j}$ = error term for role i and individual j.

The results of the regression analyses using this specification are provided in Table 2.26. The fits of the estimated equations are reasonably good, with the adjusted R^2 varying from approximately 29 per cent for the administrative role orientation variable, to 25 per cent for the partisan politician role orientation variable and to 22 per cent for the non-partisan political role orientation variable.

Let me turn to examine the specific effects estimated for the equation dealing with the administrative role orientation (see Table 2.26, col. a). Four of the five office or position variables have statistically significant effects in the variation in the acceptance of the administrative role orientation. The most marked effects of office or position are to be found for both department heads and holders of higher office. The coefficients on these terms are both large and positive, implying greater acceptance of this description of the role that these individuals play in local governance. There is a much lower coefficient for the caucus leaders' term and given the negative effect registered for council members, this means that the total impact of holding this kind of office is approximately zero. The effect of being a council member but not simultaneously a caucus leader is statistically significant and negative. No effect is registered for the office of party leader on this role orientation variable.

All of the partisan variables, with but two exceptions, those of the terms for members of the Union and the smaller parties and electoral groups, have statistically significant and negative coefficients, implying rejection of this role orientation (at

Table 2.26 Role orientation as a function of political/administrative position, party affiliation and other characteristics: regression analyses (t-statistics in parentheses)

	(a) Administrative	(b) Non-partisan political	(c) Partisan political
Position:			
Higher office	.502	−.003	−.350
	(4.28)**	(−0.02)	(−2.08)**
Department head	.728	−.909	−.890
	(5.21)**	(−6.20)**	(−4.48)**
Party leader	−.076	−.012	.714
	(−0.77)	(−0.12)	(5.04)**
Caucus leader	.198	.100	.124
	(2.50)**	(1.16)	(1.10)
Council member	−.222	−.086	.335
	(−1.97)**	(−0.73)	(2.07)**
Party affiliation:			
Greens	−.532	.204	.384
	(−4.32)**	(1.58)	(2.17)**
CDU/CSU	−.031	.106	.468
	(−0.32)	(1.03)	(3.37)**
FDP	−.272	.076	.384
	(1.88)*	(0.50)	(1.88)*
PDS	−.490	.225	.290
	(−3.66)**	(1.60)	(1.52)
Republikaner	−.788	.007	−.545
	(−2.33)**	(0.02)	(−1.11)
SPD	−.294	.185	.662
	(−3.09)**	(1.85)*	(4.48)**
Other	.094	.377	−.485
	(0.64)	(2.33)**	(−2.32)**
Other characteristics:			
Class background, higher	−.134	.089	−.092
	(−1.73)*	(1.10)	(−0.85)
Class background, lower	−.024	.054	−.042
	(0.74)	(1.60)	(−0.98)
Training – university, admin.	.547	.036	−.539
	(3.77)**	(0.24)	(−2.56)**

Table 2.26 (continued)

	(a) Administrative	(b) Non-partisan political	(c) Partisan political
Training – university, technical	.420 (3.01)**	.180 (1.23)	–.663 (–3.28)**
Training – university, social	.164 (1.15)	.306 (2.05)**	–.561 (–2.72)**
Training – non-university, admin.	.186 (1.33)	.153 (1.04)	–.474 (–2.32)**
Training – non-university, technical	.259 (1.92)**	.191 (1.35)	–.506 (–2.58)**
Training – non-university, social	.397 (1.62)	.439 (1.71)*	–.746 (–2.08)**
Region (1 = West, 2 = East)	–.063 (–0.96)	–.003 (–0.05)	–.102 (1.10)
Age	.006 (2.26)**	.005 (1.65)*	.000 (0.06)
Gender (1 = male, 2 = female)	–.251 (–3.38)**	.066 (0.85)	.099 (0.95)
Organizational ties	.040 (2.33)**	.085 (4.64)**	–.021 (–0.86)
Constant	–1.36 (–0.50)	–.698 (–2.47)**	2.43 (6.63)**

Summary statistics:

$\bar{R}^2$	.293	.225	.249
F	18.2	11.7	13.9
(significance of F)	(<.01)	(<.01)	(<.01)
Number of cases	994	994	1,036

* Significant at .05 level.
** Significant at .10 level.

Source: Democracy and Local Government in Germany, Elite Surveys.

least relative to those without any party affiliation). This is most marked among the Republikaner, the PDS and the Green partisans. Relative to these parties' members, the Social Democrats and the Liberal Democrats only moderately reject this description of their roles.

There is a weak and negative relationship between one of the class variables, that for elite members from families in the managerial/professional class and this role orientation. Among the training variables, two of the three relating to university training register a strong positive impact. Those with university training in either technical or administrative fields have a greater propensity to accept the administrative self-description role. Among those with a non-university background it is only those with technical training that register a significant and positive effect (though less than those with a comparable training at the university level) in this equation.

Interestingly, the regional variable has no statistically discernible effect. In other words, there is no difference between local elite members in the new federal states and those in the old in terms of acceptance or rejection of the administrative role orientation. However, both gender and age play a part here. Females (in part one can assume because so few actually hold administrative offices) have a discernibly lower tendency toward accepting this role orientation; and with aging there is heightening willingness to accept this orientation. Finally, it can be seen that the scope of ties one has with the community, as captured by the association membership variable, heightens the acceptance of this role orientation.

Turning to the non-partisan political role orientation (see Table 2.26, col. b), one sees that both the office and partisan affiliation sets of variables are much diminished in their impacts. Only one office variable, that for administrative department head, weighs in with an appreciable impact on the willingness to accept this role definition. In this case, one sees that this category of elite office holders is quite unwilling to view their roles in such a way. Only two of the partisan affiliation terms have coefficients that are statistically significant, at least at the .10 level. The impact registered for the Social Democrats is moderate and positive, but only weakly significant. The impact is much stronger here for those individuals connected to smaller parties and electoral groups. These latter elites seem more willing to accept this characterization as an appropriate description of the role they play in local governance.

Neither of the family-class background variables appears to influence the willingness to accept this non-partisan political role definition. With respect to the training background of these individuals, one sees that it is only those with training in the non-administrative and non-technical fields, be it at university or outside university, that register any significant difference in their acceptance of this role description; in both cases such a background appears to increase the willingness to accept this role definition.

Again, there are no differences between elites from the new federal states and those from the old. Age plays a role in the willingness to accept the characterization of a non-partisan politician with older people being more prone to accept this definition of themselves than are younger people. Finally, associational affiliation appears to play part in the willingness to see one's self as filling such a role. As with the administrative role, wider associational ties heighten the acceptance of the role of non-partisan politician.

Let me now turn to the last role orientation, that of partisan politician (see Table 2.26, col. c). The office that one holds appears to play a significant part in shaping acceptance or rejection of this role orientation. Administrative department heads are very unwilling to describe themselves in this way. While the impact of holding higher office also lowers the willingness to accept this characterization of one's role in local governance, the estimated effect is smaller than that found for departmental heads. Not surprisingly, being a local party leader pushes one toward acceptance of this role definition. This is less the case with council members. Interestingly, caucus leaders are not appreciably more willing to accept this characterization of their roles than are other council members. The willingness to accept this role definition is clearly greater for the elites belonging to political parties than it is among those with no party affiliation. This is most marked in the case of Social Democrats as well as the Christian Democrats. However, neither the Republikaner nor those affiliated with the PDS are distinguishable (at least statistically) from those aligned with no party. Members of smaller parties and electoral groups strongly reject this role definition.

Family class background again appears to have no appreciable effect. All of the training variables register relatively strong, negative impacts on the willingness to accept this role definition. None of the other background variables appears to have an effect on the willingness to accept the partisan politician role orientation.

Rating One's Own Success in Influencing Policy

Participation in politics and government stems to a major degree from a desire to influence public affairs. To what extent are these elites successful in achieving this objective? An answer to this question can be provided by examining the responses of the elites to a battery of questions about the extent of their influence in 12 policy and political areas.[29] Table 2.27 summarizes the situation in the two regions. In both regions around 20 per cent responded that they had no significant influence in any of these areas. About an equal share claimed to have significant influence in only one area. The relative frequencies with which such claims to exerting significant influence occur then taper off. Still, over 30 per cent in the West (and nearly 30 per cent in the East) claimed great influence in four or more areas, with 4 to 5 per cent claiming such influence in seven or more of these areas.

---

29 The respondents were asked whether they had a lot of influence, little influence, or no influence on the following areas in their community: (1) economic development, (2) housing, (3) environmental protection, (4) improvements in public infrastructure and services, (5) public health, (6) culture, leisure time activities and sport, (7) education, (8) the activities of political organizations, (9) taxes and spending, (10) public order and security, (11) social services and welfare and (12) employment. Of course, a local politician or administrator would not necessarily see all of these areas as within her/his province. However, the vast majority of these areas fall within the domain of local government responsibilities in the German system.

Table 2.27 Self-evaluated scope of influence on public affairs (per cent indicating significant influence on one or more of 12 areas of policy/politics)

Number of areas where significant influence claimed	East	West
None	23	20
1	22	20
2	17	14
3	11	14
4	9	11
5	8	11
6	5	6
7 or more	5	4

Source: Democracy and Local Government in Germany, Elite Surveys.

A comparison of the local elites in the two German regions with other nations' local elites on this dimension is presented in Table 2.28. By international standards, neither set of German elites does poorly in terms of the scope of influence they believe available to themselves. For example, West German elites clearly see themselves as far less restricted in the influence they exert than do the local elites in other Western nations. 48 per cent assert that they influence on none or only one of the twelve areas; this compares favorably with the range observed across the Western nations, 56 per cent to 63 per cent. The average number of policy areas where influence is claimed West German local elites is 2.6. By contrast, the Swiss and Austrian elites claim influence, on average, in 2.1 areas, while the Spanish, Dutch and American elites all average claims of 1.9. The Swedes lag behind with average of 1.6. While East German elites are slightly more pessimistic than their West German colleagues in their assessments of the scope of influence they possess, they nevertheless compare favorably with their peers in the transitional democracies of Central Europe, trailing only slightly the Polish elites and far outstripping the Hungarian, Czech and Slovak elites. In sum, by international standards, the typical member of the East and West German local elites does not betray a sense of inefficacy with respect to their influence on local policy and political issues.

There is really very little difference in the patterns across the two regions of Germany on this issue. Holders of higher office lead in terms of the scope of influence they claim to have (on average, in close to four areas), while administrative department heads trail all other categories, claiming on average to having appreciable influence in less than two areas of public affairs. In the town/city councils, caucus leaders appear to have greater scope of influence than the other members. Leaders of

Table 2.28 International comparison: local elites' self-evaluated scope of influence on public affairs (average number of policy/politics areas where significant influence claimed; 12 possible areas)

Country	Average number	Country	Average number
East Germany	2.4	West Germany	2.6
Czech Republic	2.1	Austria	2.1
Hungary	0.7	Netherlands	1.9
Poland	2.5	Spain	1.9
Slovakia	1.7	Sweden	1.6
		Switzerland	2.2
		United States*	1.9

* US figure is a weighted number based on 11 (not 12) areas.

Source: Democracy and Local Government International Data Base.

the local party organizations do not appear to assess their roles as being terribly influential.[30]

What about the levels of self-assessed scope of influence across the different partisan groupings? There are some notable differences both within and between the two regions. In the West, members of the Greens and those not affiliated with any political party trail well behind the other groupings in their assessments of the influence they claim for themselves (less than 2). The averages for the other four groups in this region are rather close to each other, ranging from 2.6 to 2.9. In the East, the PDS, the FDP and the non-partisan group fall well below the regional average in terms of the scope of influence (all below 2). In both East and West, the members of the two leading parties, the Union and the Social Democrats, clearly lead all the others in terms of the scope of influence they claim to exercise (nearly 3 on average).

One notable aspect of the scope of perceived influence among these elites is the extent to which it is tied to their assessments of how well local democracy works in their communities. Table 2.29 summarizes the situation, where it is particularly clear among the Western local elites that the greater the scope of influence an elite member claims to have, the smaller the likelihood that he or she will be dissatisfied with the performance of democracy in the community. There are at least two possible interpretations one might give to this finding.

One suggests a rather non-civic attitude: if one cannot effectively shape policy in a democracy, then, the system itself is not functioning well as a democracy. This is a

---

30 The relevant figures for council member in the East and West are, respectively, 2.4 and 2.9. Eastern caucus leaders in councils claim an average of 2.4 while their Western colleagues have an average of nearly 3. Party leaders in the East and West claim an average of about 2.1.

Table 2.29 Perceived influence and dissatisfaction with the way local democracy functions (per cent)

Number of areas where significant influence claimed	Dissatisfied with local democracy in	
	East	West
None	40	25
1	30	32
2	24	22
3	31	12
4	28	7
5	33	13
6	16	15
7 or more	14	0

Source: Democracy and Local Government in Germany, Elite Surveys.

rather self-centered way of assessing the performance of a democratic system where almost by default unless one has one's way, then one's assessment of the functioning of the system deteriorates. The alternative view would suggest that given the status of these individuals, democratically elected or else appointed to office by democratically elected officials, it is a reasonable and civic-minded point of view. If in a democracy those occupying offices of public trust are charged with carrying out the will of the electorate, then the lack of serious influence on policy matters should naturally lead the official to be disappointed in the way the supposedly democratic system is operating.

Conclusion

The findings reported here, taken in conjunction with those of Aberbach et al. (1981) and Hoffmann-Lange (1992) and Hoffmann-Lange and Bürklin (1998) suggest that local political/administrative elites are less prone than those at higher levels of government in Germany to come from privileged backgrounds. Nonetheless, they conform to the 'law of increasing disproportion' that marks the hierarchy of elites worldwide. Less privileged, more representative, at least in terms of class backgrounds, than those in analogous position at higher levels of government, these elites still have backgrounds that make it clear that they do not conform to the participatory democratic image of a governing elite. Their origins are largely working class, though not completely in conformity with the society from which they have emerged. They are much more likely, at least relative to the general population, to have had a university education. This latter characteristic is particularly pronounced in the new federal states and is becoming progressively more apparent in the older federal states.

More than the general population, though clearly less than elites at the federal level, a goodly number also come from families where the parents were involved in politics or official life. Still, these elites do not conform to an image of a local governing class where dominance of the local scene passes from one generation to the next. Indeed, most spring from places outside of the communities in which they now serve in public office. Here, again, it should be noted that at least at this level of government there is no evidence to support the notion that the East has been 'colonized' by the West. The form of government that marks cities and towns in the new federal states clearly derives from the West (indeed all five of the new federal states have adopted variants of the South German Council constitutional form for local government). Nevertheless, the personnel that have taken up elective and appointive offices at the local government level in East Germany are overwhelmingly natives of the former GDR and neither transplants nor carpetbaggers from the West. In addition, while overwhelmingly not natives of these communities, most of the members of these elites, both East and West, have spent significant proportions of their lives in these towns and cities.

In the West many members of these elites have long years of experiences in politics and/or public administration. Indeed, quite a large number have served for extensive periods of time in the offices that they presently hold. The picture in the East is starkly different for the most part. Outside of the PDS, and to some extent the two former block parties of the GDR, viz., the CDU and the FDP, the elite members are quite new to official life and have held both party membership and political/administrative office for only a short period of time.

In terms of demographic characteristics, the local government elites in both West and East share many traits with their peers in other long-established democracies (Eldersveld et al., 1995) as well in those systems that have recently emerged within the post-communist countries of Central Europe (Baldersheim et al., 1996). These elites are typically male and middle-aged. On average they have a far greater likelihood of having had a university education than their fellow citizens and are more likely to hold professional and white-collar jobs. In sum, they are not especially representative of the socio-economic patterns that characterize their communities. Nevertheless, they are clearly well-integrated within their communities. Typically long-time residents, they have a wide range of associational ties, though these more often than not reflect the political orientations of the parties of which they are members and a large number of individuals and groups within the community upon whom they rely.

It has been shown that these elite members define themselves in terms of three distinct political/administrative roles. For the most part, the constraints of the offices that they hold play an important role in this self-definition. Party affiliation is sometimes important as well. Class background seems to be unimportant is shaping role orientation but training background does play a role to varying extents. No independent effect was discovered that would allow one to distinguish between elites members in the new federal states and those from the old. An important variable in shaping orientation toward non-partisan and non-political orientations is the breadth of associational affiliation.

Chapter 3

Ideological Values of Elites and Citizens

Introduction

It is often argued that the ideologies and values that individuals bring to the political sphere greatly influence their behavior, and this in turn has important consequences for the workings of the political system. In this chapter, I examine some important aspects of the political culture of the two parts of Germany with an eye to differences and similarities in their political cultures. Barnes (1994) has suggested that one useful approach to the analysis of political culture is to distinguish among three levels: (1) directly observed things (such as symbols or behavior), (2) beliefs and values and, finally, (3) shared assumptions and meanings. The focus of this chapter is on the latter two elements with more emphasis given to beliefs and values than to the level of shared meanings. As throughout this book, much of the evidence brought to bear on this question is drawn from local elites in East and West Germany. In addition, the elites of the two regions are compared to local elites in other democratic systems as well as to the citizens within these regions.

The chapter first examines the elites in terms of the ways in which they define democracy. The examination is intended to assess the degree to which the local elites in the two regions of Germany share common assumptions about the meaning of democracy. It then goes on to identify principal ideological dimensions underlying the political cultures of the two regions. The ideologies of the local elites of East and West German local elites are then compared with those of the local elites in a number of other industrialized democracies. The elites of different political parties in terms of their ideological positions are then contrasted; a similar effort is made with respect to the citizenry in both regions. Finally, a theoretical argument that might account for individuals' ideological orientations among both the elites and the broader population is presented and empirically evaluated.

Differences in the Meaning of Democracy?

Local elites in both parts of Germany now operate under the same institutional framework of representative democracy. However, do they view this framework in the same way? Yoder (1999, pp. 124–5), in her study of Eastern state parliamentarians, summarizes the prevailing opinion that, while there is no fundamental difference in views on basic political rights between the elites in both regions of Germany, there is far greater belief in a social-egalitarian and participatory view of democracy among

Eastern elites. Robert Rohrschneider's work (1994, 1996a, b; 1999) on local government elites in the two parts of reunited Berlin studied this question in some detail.

Rohrschneider produced his evidence from personal interviews with city parliamentarians of Berlin in 1992 and 1995. Taking the responses to the open-ended question ('The term democracy is frequently used without further specification these days. What seem to you personally the essentials of democracy?'), he coded these in accordance with a scheme originally developed by Putnam (1973) in his study of British and Italian national elites. These were then selectively grouped into ten broad categories.[1] Attempting to assess two models of the sources of political values, Rohrschneider evaluated elite responses to this question. He was particularly interested in inter-regional as well as inter-generational differences. The concern for these differences arose out of two models of value generation, the one model one emphasizing socialization and the other value diffusion.

His results led him to conclude that there were important differences in how these elites of the two regions conceived of democracy. As it turned out, there were two areas of democratic values where elites in the two parts of the city differed appreciably. These were the same views Yoder mentions: social equality and direct democracy. East Berlin elites were particularly more prone to state that to them personally both social equality and direct democracy are essential elements of democracy. Furthermore, there were clearly generational differences on these two elements among the elites in East Berlin, with those of the post-war generation far more likely to see these two elements as essential elements of democracy.

Here we can take advantage of the broader sample developed for this study to look once again at this issue. A similarly worded open-ended question ('There are different views about democracy. What does it mean to you?') was posed to the elite respondents. The answers to these questions were then coded into a large number of different categories. The results from this coding effort are presented in Table 3.2 along with the results developed by Rohrschneider (1994, 1999) in his study of East and West Berlin city council members in 1992 and the follow-up study of East Berlin council members in 1995.

---

1   Table 3.1 contains the coding scheme. It is based on a scheme originally developed and employed by Putnam (1973) and modified by Rohrschneider (1994, 1999).

The data in Table 3.2 are based on coding of the responses to the open-ended question. The first five responses were coded, thus the figures may add up to more than 100 per cent. Note, although Rohrschneider's (1994) tabulations for East and West Berlin elites in 1992 are the same as those reported in his 1999 publication, he reports in 1994 that the percentages were based on up to five responses and in 1999 that they are based on up to six responses. Here is the pattern in the number of responses provided by the elites in this study:

Number of responses	0	1	2	3	4	5+
Percentage of respondents	6.1	30.8	21.8	18.4	8.7	14.2

Table 3.1 Categories and coding schemes for respondents' conceptions of democracy*

Rohrschneider's categories	Putnam's categories	Item numbers	Titles of Putnam's categories / Descriptions of items
			Government by the people
Government by the people	1	11	Government by the people (popular control, control by the people)
Government by the people	1	12	Popular interest in and awareness of politics
Government by the People	1	13	Government based on consent (responsibility or answerability of government to the people, electoral mandate)
	1	14	Dialogue between the government and the people (with both taking an active role in decision-making)
Active participation	1	15	Popular participation (an active role for the people; popular-decision-making, direct democracy in the context of parliamentary democracy, 'Mitsprache')
Direct democracy	1	16	Direct democracy (referenda for important decisions, 'Runde Tische')
	1	17	Government close to the people (decentralized government, communal self-government)
	1	18	Decisions taken in public (no secrecy, public informed about policy, public debate)
	1	19	Other aspects of government by the people (frequently actions taken in the interest of citizens)
			Equality and social democracy
Social equality	2	21	Equality in general
Social equality	2	22	Political equality (one person, one vote)
Social equality	2	23	Equality of opportunity (each person has the possibility to develop herself/himself as far as possible)

Table 3.1 (continued)

Rohrschneider's categories	Putnam's categories	Item numbers	Titles of Putnam's categories / Descriptions of items
			Equality and social democracy (continued)
Social equality	2	24	Just standard of living (freedom from want; social and economic security for all, social justice)
Social equality	2	25	Classless society (less social distance, fewer rich and poor, less social privilege)
Social equality	2	26	Social ownership/control over the economy (industrial democracy)
Social equality	2	27	Minimum social security (right to a job)
Social equality	2	28	Gender equality
Social equality	2	29	Other equality (among others: multiculturalism)
			Liberty
Civil rights/limited government	3	31	Liberty (freedom in general)
Civil rights/limited government	3	32	Political or civic liberties in general
Civil rights/limited government	3	33	Freedom of expression (speech, press, etc., as well as freedom of thought)
Civil rights/limited government	3	34	Minority rights
Civil rights/limited government	3	35	Limited government (checks and balance, no arbitrary power, separation of powers)
Civil rights/limited government	3	36	Laissez-faire, socially and economically (freedom from government interference in socio-economic affairs, market economy)
	3	37	Religious liberty
	3	39	Other aspects of liberty

Table 3.1 (continued)

Rohrschneider's categories	Putnam's categories	Item numbers	Titles of Putnam's categories / Descriptions of items
			Government institutions and procedures
Political competition	4	41	Elections
Political competition	4	42	Majority rights
Political competition	4	43	Representative or parliamentary government in general
Political competition	4	44	Parliamentary or legislative control over the executive
Political competition	4	45	Rule of law
	4	46	Constitutionalism
	4	48	Independent judiciary
	4	49	Other aspect of government institutions and procedures (including justice)
			Political competition and choice
	5	51	Possibility of government changes (majority may become the minority)
Political competition	5	52	Party competition (more than one party)
Political competition	5	53	Strong, critical opposition
Political competition	5	54	Elite competition
	5	55	Possibility of removal (of individual execute or representative disapproved of by the electoral)
	5	59	Other aspects of political competition
			Societal conditions
Social competition	6	61	Pluralism (variety of private associations and institutions)
Social Competition	6	62	Consultation (by the government with groups and organizations)

Table 3.1 (continued)

Rohrschneider's categories	Putnam's categories	Item numbers	Titles of Putnam's categories / Descriptions of items
			Societal conditions (continued)
	6	63	Parties (as centers of representation and participation)
	6	64	Absence of party discipline
	6	65	Decentralized institutions
	6	66	Ecologically sound politics
	6	69	Other social conditions (including pluralism of views, welfare, compromises among groups)
			Characteristics of citizens
Citizens' responsibility	7	71	Mature, educated, intelligent citizens
Citizens' responsibility	7	72	Liberty, not license (freedom to do what is right, individual self-control)
Citizens' responsibility	7	73	Assumption of responsibilities and duties
Citizens' responsibility	7	74	Action in interest of the collective (solidarity)
Citizens' responsibility	7	75	Reciprocal respect and tolerance
	7	79	Other characteristics of citizens
			Other
	8	81	Strong, stable, effective, disciplined government
	8	82	National tradition
	8	83	Best/only form of government
	8	84	Best possible form of government despite its flaws
	8	85	Peaceful, secure, non-violent form of government

Table 3.1 (continued)

Rohrschneider's categories	Putnam's categories	Item numbers	Titles of Putnam's categories Descriptions of items
			Other (continued)
	8	86	Competent (people have a chance to make technically correct decisions, even if citizens oppose this)
	8	89	Other

* This coding scheme based on that originally developed by Putnam (1973) and modified by Rohrschneider (1994). The following should be noted:

- Putnam category 1: Rohrschneider dropped 14 ('dialogue') and combined 'popular participation' and 'direct democracy'; these latter two are treated here as two distinct answers; 17 ('decentralized government') and 18 ('public decisions') added.
- Putnam category 2: Following Rohrschneider Putnam's 'equality of respect' has been dropped and 27 ('social security') as well as 28 ('gender equality') have been added.
- Putnam category 4: Following Rohrschneider Putnam's 'administrative due process' has been dropped. Unlike Rohrschneider Putnam's 'constitutionalism' has been reinserted; furthermore, Rohrschneider's 'defensible democracy' has been eliminated and 48 ('independent judiciary') has been added.
- Putnam category 5: Rohrschneider dropped 55 ('possibility of removing individual') from Putnam's list; it has been retained here. As did Rohrschneider, Putnam's 'elected oligarchy' has been deleted.
- Putnam category 6: Following Rohrschneider, Putnam's 'discussion' and 'pluralism of press' have been deleted and 66 ('decentralized institutions') as well as 66 ('ecologically sound politics') have been added.
- Putnam category 8: 82 through 86 are in neither Putnam's nor Rohrschneider's lists.

Sources: Putnam (1973); Rohrschneider (1994; 1999); Democracy and Local Government in Germany, Elite Surveys.

Table 3.2 Conceptions of democracy*: regional and generational differences – a comparison between Rohrschneider's Berlin local elites and local elites included in this study (per cent expressing view)

	This study		Berlin study		
	East	West	East (1995)	East (1992)	West (1992)
Government by the people	10.6	11.5	13.9	26.6	25.8
Pre-war	12.4	10.3	20.0	24.4	26.1
Post-war	9.2	12.7	6.7	29.4	25.6
Social equality	9.2	6.4	46.2	35.4	7.9
Pre-war	12.0	7.4	40.0	28.9	10.9
Post-war	7.3	5.4	53.3	44.1	4.7
Active participation	21.8	19.2	6.2	17.7	12.4
Pre-war	19.1	13.5	8.6	13.3	13.0
Post-war	23.7	24.8	3.3	23.5	11.0
Direct democracy	3.5	1.6	35.4	25.3	2.2
Pre-war	4.0	0.6	25.7	13.3	0.0
Post-war	3.2	1.5	46.7	41.2	4.7
Equality of opportunity	14.6	12.8	1.5	3.8	7.9
Pre-war	15.1	11.3	–	2.2	4.3
Post-war	14.2	14.3	3.3	5.9	11.6
Civil rights/limited government	36.6	46.5	80.0	64.6	73.0
Pre-war	36.0	47.4	77.1	77.1	69.6
Post-war	37.0	45.5	83.3	55.9	76.7
Institutions	24.0	21.6	56.9	40.5	60.7
Pre-war	24.0	21.6	57.1	51.1	58.7
Post-war	24.2	21.7	56.7	26.5	62.8
Political competition	5.2	2.2	9.2	20.3	30.3
Pre-war	5.3	2.6	11.4	22.2	32.6
Post-war	5.1	1.9	6.7	17.6	27.9
Societal competition	2.2	1.7	4.6	17.7	19.1
Pre-war	2.2	1.4	8.6	17.8	15.2
Post-war	2.2	1.9	–	17.6	23.3
Citizen's responsibility	14.6	19.2	18.5	8.9	7.9
Pre-war	14.2	17.1	28.6	6.2	13.0
Post-war	14.9	21.3	6.7	11.8	2.3

* The dimensions used here are based on Rohrschneider's (1994, 1999) reformulations of Putnam's (1973) categories. Note that the sum of the columns add up to more than 100 because of the possibility of including up to three responses for each individual.

Sources: Rohrschneider (1994; 1999); Democracy and Local Government in Germany, Elite Surveys.

As noted above, Rohrschneider found some significant differences between East and West Berlin local government elites. East Berlin parliamentarians were particularly more prone to see democracy in terms of social equality and direct democracy. For example, in 1992, more than a third of the Easterners defined democracy in terms of social equality while less than one in twelve of the Westerners held similar views. Simultaneously a quarter of the Easterners defined democracy in direct democratic terms while only 2 per cent of the Westerners did so.

Such differences in the meaning of democracy are not evident among the broader group of East and West German local elites included in the present study. Here one sees that by far fewer Easterners suggest that social equality is a part of their definition of democracy; indeed there is very little difference between the elites of the two regions on this point. The same absence holds for the other difference in essentials, direct democracy.

Indeed, this definition of democracy hardly registers at all among the local elites in either region. The only appreciable difference that does emerge between the elites of the two regions is with respect to civil rights/limited government. While this item appears to be the category most likely to be named by either elite group, there is a tendency for Westerners to give it more emphasis in their definition of democracy. Note that the absence of the marked differences in definitions of democracy in this broader study of local elites is not the product of sampling differences in terms of party affiliation between this study and Rohrschneider's.[2] Rather, it may be the case that the extraordinary situation of both parts of Berlin prior to the collapse of the GDR promoted rather peculiar elite political cultures on both sides of the Berlin Wall.

Five dimensions stand out in terms of local elites definitions of democracy. These include civil rights/limited government, institutions, active citizen participation, citizen responsibility and equality of opportunity. On none of these dimensions is there a large difference between the positions of the two regions' local government/political elites. If sum, there appears to be a shared set of conceptions about the meaning of democracy in the political cultures of the local elites in the two regions. While this community of meaning holds, is it also the case that ideological values are also shared across the two regions? We turn next to evidence on this question.

Ideological Values: A First Cut

As noted in the introductory chapter, this study was conducted in conjunction with the International Project on Democracy and Local Governance. One of the principal aims of the project has to been uncover the main ideological divisions that characterize local government elites. In a number of studies (Jacob et al., 1966; Jacob, Ostrowski

---

2 Information on the samples is to be found on page 57 of Rohrschneider (1999) and the Appendix to this book.

Table 3.3 Democracy and Local Governance Project's ideological dimensions

Political	Economic	Miscellaneous
Necessity and legitimacy of political opposition and conflict	Importance of economic development	Importance of honesty in public affairs
Commitment to meaningful citizen particiation in political process	Support for capitalism	Local versus national concerns
Support for political equality	Support for economic equality	
Support for minority rights		

Source: International Project on Democracy and Local Governance questionnaire.

and Teune, 1993; Eldersveld, Strömberg and Derksen, 1995), use has been made of a large cluster of scales that putatively capture many of the intrinsically important ideological characteristics of local elites. Of central concern has been the extent to which consensus and diversity prevail with respect to these ideological traits. The scales embodying these ideological dimensions are presented in Table 3.3.[3] Indeed, the standardized international questionnaire contains over 50 items that have been employed to capture this array of ideological values.

Let us examine each of the principal dimensions in some detail.[4] The first deals with acceptance of the necessity and legitimacy of political opposition and conflict. The core of this ideological concept is the idea that elites (and citizens) will have very different preferences as to whether they hold that conflict should be avoided or, alternatively, believe that conflict is normal and necessary part of democratic politics (Eldersveld et al., 1995, p. 179). Items meant to capture this ideological dimension include queries regarding the necessity for unanimity on public decisions and the need for the preservation of harmony even at the cost of failing to implement necessary community programs. Also included are questions dealing with whether leaders

---

3   Note that in the 1990s a tenth putative dimension based on a number of different questions dealing with respect for the 'Rule of Law' was added to the international project's questionnaire.
4   At the time of this study, there were indeed 53 items in the international project's standardized questionnaire. The elite survey conducted in Germany reduced this number to 43. In the presentation of results on the international project's scales, four items related to a new scale, dealing with the 'rule of law' are excluded as are three other items that are connected to one or another of the nine scales presented.

should refrain from making necessary and important proposals if these might divide the community, as well as whether community leaders who focus heavily on resolving conflicts are prone to be remiss in carrying out effective and successful policies.

The second major dimension of ideology relates to popular political participation. The focus of the questions tapping this dimension is on the commitment to meaningful citizen participation in the political process. It should be pointed out, however, that the items that supposedly tap this dimension are heterogeneous mixture of concerns with self-management and citizen participation (Jacob et al., 1971, pp. 74–5). The items here focus on the desirability of leaving decisions to experts as well as the lack of necessity for popular participation in decision-making when choices can be placed in the hands of trusted and competent leaders. In addition, attention also centers on the belief that widespread political participation leads to undesirable conflict as well as the belief that voting rights should be restricted to only those who are fully informed on public issues.

The third dimension focuses on the support for political equality. In reality, it would appear that there are striking similarities to the focus found in the questions dealing with the political participation dimension. Thus, one finds items concerned with whether all people really know their own best interests and questions that trace agreement or disagreement with the need to restrict decision-making to traditional, meritocratic, or strong leaders.

The fourth dimension concerns itself with support for minority rights. Here emphasis is on such issues as restrictions on the rights of a majority to impose its will on the minority, the responsibility of government to see that all the rights of minorities are protected, guaranteeing the prerogatives of minorities to organize and resist government initiatives, as well as the minimum right of the minority to oppose but not resist majority decisions.

The fifth through seventh dimensions shift focus away from concerns about democratic values and concentrate on economic ideology. The first of these dimensions centers on the importance of economic development. Most of the items here emphasize tradeoffs between the importance of economic development and other concerns. In addition, one item emphasizes the value of such development in promoting the general welfare. The sixth dimension is meant to tap support for capitalism as an economic system. In addition to two items measuring normative evaluations of the capitalist system, two other items deal with beliefs about the role that government should or should not play in the operation of the economy. The last of the three economic dimensions deals with support for economic equality. The different items focus on normative evaluations of positions on distributional and redistributional issues.

Finally, there are two other dimensions, one dealing with localism and the other with honesty. The first of these focuses on the relative priority of local affairs over national affairs. The items here deal with such issues as the willingness to tolerate costs to the local community in order to achieve national goals and the priority to be given to national concerns given that there are significant local problems.

Table 3.4 An international comparison of local elites' ideological values: international project scales (average positions*)

	East Germany	CZ	H	PL	SK	West Germany	A	NL	E	S	CH	US
Conflict	0.65	0.58	0.60	0.55	0.57	0.66	0.52	0.68	0.50	0.65	0.58	[0.60]
Participation	0.68	0.56	0.50	0.43	0.55	0.72	0.62	0.69	[.66]	0.80	0.71	0.70
Minority rights	0.55	0.52	0.48	0.53	0.50	0.56	0.59	0.59	[.56]	0.58	0.56	0.59
Political equality	0.56	0.51	0.43	0.47	0.53	0.59	0.50	0.44	[.58]	0.75	0.50	0.65
Economic development	0.74	0.61	0.70	0.67	0.64	0.66	0.60	0.51	0.59	0.63	0.64	–
Capitalism	0.54	0.65	0.57	0.64	0.62	0.63	0.55	0.51	0.41	0.58	0.64	0.66
Economic equality	0.49	0.44	0.41	0.34	0.46	0.39	0.49	0.34	0.65	0.52	0.37	0.32
Honesty	0.76	0.68	0.62	0.74	0.70	0.76	0.70	0.53	0.66	0.77	0.69	–
Localism	0.62	[0.56]	0.57	0.59	[0.58]	0.60	0.54	0.42	0.52	0.54	0.47	–

CZ: Czech Republic; H: Hungary; PL: Poland; SK: Slovakia; A: Austria; NL: Netherlands; E: Spain; S: Sweden; CH: Switzerland

* Using four common items per scale. Final score = (sum of scores – #questions) / (#questions * 4). Range for Final Score = 0 – 1.0. Each item has four responses.

Source: Democracy and Local Government International Data Base.

The last ideological dimension is concerned with the importance of honesty in public affairs. Items here concentrate on the importance of truthfulness, the appropriateness of concealing information about policy failures and the legitimacy of not engaging in full disclosure.

Table 3.4 provides an overview of how the two German regions' local government elites line up on these nine ideological value dimensions and contrasts these positions with those of local elites in other long-established and transitional democracies. The number presented in each cell is the average for the dimension which itself is captured by a summated scale ranging from 0 to 1.0, with a higher score standing for greater support for the ideological value. A value of .5 can be interpreted as neutrality with respect to the ideological value and a value below that score can be seen as indicative of lack of commitment or, indeed, opposition to the ideological goal.

The East German elites appear to be relatively more attached to libertarian political rights than do their peers in the transitional democracies in Central Europe. They clearly score higher than these elites in their support for the legitimacy of conflict and popular participation and are slightly more supportive of minority rights and political equality. In this, they display a great similarity to their West German colleagues who themselves are generally among the highest scoring of the local elites on these dimensions in the more established democracies. The East German local elites stand in marked contrast to the Hungarian local elites who are far less favorably disposed toward popular participation, minority rights and political equality.

Simultaneously, the East German local elites also appear to be wedded to a more 'non-capitalistic' and, simultaneously, 'egalitarian' ideology than the elites from the other former Communist states. In this, though, they are not very different from the local elites of some of the more established democracies, in particular, Austria and Sweden. By contrast, the West German elites are far and away more supportive of the capitalist system and much less enamored of the ideal of economic equality.

On the two miscellaneous ideological dimensions, the local elites in both East and West Germany stand out. They appear to be among the most committed to honesty in public affairs and are also among the most supportive of giving priority to local over national affairs.

A more differentiated view of the local elites in the two regions of Germany can be found by examining the positions held by members of the various political parties. Data on these positions are provided in Table 3.5. In the broadest terms, across the two regions, there is very little difference between the two sets of elites on the political ideological values as well as the two miscellaneous dimensions of 'honesty' and 'localism'. It is in the area of economic ideology where one sees indications of substantive difference. On the whole, the Eastern elites value 'economic development' as well as 'economic equality' more highly than their peers in the West do. Similarly, they manifest far less support for 'capitalism' than their colleagues do in the other region.

There are, moreover, some radical differences across the parties in the two parts of Germany. In both regions, for example, partisan-based differences on the valuation

Table 3.5 Germany: party-regional differences on international project scales (average scale positions*)

East Germany:	Total	Greens	CDU/CSU	FDP	PDS	SPD	Other	Non-partisan
Conflict	0.65	0.65	0.63	0.66	0.64	0.67	0.64	0.68
Participation	0.68	0.73	0.63	0.66	0.77	0.68	0.71	0.64
Minority rights	0.55	0.67	0.46	0.44	0.70	0.55	0.66	0.48
Political equality	0.56	0.62	0.46	0.54	0.67	0.58	0.53	0.53
Economic development	0.74	0.54	0.80	0.84	0.68	0.76	0.80	0.77
Capitalism	0.54	0.48	0.67	0.65	0.34	0.51	0.53	0.58
Economic equality	0.49	0.57	0.37	0.27	0.74	0.49	0.52	0.40
Honesty	0.76	0.81	0.70	0.72	0.90	0.72	0.76	0.75
Localism	0.62	0.55	0.60	0.53	0.66	0.65	0.58	0.62
West Germany:								
Conflict	0.66	0.68	0.66	0.62	–	0.66	0.64	0.65
Participation	0.72	0.82	0.69	0.65	–	0.75	0.68	0.69
Minority rights	0.56	0.72	0.47	0.55	–	0.61	0.55	0.49
Political equality	0.59	0.72	0.53	0.46	–	0.64	0.53	0.58
Economic development	0.66	0.44	0.74	0.74	–	0.65	0.66	0.69
Capitalism	0.63	0.49	0.73	0.75	–	0.54	0.72	0.69
Economic equality	0.39	0.57	0.26	0.25	–	0.51	0.34	0.31
Honesty	0.76	0.83	0.72	0.69	–	0.76	0.82	0.74
Localism	0.60	0.52	0.61	0.60	–	0.60	0.70	0.59

* Using four common items per scale. Final score = (sum of scores − #questions) / (#questions * 4). Range for Final Score = 0 − 1.0. Each item has four responses.

Source: Democracy and Local Government in Germany, Elite Surveys.

of economic equality are very sharp. In the East, both the SPD and the PDS stand out in their commitment to the goal of 'economic equality' while the FDP and the Union elites are quite unsupportive of this goal. Interestingly, while there are also sharp differences amongst elites on this goal in the West, the two partisan groupings with the highest scores on this dimension, the SPD and the Greens are rather neutral in terms of their commitment to this goal.

In the political area, as well, partisan differences are particularly pronounced when one examines the profiles of the Greens and the PDS on one side and the Union and FDP on the other. The elites in the first two parties are particularly supportive of 'participation', 'minority rights' and 'political equality', while the Union and FDP elites generally hold more neutral positions, particularly with respect to 'minority rights' and 'political equality'. Note as well that not only do the PDS elites stand out on their stated commitment to democratic political rights and leftist economic values, they seem to value 'honesty' more highly than any other partisan grouping.

Ideological Values: A More Refined View

Further analyses of the ideological values data for the German as well as the other nation's local elites, however, indicates that these scales are really not as strong as has generally been assumed by the DLG research group. Indeed, quite a few items line up in ways that differ from what have been taken for granted in earlier studies.[5] This point can be illustrated with the results from an analysis of the data drawn from the German study. Initially a principal components analysis of the entire battery of the 43 'values' items in the German elite survey questionnaire was undertaken. This identified eleven underlying dimensions (using as the criterion an eigenvalue of 1.0 or greater). Those items which did not have a loading of .5 or greater on any of the dimension were then dropped; this reduced the number of items by eleven. The remaining 32 items were again subjected to a principal components analysis and this produced a set of nine factors. The results from this analysis are presented in Table 3.6 where for purposes of clarity only the largest factor loading of each of the 32 items is reported. Here one can see that the two strongest dimensions do not conform to any of the nine DLG scales. The first of these two is a combination of elements from two different DLG scales, namely 'economic equality' and 'capitalism'. The second is similar to the first in that it is composed of items from two scales, in this case 'political equality' and 'participation'.

Less problematic are four other reputed scales. Thus, the 'localism' dimension (3rd factor) is generally reproducible in the analysis of the German data, as is 'economic development' (4th factor), 'conflict' (the 7th factor) and the new dimension in the DLG battery, 'rule of law' (the 8th factor). However, the fifth and sixth factors produced in the analysis of the German elite data, which are labeled 'openness to citi-

---

5   See the country studies included in Jacob, Ostrowski and Teune (1993).

Table 3.6 Basic political values: results from principal component analysis*

Variables with principal loading on factor I	Loading on factor
V242 – There should be an upper limit on income so that no one earns very much more than others**	.78
V266 – Discrepancies in salaries should be continually reduced	.75
V247 – The government has the responsibility to see that nobody lives well when others are poor	.72
V243 – Competition is often wasteful and destructive	.63
V239 – The government hast the responsibility to see to it that everybody can find a job	.62
V261 – The private enterprise system is generally a fair and efficient system	−.60
V229 – Rich people should pay more for the support of community projects than poor	.55
Variance explained	13.6
Eigenvalue	4.3

Variables with principal loading on factor II	Loading on factor
V241 – Most decisions should be left to the judgement of experts	.70
V268 – In this complicated world the only way to we can know what is going on is to rely on leaders or experts who can be trusted	.65
V254 – It will always be necessary to have a few strong, able people actually running everything	.63
V252 – Participation by the people is not necessary if decision-making is left in the hands of a few trusted and competent leaders	.60
Variance explained	9.2
Eigenvalue	2.9

Variables with principal loading on factor III	Loading on factor
V246 – We should not worry so much about national problems when we have so many in our own community	.76
V236 – Although national affairs are important, people here should first worry about their own communities problems	.73
V240 – Community progress is not possible if national goals always have priority	.67
Variance explained	5.9
Eigenvalue	1.9

Table 3.6 (continued)

Variables with principal loading on factor IV	*Loading on factor*
V250 – After obtaining a certain standard of living further concern with economic growth is not required	.66
V256 – Only economic development will ultimately provide for the welfare and happiness of the people	–.63
V248 – Economic development should not be pursued if it means hardships for the people	.61
Variance explained	5.1
Eigenvalue	1.6

Variables with principal loading on factor V	*Loading on factor*
V265 – Local leaders should always publicly and truthfully speak the facts about their failures in performing social affairs	.67
V236 – Leaders should present the truth no matter what the consequences are	.66
V245 – When important problems are discussed, a politician should speak his/her mind, even when the majority of citizens within the community are of a different opinion	.58
V231 – The most important thing for the leader is to follow his convictions even if this is different from what the constituency expects	.29
Variance explained	4.4
Eigenvalue	1.4

Variables with principal loading on factor VI	*Loading on factor*
V230 – Every individual and group should have the right to sue the authorities	.72
V233 – Any individual or an organization has the right to organize opposition or resistance to any governmental initiative	.63
V235 – All decisions should be subject to appeal to an independent authority for review	.52
Variance explained	4.0
Eigenvalue	1.3

Table 3.6 (continued)

Variables with principal loading on factor VII	Loading on factor
V258 – A good leader should refrain from making proposals that divided the people even if these proposals are important for the community	.63
V267 – A leader is obligated to follow the wishes of the community even if he thinks the citizens are mistaken	.48
V260 – The minority has a right to oppose but no right to resist decisions taken by the majority	.46
V255 – Preserving harmony in the community should be considered more important than successfully carrying out community programs	.45
Variance explained	3.5
Eigenvalue	1.1

Variables with principal loading on factor VIII	Loading on factor
V253 – There are no circumstances where provisions of the constitution can be ignored by the authorities	–.73
V257 – It is appropriate for local leaders to disobey the law if such an action is in the interest of the community	.54
Variance explained	3.5
Eigenvalue	1.1

Variables with principal loading on factor IX	Loading on factor
V226 – The economic development of the nation should take precedence over immediate consumer gratification	.55
V259 – In order to achieve community goals, it is permissible for leaders to present facts in a one-sided way	.46
Variance explained	3.3
Eigenvalue	1.1

* Factors loadings given only for the factor where the variable had its strongest loading.
** Each statement has four corresponding possible answers: strongly agree (1), agree somewhat (2), disagree somewhat (3), or strongly disagree (4).

Source: Democracy and Local Government in Germany, Elite Surveys.

zenry' and 'citizens rights', do not tightly correspond to the presumed set of dimensions in the DLG battery, nor, of course, does the ninth identified factor, which is an amalgam of a concern for economic development and commitment to honesty.

One encounters similar problems in almost all of the other DLG country elite data sets used in this volume. Generally, only a few of the putative scales could be uncovered with the use of factor analysis. Indeed, the only national data set that conforms to the DLG project's expectations in terms of the underlying ideological dimensions is that of Poland.

Part of the design of this project was to compare the ideological values of local elites and citizens. However, limited resources required that one be selective in terms of ideological items that could be included in the survey of citizens. This forced a decision on which items to include. Two primary options were available: either a reproduction in a reduced form of the many putative scales included in the elite questionnaire (that is a sample of the questions that make up the putative scales) or the use of the items from the primary dimensions of ideological values found in the elite data. The latter option was selected.

Grounds for this choice are two-fold. First, as noted above, the analyses of both the German elite data and the other nations' local elite data indicate that there seems to be no strong basis upon which one can assume the DLG scales hold at the elite level. Comparisons with data from the citizenry level based on these scales would then appear to be of little empirical value. Second, and perhaps more importantly, there are strong theoretical reasons for believing that the socialism-capitalism and libertarian-authoritarian scales are among the most significant ideological dimensions in modern democratic societies. As Kitschelt has argued (Kitschelt, 1993, 1997) these two dimensions have become critical ideological divides within modern industrialized societies along which significant elements of the population place themselves. Kitschelt's empirical work, as well as that of others, is also supportive of this operating assumption.[6]

At the elite level, the eleven items found to constitute the two primary dimensions of ideological values were thus included in the questionnaire used in polling the citizens. Factor analysis of the data from the citizen survey suggested that, with one exception, the items lined up similarly to the way in which they did in the elite data. The exception was the item dealing with whether the private enterprise system is viewed as 'fair and efficient'. This item loaded almost equally on both scales. This item was dropped from consideration and further analysis confirmed the existence of two dimensions at both the elite and citizen levels (see Tables 3.7a and 3.7b). Addition-

---

6 See, for example, the extensive work by Heath and Evans (Heath, Evans and Martin, 1993; Evans and Heath, 1995; Evans, Heath and Lalljee, 1996) on formulating operational measures of these concepts. The application of this general approach can be found in numerous studies, for example, that by Knutson (1997), McIntosh et al. (1994) and Miller et al. (1995) as well as studies on the populations of the two regions of Germany (e.g., Welzel, 1999; Zelle, 1999).

Table 3.7a Principal component analyses of elites' values

	All n = 1,162		West n = 599		East n = 510	
	I	II	I	II	I	II
Upper limits on income	0.81	0.01	0.80	.04	0.81	0.03
Reduced inequality	0.77	−0.11	0.74	−0.16	0.78	−0.10
Government assure equality	0.76	0.05	0.73	0.07	0.79	0.01
Government responsible for employment	0.67	−0.03	0.64	−0.10	0.68	0.06
Competition is bad	0.63	0.13	0.58	0.14	0.65	0.08
Rich should pay more	0.57	−0.21	0.56	−0.20	0.59	−0.18
Only leaders trusted	0.07	0.69	0.07	0.67	0.08	0.71
Leave decisions to experts	0.11	0.68	−0.03	0.69	0.12	0.66
Need few strong leaders	−0.16	0.65	−0.15	0.63	−0.22	0.66
Leave decisions to few	−0.09	0.65	.06	0.69	−0.06	0.63
Percentage of variance	30.6	18.5	29.0	17.9	31.9	18.1

Source: Democracy and Local Government in Germany, Elite Surveys.

Table 3.7b Principal component analyses of citizens' values

	All n = 2,011		West n = 991		East n = 1,020	
	I	II	I	II	I	II
Upper limits on income	0.76	0.10	0.72	0.12	0.76	0.04
Reduced inequality	0.71	0.09	0.70	0.08	0.67	0.07
Government assure equality	0.71	0.08	0.70	0.08	0.70	0.06
Government responsible for employment	0.66	0.14	0.65	0.19	0.58	0.04
Competition is bad	0.55	0.17	0.56	0.22	0.48	0.09
Rich should pay more	0.55	−0.03	0.51	−0.08	0.50	0.00
Only leaders trusted	0.15	0.70	0.14	0.68	0.17	0.71
Leave decisions to experts	0.03	0.69	0.03	0.71	−0.06	0.67
Need few strong leaders	0.01	0.66	0.01	0.65	−0.07	0.65
Leave decisions to few	0.15	0.50	0.15	0.50	0.22	0.49
Percentage of variance	29.2	14.5	28.6	14.3	25.3	15.2

Source: Democracy and Local Government in Germany, Citizen Survey.

Table 3.8a Principal component analyses of Central European local elites' values

	Czech Republic		Hungary		Poland		Slovakia	
	I	II	I	II	I	II	I	II
Upper limits on income	0.80	0.09	0.81	0.09	0.80	0.09	0.80	0.10
Reduced inequality	0.63	0.09	0.67	0.10	0.72	-0.02	0.73	-0.11
Government assure equality	0.78	0.07	0.73	0.07	0.73	0.08	0.73	-0.02
Government responsible for employment	0.75	-0.04	0.48	0.24	0.60	0.12	0.54	0.10
Competition is bad	0.59	0.07	0.63	0.01	0.71	0.12	0.60	0.14
Rich should pay more	0.46	-0.18	0.20	-0.11	0.44	0.21	0.42	0.05
Only leaders trusted	0.08	0.65	-0.01	0.77	0.08	0.70	0.10	0.60
Leave decisions to experts	0.10	0.64	0.07	0.55	0.22	0.57	0.13	0.47
Need few strong leaders	-0.13	0.71	-0.02	0.74	0.07	0.68	-0.09	0.72
Leave decisions to few	0.01	0.72	0.29	0.38	0.03	0.62	0.01	0.61
Percentage of variance	28.2	18.9	25.8	14.9	31.0	14.8	26.1	15.0

Source: Democracy and Local Government International Data Base.

Table 3.8b Principal component analyses of Western local elites' values

	Austria		Netherlands		Spain		Sweden		Switzerland		USA	
	I	II	I	II	I	II	I	II	I	II	I	II
Upper limits on income	0.81	−0.05	0.78	−0.05	0.72	−0.22	0.71	0.08	0.82	−0.04	0.63	−0.08
Reduced inequality	0.74	−0.21	0.09	0.64	0.70	0.01	0.75	−0.25	0.80	−0.12	0.57	0.09
Government assure equality	0.65	0.22	0.59	0.13	0.78	0.07	0.66	−0.16	0.77	−0.02	0.62	0.12
Government responsible for employment	0.52	0.26	0.47	0.09	0.41	0.21	0.68	−0.14	0.62	0.23	0.76	−0.11
Competition is bad	0.65	0.09	0.60	−0.10	0.66	−0.18	0.56	0.28	0.67	0.03	0.53	0.34
Rich should pay more	0.62	−0.24	0.68	−0.03	0.41	−0.32	0.58	−0.03	0.57	−0.14	0.40	−0.36
Only leaders trusted	0.03	0.66	−0.12	−0.39	0.00	0.80	−0.06	0.67	0.11	0.67	−0.04	0.62
Leave decisions to experts	0.09	0.69	0.08	0.76	−0.05	0.79	−0.07	0.70	0.06	0.72	−0.01	0.68
Need few strong leaders	−0.08	0.65	−0.17	0.35	n/a	n/a	−0.04	0.74	−0.24	0.50	0.04	0.71
Leave decisions to few	0.01	0.57	−0.10	0.64	n/a	n/a	−0.19	0.75	−0.03	0.69	0.17	0.71
Percentage of variance	27.2	18.8	20.9	16.9	31.0	17.5	28.2	20.6	31.5	17.9	22.9	20.1

n/a not available.

Source: Democracy and Local Government International Data Base.

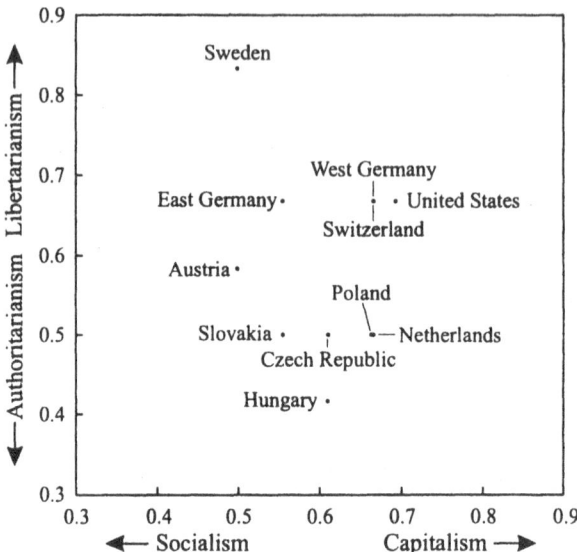

Figure 3.1   Elites' values: an international comparison

ally, analyses of the elite data from other national surveys of local elites are generally supportive of the thesis that 'socialism-capitalism' and 'authoritarianism-libertarianism' constitute two very important dimensions of ideological values across all of these nations (see Tables 3.8a and 3.8b).

Overall, then, how do German local elites compare to those in other nations on these two dimensions? Figure 3.1 compares the median positions of local elites in the two German regions with the positions of local elites in nine other countries on the two ideological dimensions. West German elites on the whole are among the most supportive of capitalist values and simultaneously equally highly placed in their support for libertarian values. In this, they appear to be quite similar to the local elites of two other Western democracies, namely, Switzerland and the United States. East German elites, while equally high in their support for libertarian values, are among the least supportive of capitalist as opposed to socialist values. In this overall position they differentiate themselves from the local elites of other Central European transitional democracies who, while generally more supportive of capitalist values (Slovakian elites being the exception on this dimension), are clearly more authoritarian as well.

A number of other comparisons provide further insight to the ideological situation in Germany. First, take the populations of the two regions. Figure 3.2a describes how the two regions' populations distribute themselves along the socialism-capitalism dimension. One sees there that the two populations are markedly different in their orientations toward the organization of economic life. Easterners are far more favorably inclined toward socialistic organizing principles than are their Western colleagues. Indeed, the median of the distribution of the Eastern population is far to the left of the median position in the Western population. Simultaneously, the overall distribution of the two populations in terms of their orientation toward authoritarianism-libertarianism (Figure 3.2c) is quite similar. Furthermore, the median position along this dimension is the same in both regions.

Second, a comparison of the elites in both regions shows a somewhat parallel situation. Eastern elites are less favorably oriented toward capitalism than the Western elites (Figure 3.2b), while elites in both regions are very similarly distributed along the authoritarian-libertarian scale (Figure 3.2d). Third, the elites in both regions are clearly more favorably oriented toward both capitalism and libertarianism than are their respective populations.[7]

Seen from the viewpoint of representation a markedly complex picture emerges. Figures 3.3a and 3.3b depict the relative positions in the two dimensional ideological space of the elites and citizens by their partisan affiliations. In both regions, one sees relatively smaller distances among the partisan voter groups than are to be found among the partisan elite groups. In the East, this is particularly salient in the way the partisan elite groups distinguish themselves along the socialism-capitalism dimension. The difference between the two extremes at the elite level on this dimension is four times the gap between the two extreme positions among partisan supporters at the citizen level.

While large as well in the West, the gap between the two extremes on the socialism-capitalism scale at the elite level is only about half that seen in the East. Interestingly, the positions of the Western citizen partisan groupings on this dimension are far more heterogeneous than those in the East where support for socialist principles is widely shared across the partisan groupings. With respect to the other dimension, authoritarianism-libertarianism, Western partisan elites again position themselves across a far wider span of the spectrum than do the Eastern elites; a similar tendency is to be seen at the voter level, though, again, the breadth of positions is narrower than at the elite level.

Are the party elites representative of their voters in terms of how they position themselves in this two dimensional ideological space?[8] The patterns in both regions present a mixed picture. In the East, it turns out that both the PDS and the SPD elites position themselves most closely to their own voters. At the same time, however, the SPD elites are actually closer to the voters of the Greens, FDP and CDU voters than are the elites of these parties. In two of these three cases, the Greens and the CDU, however, the relative degree of separation between the parties' voters and elites is not that

---

7 Comparable differences in ideological values between regional elites and citizens have been found using the Potsdam German National Elite survey (see Welzel, 1998).

8 Representation here is operationalized as the relative distance between party voters and party elites. The distance measure is the unweighted Euclidean distance between the median of the party voters positions on the two scales and the medians of the party elites positions (Enelow and Hinich, 1984). This does not take into account other theoretical models of representation, for example, those based on directional or leadership theories (see Iversen, 1994).

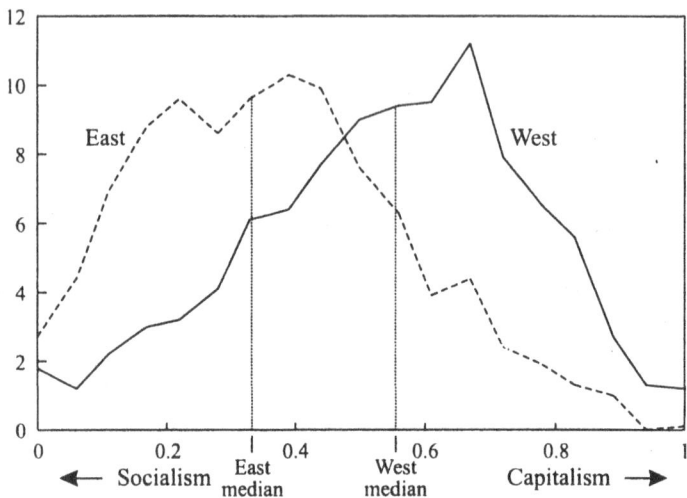

Figure 3.2a Socialism-capitalism, citizens, East and West Germany

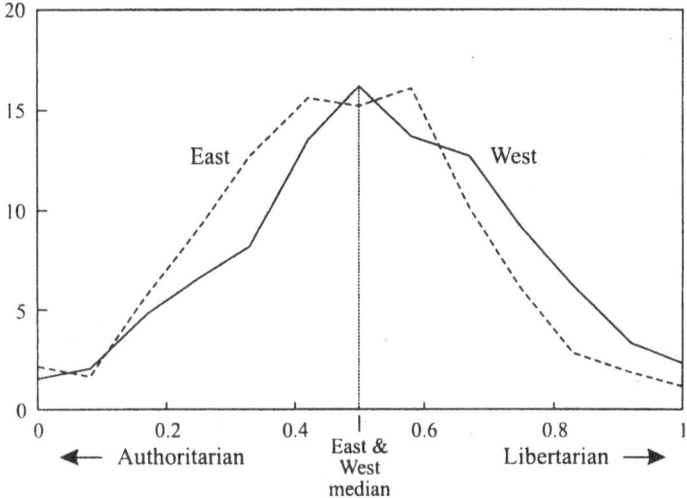

Figure 3.2b Authoritarianism-libertarianism, citizens, East and West Germany

pronounced. FDP voters, however, have the rather peculiar characteristic of supporting the party whose elites are actually the furthest from them in the ideological space.

In the West, the SPD party elites once again position themselves more closely than other elites to their own voters. Moreover, as in the East this party's elites also are closer to the Greens voters than are the elites of that party. Unlike in the East, the

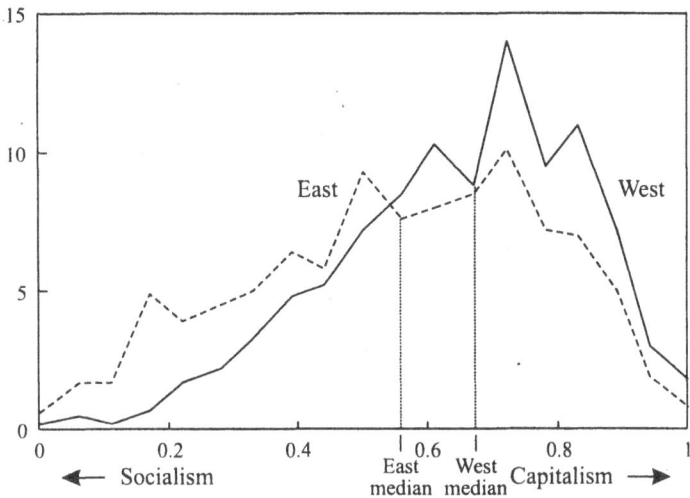

Figure 3.2c Socialism-capitalism, elites, East and West Germany

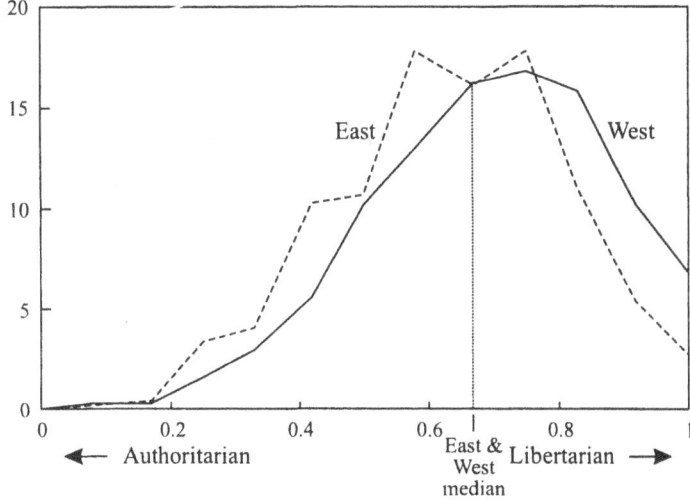

Figure 3.2d Authoritarianism-libertarianism, elites, East and West Germany

FDP party elites in the West are the nearest of all the party elites to their own voters. CDU party elites turn out to be slightly more distant from their own voters than are the FDP elites.

The patterns among the citizenries of the two regions revealed using the socialism-capitalism scale seem to accord rather well with independently generated data on the

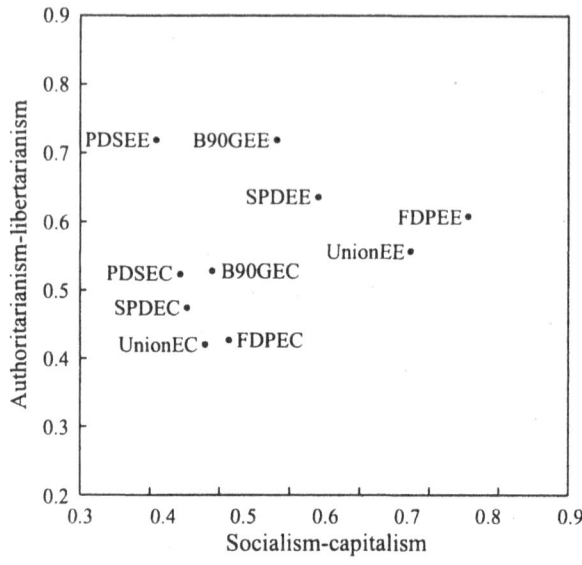

Figure 3.3a Citizens and elites: socialism-capitalism and authoritarianism-libertarianism, East Germany

economic role of the state developed by the International Social Survey Project (see Table 3.9). First, from an international perspective, East German citizens indeed appear to be quite supportive of the socialist model when compared to citizens in West Germany as well as those in both the transitional and more established democracies. And, using data from an earlier year, 1990, this position seems to have changed hardly at all. Second, the narrower differences amongst supporters of the different political parties in the East as opposed to the West show up here as well (Table 3.10).

The Sources of Ideological Values

Attention now turns to the sources of individuals' ideological positions. This is a particularly interesting issue in the German context with the on-going effort to integrate more than fifteen million former citizens of the former socialist regime of the

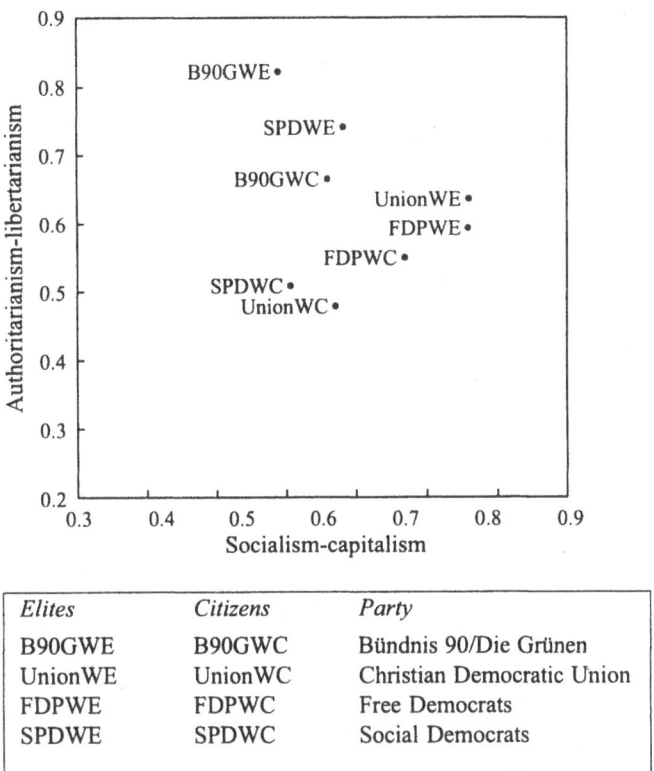

Figure 3.3b Citizens and elites: socialism-capitalism and authoritarianism-libertarianism, West Germany

German Democratic Republic into the democratic and market-based regime of the Federal Republic. The previous section mapped out the differences on two major ideological axes amongst local elites and citizens across both regions of Germany. In that section it was shown that there is an appreciable gap between elites and citizen on one axis, authoritarianism-libertarianism. However, this gap is of the same size in each of the two regions. Thus, the median elite position on authoritarianism-libertarianism is the same in both East and West Germany. So, too, are the median positions of citizens in the two regions the same on this dimension. What was particularly outstanding, however, were the differences between regions at both the elite and citizen level on the socialism-capitalism axis. Here there are significant gaps between the median positions of the two regional elites, even larger gaps between the median positions of citizens in the two regions and, as a consequence, appreciable gaps between the median positions of citizens and elites in each region. For this reason, I will concentrate on effort to explain why these differences exist.

Table 3.9 An international comparison of partisans' attitudes towards government's role in the economy based on data from the 1990 and 1996 ISSP surveys on the role of government (per cent)*

		East Germany		Czech Rep.	Hungary	Poland	West Germany		Spain	Sweden	United States
		(a)	(b)				(a)	(b)			
Gov't should reduce differences between people with high and low incomes	Agree not Disagree	74.5 14.4	75.7 11.9	60.3 22.1	66.8 14.9	78.1 10.2	56.4 19.8	49.4 28.7	77.3 12.4	59.6 20.6	32.6 43.0
Gov't should control wages by law	Favour Against	78.7 12.5	68.6 14.7	47.1 33.1	50.7 30.1	60.7 19.7	33.1 46.3	27.3 49.2	67.1 18.1	28.3 48.9	28.2 50.3
Gov't should control prices by law	Favour Against	87.8 7.5	81.7 9.4	72.0 13.8	63.8 21.4	75.6 12.5	51.0 32.1	50.4 32.7	86.5 6.8	58.0 24.9	35.0 42.4
Gov't responsibility to provide jobs for everyone who wants one	Should Should not	94.9 5.1	91.9 8.1	76.3 23.7	86.9 13.1	89.6 10.4	74.2 25.8	74.5 25.5	90.8 9.2	65.1 34.9	39.4 60.8
Gov't responsibility to provide decent standard of living for unemployed	Should Should not	92.2 5.8	91.6 8.4	44.7 55.3	62.8 37.2	81.2 18.8	78.3 21.7	80.4 19.6	93.9 6.1	90.3 9.7	47.7 52.3
Gov't responsibility to reduce income differences between rich and poor	Should Should not	84.3 15.7	83.7 16.3	61.7 38.3	78.7 21.3	84.1 15.9	63.6 36.4	62.5 37.5	90.1 9.9	70.6 29.4	47.9 52.1

* Note that the data are generally for 1996. In addition, data for East and West Germany are provided for 1990 (a) and 1996 (b).

Source: Data in this table drawn from the International Social Survey Project (ISSP 1990 and 1996) Studies on the Role of Government, II and III (ZA Studies 1950 and 2900). Data sets supplied by the Zentralarchiv für Sozialforschung an der Universität zu Köln.

Table 3.10 Cross-regional comparison of partisans' attitudes towards government's role in the economy based on data from the 1990 and 1996 ISSP surveys on the role of government (per cent)

		Greens	CDU/CSU	FDP	PDS	SPD	Other	Non-voter
East Germany								
Gov't should reduce differences between people with high and low incomes	Agree	61.3	67.3	67.7	81.9	83.4	66.7	75.4
	Disagree	18.8	18.5	17.6	9.5	6.9	33.3	7.4
Gov't should control wages by law	Favour	58.5	61.0	72.5	78.2	70.5	83.3	70.2
	Against	23.2	22.4	10.0	8.4	13.3	16.7	13.7
Gov't should control prices by law	Favour	73.2	80.0	90.0	88.2	81.0	66.7	80.9
	Against	14.6	10.5	10.0	5.0	9.0	16.7	7.6
Gov't responsibility to provide jobs for everyone who wants one	Should	85.4	85.8	97.4	95.7	94.2	100.0	92.8
	Should not	14.6	14.2	2.6	4.3	5.8	0.0	7.2
Gov't responsibility to provide decent standard of living for unemployed	Should	91.3	86.3	92.5	92.4	93.7	100.0	89.3
	Should not	8.8	13.7	7.5	7.6	6.3	0.0	10.7
Gov't responsibility to reduce income differences between rich and poor	Should	76.9	76.6	82.4	86.1	90.0	66.7	86.6
	Should not	23.1	23.3	15.8	13.9	10.0	33.3	13.4

Table 3.10 (continued)

West Germany		Greens	CDU/CSU	FDP	PDS	SPD	Other	Non-voter
Gov't should reduce differences between people with high and low incomes	Agree	50.4	41.4	34.6	—	52.4	59.1	59.0
	Disagree	27.1	34.6	38.9	—	25.5	22.7	21.8
Gov't should control wages by law	Favour	27.9	26.5	22.1	—	27.0	43.5	34.8
	Against	50.6	53.6	15.3	—	50.9	39.1	38.1
Gov't should control prices by law	Favour	40.4	47.9	42.9	—	53.2	68.2	61.3
	Against	41.2	36.8	42.9	—	32.0	22.7	19.9
Gov't responsibility to provide jobs for everyone who wants one	Should	77.0	69.1	53.8	—	78.6	68.2	81.1
	Should not	23.0	30.9	46.3	—	21.4	31.8	18.9
Gov't responsibility to provide decent standard of living for unemployed	Should	84.0	76.8	70.4	—	82.4	69.6	84.9
	Should not	16.0	23.3	29.6	—	17.6	30.4	15.1
Gov't responsibility to reduce income differences between rich and poor	Should	69.1	53.5	42.7	—	67.4	66.7	69.5
	Should not	30.9	46.5	57.3	—	32.6	33.3	30.5

Source: Data in this table drawn from the International Social Survey Project (ISSP 1996) Studies on the Role of Government, III (ZA Study 2900). Data set supplied by the Zentralarchiv für Sozialforschung an der Universität zu Köln.

Among political scientists, there has been fairly widespread pessimism about the prospects for the short- or medium-term success of the German integration effort. This pessimism has been founded on the assumption that the processes of socialization instill in people sets of permanent ideological values. This then makes it difficult for these people who have long experienced a system founded on very different principles to adopt ideological values that accord with a democratic and market-based system. Given that the citizens of the GDR have been exposed to the ideological drumbeat of communism for more than forty years, it was expected that this would have hardened their attitudes on political and economic questions in ways quite unfavorable to the values commonplace within the West German population.

This pessimism is somewhat difficult to understand. Numerous research reports in the early 90s examined the political values of populations in the former communist systems of central and eastern Europe and discovered a surprisingly high level of pro-market and pro-democratic values and attitudes (see, e.g., Dalton, 1994; Gibson et al., 1992). However, as the decade proceeded, a great deal of this popular pro-democratic and pro-market sentiment dissipated. The general decline in positive feelings about the economic and political system in both regions of Germany is quite apparent in Table 3.11. In part, researchers were willing to concede that the disappointments produced by the both the political and economic system made a contribution to this decline (e.g. Fuchs, 1999; Klugel et al., 1999). But more frequently than not the initial presence was attributed to the euphoric atmosphere of the period and its abatement was accredited to the permanence of the values that had been instilled by the previous regime.[9] The long-term exposure to a hegemonic culture of socialism had irrevocably shaped individuals' ideological political-economic preferences and this would only pass with generational replacement (Roller, 1997).

In attempting to illuminate the sources of individuals' ideological preferences with respect to socialism-capitalism, I proceed on the basis of an alternative theoretical model founded on the principle that material self-interest is at the root of these preferences. The basic idea here is that with exposure to the disciplines and rewards of the market economy, it is rational on the part of an individual to develop and maintain ideological preferences that accord with the relative rewards one receives or is denied by one's position in the market system.[10] This is a very traditional argument stretching back at least to de Tocqueville (1835/1945). In its more modern shape, the most representative formulation stems from Meltzer and Richard's work (1979, 1981).

---

9 An alternative and more elaborate explanation based on socialization has also been put forward (e.g., Rohrschneider, 1994, 1996a, b, 1999; Fuchs, 1998; Roller 1994; 1997) which casts the learning involved as both intra-systemic and extra-systemic. The latter is thought to have been at work in promoting the favorable attitudes toward market ideas and liberal democracy in East Germany through the widespread availability of West German media (particularly television) in the period prior to the collapse of the GDR.

10 For somewhat similar arguments, see Kuhlberg and Zimmerman (1999) and Liebig and Verwiebe (2000).

Table 3.11 Opinion about the Federal Republic's economic and political systems in East and West Germany (per cent)

	Positive opinion about Federal Republic's			
	economic system*		political system**	
	East	West	East	West
1990	73	–	41	81
1991	53	–	34	77
1992	44	–	41	78
1993	35	–	32	75
1994	38	57	33	79
1995	32	55	28	70
1996	19	45	–	–
1997	25	42	23	69
1998	22	44	–	–

* The original source for these data is the Allensbacher Institiut für Demoskopie. Data are drawn from Rohrschneider (1999, Figure 8.21). Values given for 1990, 1991, 1995 and 1997 are averages of the separate values listed for those years. Question posed was: 'Do you have a good or bad opinion of the Federal Republic's economic system?'. Values listed are the percentages reporting a good opinion.

** Data drawn from Noelle-Neumann and Köcher (1997, p. 657). Question posed was: 'Do you believe that the democracy we have in the Federal Republic is the best political system, or is there another political system that is better?'. Values listed are the percentages responding that the Federal Republic's system is best.

In very recent work on individual political preferences, the basic line of argument has been described as the 'homo oeconomicus effect' whereby an individual's rational calculation of personal gains or losses from a general economic policy leads that individual to support or oppose that policy (Corneo, 2000; Corneo and Grüner, 2001; Alesina and La Ferrara, 2001).

Actual experience and expectations are the bases of this process. For example, individuals with a great deal of human capital can expect to do better in the market system than those with relatively little human capital (see, for example, Psacharopoulos, 1985 and Card, 1999). As a consequence, one would anticipate that people in the former group are more supportive of market principles while those in the latter group would have good self-interested reasons are more supportive of the egalitarian characteristics of socialist systems. Simultaneously, the actual rewards one receives from the market system should shape how one orients oneself: those who receive high rewards from the market system have strong reasons to favor the capitalist system while those who receive very few or no rewards should be equally predisposed to support the socialist alternative.

Table 3.12 provides an overview of how a set of important socio-economic characteristics of citizens are linked to preferences with respect to socialism-capitalism. The breakdown of orientations toward socialism-capitalism by age groups across the two regions is supportive of the socialization hypothesis. First, one sees that there is no clear systematic relationship between age and ideological orientation in the West, a region where capitalism has reigned continuously since World War II. This pattern is what one would expect in a system that has not undergone any major change in its social institutions. Second, in the East, the pattern is markedly different. In that region, one sees a very distinctive pattern. Here, younger cohorts are less socialistically oriented, while older cohorts are strongly socialist in orientation. Given the socialization hypothesis, one might expect such a profile. Simply put, those with long exposure to a socialistic system would tend to have internalized its values far more deeply than those with a brief exposure.

Nevertheless, the self-interest hypothesis is another and at least equally plausible interpretation of these data. This view rests on the prospects an individual has under a capitalist system. Those who have spent most of their life in such a system have had the opportunity to make choices in the past consistent with the structure of incentives found in such a system. This characterizes the citizens in the West and therefore it is not surprising that one finds no correspondence between age and socialist-capitalist ideological preferences. Those who have spent much of their life in a socialist system, a system with a very different set of incentives, will have made many choices and investments that most likely would not align very well with a capitalist system. Thus, people who have lived longer in the socialist system, the older part of the population, are therefore more likely to be in the position of having made more 'wrong choices and investments' than are younger people. The latter, simply through the lack of opportunity to have made such decisions and commitments in the past, are afforded the chance to orient their actions in a way that rationally accords with the incentive structures of a capitalist system. All of this would lead one to expect the lack of any correlation between age and socialist-capitalist preferences in the West and a fairly strong and negative correlation between the two in the East. This is exactly the pattern that emerges in Table 3.12.

Looking at income, one sees that in both regions, there is a strong and nearly monotonic relationship between income and self-placement on the ideological dimension. Consistent with the self-interest hypothesis, people with lower incomes, hence those who benefit least from a capitalist market system, favor socialistic values while those with higher incomes, and thus the principal beneficiaries of the prevailing system, prefer capitalistic values.

Similarly, the relationship between education and preferences with respect to socialism-capitalism is consistent with the self-interest hypothesis. Individuals with higher levels of education or human capital and, therefore, greater capacity to gain from capitalist structured markets, are more pro-market oriented than are individuals with lower levels of education.

Table 3.12 Socio-economic characteristics and average position on socialism-capitalism scale

Socialism-capitalism scores, across regions	East Germany	West Germany
By age categories:		
1: 18–24	.47	.52
2: 25–34	.45	.57
3: 35–44	.38	.56
4: 45–54	.37	.55
5: 55–64	.29	.50
6: 65+	.31	.50
By households' income categories: (monthly net income, in D-Mark)		
1: under 1,000	.30	.47
2: 1,000–1,799	.30	.44
3: 1,800–2,499	.31	.48
4: 2,500–3,499	.36	.54
5: 3,500–4,499	.38	.54
6: 4,500–5,499	.46	.54
7: 5,500–6,499	.50	.62
8: 6,500–7,499	.55	.64
9: 7,500 or more	.59	.68
By education levels:		
1	.35	.41
2	.28	.47
3	.36	.57
4	.45	.60
5	.45	.61
By gender:		
– Female	.35	.50
– Male	.39	.58
By union membership:		
– Member	.36	.53
– Non-member	.37	.54

Source: Democracy and Local Government in Germany, Citizen Survey.

The other two variables, gender and union membership, apparently have either a weak or no relationship to individuals' orientations toward socialism-capitalism. The self-interest hypothesis would be that women, given their greater degree of dependency in the German system, would have more sympathy toward socialism than men would have.[11] While this seems to be the case, the differences between the two genders in both regions are not very substantial. Finally, the self-interest hypothesis suggests that union members would be more socialist oriented than non-union members (see, e.g., Kitschelt, 1994; Boeri, Börsch-Supan and Tabellini, 2001). However, in both regions the differences between members and non-members is minuscule, though it is in the expected direction.

Six characteristics are drawn together in a linear additive regression model meant to capture the variation in individuals' positions on the socialism-capitalism scale.[12] The model takes the following form:

$$SC_i = a + b_1 G_i + b_2 E_i + b_3 I_i + b_4 A_i + b_5 R_i + b_6 A_i R_i + b_7 U_i + e_i$$

In light of the self-interest principle and given the reasoning laid out above, the expectations regarding the coefficients in this model are as follows. First, women have a greater self-interest in an economic order governed by socialist as opposed to capitalist principles, thus, b1 < 0. Second, since higher education endows the individual

---

11 Esping-Andersen (1999) characterizes the German system as one that establishes significant barriers to female employment. At the same time, its welfare state regime, while generous and comprehensive, is strongly linked to one's employment record; this obviously disadvantages women. In addition, the regime is structured in such a way as to maintain the family's role in tradition caring functions, a role that places a far heavier burden on women than men (Esping-Andersen, Assimakopoulou and van Kersbergen 1993). Together with its under-funded publicly provided social services, all of this would promote among females in Germany a real incentive in advocacy of greater government activism.

12 For purposes of the regression analyses, the socialism-capitalism scale scores (SC) have been rescaled. The rescaling involves multiplying the original scores (which theoretically range from 0 to 1.0) by 100. Note that the gender variable (G) in the equation is a dummy variable coded 1 for females and 0 for males. Education (E) is operationalized differently in the two data sets. It ranges from 1 to 5 in the citizenry data, with a 1 standing for incomplete primary education in and a 5, the highest category, standing for completion of the secondary education track required for admission to university. The elite data on education ranges from 1 to 7 with 1 standing (as in the citizenry data) for incomplete primary education and 7 standing for completion of university education. Income (I) has the same nine categories displayed in Table 3.12. Similarly, age (A) has the six categories used in that Table but the variable in the regression equation is recoded so that it ranges from a low of 0 (for the age category 18–24) to a high of 5 (those aged 65 and over). This transformation is necessitated by the introduction of the interaction between age and region in the equation. Both region and union membership are dummy variables. Region (R) is coded 0 for Westerners and 1 for Easterners. Union membership (U) is coded zero for non-members and 1 for members.

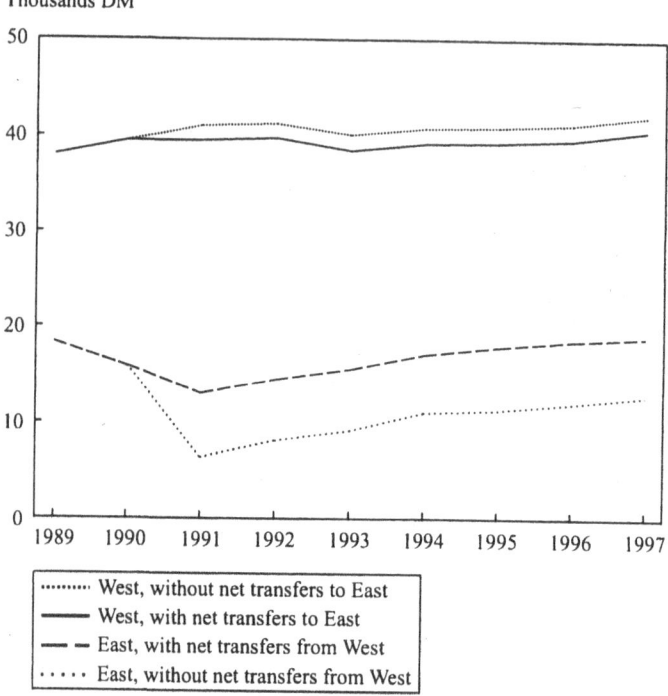

Sources: Based on data from Brinkmann (1995); Statistisches Bundesamt (1999; 2000).

Figure 3.4 Regional economic development and net transfers to the East, 1989–1997 (gross domestic product per capita in 1991 DM)

with greater human capital and therefore increases the rewards one can expect in a system based on capitalist principles, then individuals with higher education are more favorably disposed toward capitalism, that is, $b2 > 0$. Third, an individual with higher income actually reaps greater rewards from the prevailing capitalist system. This will promote that individual's regard for capitalist principles and therefore one can expect $b3$ to be positive.

Given the specified interaction between age and region in the model, the expectations regarding the parameters for the constituent and joint terms, i.e., $b4$, $b5$ and $b6$, need to be dealt with together. A fundamentally clear prediction based on the self-interest principle is that $b6$, the parameter on the interaction between age and region, should be negative. This is consistent with the argument that older people in the East, saddled with the problem of unwittingly having made the 'wrong choices and investments', are therefore more likely to see their self-interest in an economic order governed by socialist as opposed to capitalist principles. With regard to $b5$, the expectation is that this parameter will be negative. This follows from the extremely high dependence of the Eastern region on government transfers. Five years after unification, East German domestic product per capita, which had witnessed a dramatic collapse with integration into the Federal Republic's economic system, was still less than half the level of that prevailing in the West (see Figure 3.4). And, most importantly, a significant share of that (36 per cent) was financed out of net transfers by the government to the region. Such a heavy dependence on the 'generosity' of government can have only made East Germans more favorably disposed to activist policies by government in the economic sphere and therefore more likely to arrange themselves further toward the socialist end of the scale than their West German colleagues.[13] As to the parameter on the other constituent term (age) involved in the interaction, that is b4, the expectation is that other things being equal, there should be no effect of age on ideological position and thus the parameter should not be significantly different from zero. Finally, as noted above, the expectation is that union members are more supportive of socialist principles than non-union members. It follows, then, the parameter b7 will be negative.

Analysis of the model specified above has been undertaken using three different data sets. The first two data sets are based on the citizen and elite surveys conducted for this project. The third data set is drawn from the International Social Survey Project's third 'Role of Government' survey conducted in 1996. Results from the first two data sets are presented in Table 3.13a and those from the ISSP survey are presented in Table 3.13b.

In Table 3.13.a one sees that the model does reasonably well in accounting for the variance in both citizens' and elites' positions on the socialism-capitalism scale. In addition, the predictions based on the self-interest hypothesis with respect to the parameters generally find strong backing. Thus, the expectation regarding gender is supported. Women tend to be more supportive of socialist values than are men. This effect is particularly salient among the female local elites where the impact is more than twice as large as the impact among the citizenry.

Education has the predicted effect among both elites and citizens. The higher the level of education, the greater is the support for capitalist principles. The coefficients on the education variables, however, are not directly comparable because of the coding differences between the two data sets. Still, it is clear from the results that people with greater human capital and, therefore, with greater potential rewards from the capitalist system, give less support to socialist values than do those with relatively little human capital. Given the data from the citizen survey and the statistics estimated with the regression equation, what does the parameter on education imply about the substantive relationship between this measure of human capital and an individual's position on the socialism-capitalism scale? To answer this question, Monte Carlo

---

13 Of course, one could also interpret a negative parameter here as supportive of the socialization approach.

Table 3.13a Regression analyses: socialism-capitalism*

	Citizens	Elites
Gender	−3.90 (−4.02)	−8.40 (−5.21)
Education	3.50 (5.86)	1.00 (2.76)
Income	2.40 (8.30)	not available
Age	−.60 (−1.31)	.90 (1.17)
Region	−7.10 (−2.80)	8.70 (1.86)
Region * age	−2.20 (−3.46)	−4.90 (−4.20)
Union member	−2.50 (−2.20)	−13.90 (−10.55)
Constant	42.10 (12.84)	61.20 (14.85)
Summary statistics:		
$\bar{R}^2$	.25	.18
Number of cases	1,764	1,025

* Note that the socialism-capitalism scale has been multiplied by 100. Parameters reported in the table are non-standardized regression coefficients. The t-statistics are given in parentheses.

Source: Democracy and Local Goverment in Germany, Elite and Citizen Survey.

simulation was used to provide an estimate of the substantive relationship and the uncertainty surrounding it.[14]

---

14 It was possible to carry out these simulations using the Tomz, Wittenberg and King (1999, 2000) program clarify in conjunction with the Stata statistical package. These and each of the other sets of results reported from the simulation exercises are based on 1,000 experiments. The level of the confidence intervals employed is 95 per cent. In addition, all other variables in the equation are set to their mean values.

Table 3.13b Regression analysis: socialism-capitalism from ISSP, 1996*

	Citizens
Gender	−3.35
	(−4.63)
Education	−.46
	(1.55)
Income	2.64
	(13.38)
Age	.07
	(0.26)
Region	−13.00
	(−8.58)
Region * age	−1.74
	(−3.62)
Union member	−1.69
	(−1.34)
Constant	28.90
	(15.97)
Summary statistics:	
$\bar{R}^2$	.27
Number of cases	2,644

* Note that the socialism-capitalism scale has been multiplied by 100. Parameters reported in the table are non-standardized regression coefficients. The t-statistics are given in parentheses.

Source: Data in this table drawn from the International Social Survey Project (ISSP 1996) Studies on the Role of Government, III (ZA Study 2900). Data set supplied by the Zentralarchiv für Sozialforschung an der Universität zu Köln.

Figure 3.5a presents the results from the simulation experiments for the relationship between education and socialism-capitalism among the citizens of each of the two regions. The unbroken lines with markers are the mean expectations for the two regions. The two broken lines (dots for the West and bars for the East) surrounding each unbroken line represent the upper and lower limits of the 95 per cent confidence interval for the estimates. Looking at the average expected positions one sees that in

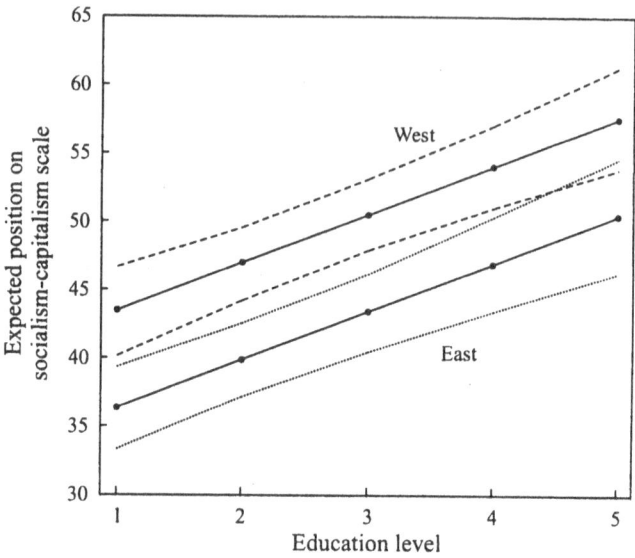

Figure 3.5a Education and expected position on socialism-capitalism scale

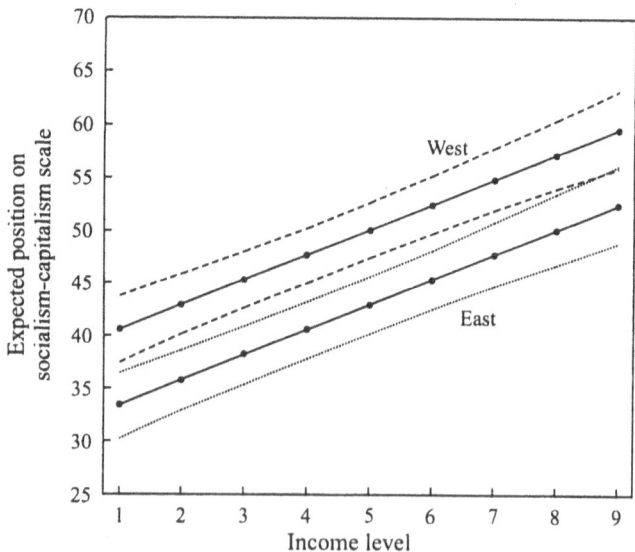

Figure 3.5b Income and expected position on socialism-capitalism scale

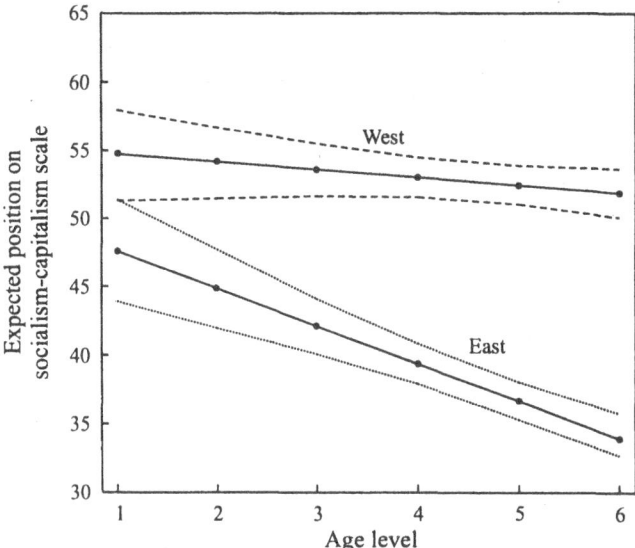

Figure 3.5c Age and expected position on socialism-capitalism scale

both regions they climb by 14 points on the socialism-capitalism scale as one moves from the lowest to the highest level of education. And while the gap between the two regions is about 7 points, the confidence intervals on both sets of estimates are significantly wide enough to call into question whether one can with complete certainty say that there is a large inter-regional difference in the correspondence between an individual's level of education and that individual's position on the socialism-capitalism scale. This is particularly the case at the highest level of education where the confidence intervals for the two regions' relationships slightly overlap.

Since no income variable is available from the elite survey, it was not possible to include such a term in the equation for the elites. Nevertheless, the resulting estimate of the parameter in the equation for the citizen data is fully supportive of the self-interest hypothesis. Thus, it is positive (as well as highly statistically significant) and thereby signifies that those who achieve greater rewards from the market system are more supportive of capitalist principles than are those who receive fewer such rewards. The effect registered is very pronounced. Other things being equal, moving from the lowest to the highest income category prompts a shift upward in the statistical expectation regarding the position equivalent to about 19 per cent of the socialism-capitalism scale's total distance (see Figure 3.5b). Once again, given the average expectation of the position on the socialism-capitalism scale and the width of the confidence intervals, it cannot be said with complete certainty that the size of the gap between the two regions' relationships is large.

The parameters on age, region and the interaction between age and region are best examined together. In conformity with expectations, age alone has no statistically significant effect on an individual's preferences with respect to socialism or capitalism.

Region registers contradictory effects across the two samples. Among citizens, the impact is, as expected, negative and statistically significant. This implies that citizens in the East in the youngest age category are more favorably inclined toward socialism than their age-peers in the West. At the elite level, however, the effect that is registered is positive, although the statistical significance of the coefficient is only .10 using a two-tailed test, which, given the construction of the variables involved in the interaction between age and region, implies that Eastern elites in the youngest age category, are more favorably inclined toward capitalism than are those of the same cohort in the West.

What is theoretically and substantively more interesting are the coefficients on the interaction between age and region. In both equations they are statistically significant and in the predicted negative direction. This means that age in the East alone works a negative effect on the support for capitalism at both the citizen and elite levels. Given the magnitude of the parameters in the two equations, the impact is large among both citizens and elites, with the impact being more than twice as high among the elites as it is among citizens.

Looking once again at the simulation results for citizens, one can detect very clear differences in the expected position on the socialism-capitalism scale for the different age groups in the two regions (see Figure 3.5c). Within the youngest age category, 18–24, West Germans score on average 7 points higher on the socialism-capitalism scale. Note that within this age group, the confidence intervals actually meet and one cannot with complete confidence reject the idea that there is little difference between the two regions' in terms of their position on the scale. However, the gap widens significantly as age increases and among the oldest age group, 65 and over, the average difference between the two regions is nearly 18 points. Given the size of confidence intervals for the set of estimates, one can be almost completely assured that the difference between the two regions' oldest age group is at least 14 points and may be as high as 21 points.

The parameter on the union membership variable is, as predicted, negative and statistically significant. Thus, membership in unions entails greater support for socialist values than does non-membership. As with most of the other elements' effects revealed in the analyses of citizens and elites, the impact of this factor is far greater among elites than it is among citizens.

To further assess the validity of the approach, a parallel effort was undertaken using a different data set for citizens drawn from the ISSP Role of Government (III) surveys conducted in Germany during 1996. It should be noted that it was not possible to operationalize all of the elements of the model in the same way as done with the citizen survey conducted in conjunction with the Democracy and Local Government Study. Two variables in the analysis of the ISSP had to be operationalized differently, with the most important difference being in the components of the socialism-capitalism scale.[15]

As it turns out, the results (see Table 3.13b) are quite similar to those reported above. Gender is important in that females have a greater tendency to be supportive of socialist principles than do males. The impact of education is positive; however, in this case the estimated parameter is not statistically significant. Income again has a positive and statistically significant parameter indicating that those with higher incomes are more supportive of capitalist values. The signs on the parameters on age, region and interaction of the two terms are similar to those reported for citizens in the analysis above. Note, however, the regional terms parameter is much larger here, suggesting a very strong tendency among younger East Germans to be supportive of socialist values. Once again, age has no discernible impact by itself, but when combined with region has a negative effect, thus indicating that older citizens in the East provide greater support for socialist principles and that this tendency increases with age in the region. The impact of union membership is again negative, but in this case, the parameter is not statistically significant.

Overall, the evidence suggests that self-interest plays an important role in the way individuals orient themselves along the ideological dimension of socialism-capitalism. While socialization, in whatever form, may have an effect on how people align themselves on this major ideological axis within German political culture, the finding that East Germans have a greater affinity for socialism than do their West German fellow citizens can also be understood on the basis of objective economic conditions and the self-interest of individuals.

If an individual stands to benefit from a less capitalist and more active and interventionist government, support for such policies reflect a rational calculation on the part of that person. The East German region lags well behind the West in terms of income and wealth as well.[16] In addition, a significant part of East Germany's income derives from direct government transfers. These transfers constitute one third of the region's gross domestic product. It is in the self-interest of Eastern Germans, then, to be supportive of a more socialist economic order and for West Germans, who actually bear the direct costs of that order, to be less supportive.

---

15 The components of the scale are the variables used in Tables 3.9 and 3.10. Factor analysis of the items strongly supports the idea that the items do tap a single underlying dimension. Again, as with the socialism-capitalism measure used with the German data from the local elite and citizenry data the measure used is a summated scale ranging from 0 to 1.0, which is then multiplied by 100.

Again, the coding of the education variable differs. This time while seven categories are used, and while the first and the last are the same as those in the elite data, the intermediate categories differ from those in the elite data.

16 An extensive study of living situations in Germany produced under the auspices of the Federal Ministry of Labor shows that in 1998 the average level of per capita net wealth in East Germany was only 35 per cent of that to be found in West Germany (BMA, 2001, Table 1.45).

Information from the 1992 ISSP Survey on Social Inequality helps reinforce this argument. In that survey respondents were presented with the following situation: 'If income became more equal in Germany, some people would get higher income and some would get lower incomes.' They were asked to respond in terms of their expectations about what would happen to their own income in such a situation. Nearly 42 per cent of the West Germans responded that they thought their own incomes would definitely or probably increase. On the other side of the former Wall, nearly 86 per cent of the East German respondents indicated that they expected that their own incomes would definitely or probably increase as a consequence of such an egalitarian redistribution.

There are clearly conflicts of interest and differences in perceptions between the populations of the two regions. In the richer of the two regions, only a minority (but still a large one) of the people see themselves as gaining from an egalitarian redistribution of income in Germany. In the poorer of the two regions, an overwhelming majority expects that they would all individually gain from the implementation of such a policy.

However, there may be even more to this than the straightforward and objective disparity between the two regions in terms of economic prosperity. An individual may be poorly informed. And this misinformation or lack of information could prompt individuals to prefer some strategic alternative in the false belief that this will achieve a favorable result for her- or himself.[17] This can best be illustrated by examining the effect of individuals' actual income levels on their expectations regarding whether they would gain financially from an egalitarian redistribution of income within their society. A logit model, with the expectation of individual economic gain from an egalitarian redistribution of income within the country as the dependent variable, has been estimated using the same set of independent variables employed to explain positions on the socialism-capitalism scale.[18] All of the data are taken from the 1992 ISSP study. The estimation results are presented in Table 3.14.

The model does a good job in capturing the actual distribution of responses on whether people expect to gain or not from such a policy. Seventy per cent of the responses are correctly predicated. The chi-square statistic based on the log-likelihoods of the model and the null model is quite large and statistically significant. The parameters are in the expected direction and are generally statistically significant. What is of particular interest here is the substantive implications of the parameter on

---

17 Another factor at work may be that experience in similar situations has led some individuals to suspect that the application of a policy that should favor them or at least leave them unaffected may be so distorted as to injure them.

18 This simpler specification works as well as the logit model with the interaction between age and region. Indeed, the interaction term is only marginally substantively and statistically significant (unlike the formulation predicting position on the socialism-capitalism scale). The change in effects of income on the predicted values of expected gain, to be discussed below, is quite small.

Table 3.14 Logit analysis: expectations about changes to one's income as a consequence of an egalitarian redistribution*

	Coeff. (z-stat.)
Gender	.15
	(1.54)
Education	−.31
	(−6.93)
Income	−.22
	(−7.73)
Age	.23
	(−7.73)
Region	1.80
	(15.06)
Union member	.04
	(0.37)
Constant	2.79
	(10.26)
Summary statistics:	
$LL_{nullmodel}$	−1,652
LL_{model}	−1,367
χ^2	568
p	.001
Number of cases	2,466

* 1 = expect income to increase; 0 = expect income to decrease or remain the same.

Source: Data in this table drawn from the International Social Survey Project (ISSP 1996) Studies on the Role of Government, III (ZA Study 2900). Data set supplied by the Zentralarchiv für Sozialforschung an der Universität zu Köln.

the income term in the equation. What does it imply for the relationship between an individual's income level and that person's expectation of income gain as a consequence of an egalitarian redistribution of income within society? Figure 3.6 provides estimates of this relationship in both regions of Germany.

It is important to remember that the categorization scheme for income is the same across both regions. Furthermore, East Germans are far more concentrated in the

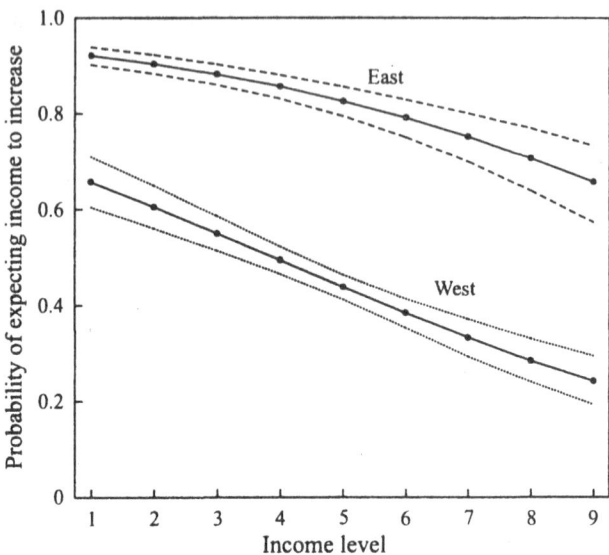

Figure 3.6 Effect of income level on expected gain from an egalitarian redistribution of income

lower income categories than are the West Germans.[19] Indeed, while 60 per cent of the East Germans are in the three lowest income categories in this data set, slightly less than 30 per cent of the West Germans fall into these low-income groupings. Such different distributions would account for part of the relatively larger share of East Germans expecting to benefit financially from redistribution. Nevertheless, it does not account for all of this as shown clearly in the graphic. At every income level, there is an appreciable difference between the two regions' populations and their expectations of financial gain from an egalitarian redistribution of income. For example, within the lowest income category on average about 66 per cent of West Germans expect to benefit from such a redistribution, 92 per cent of East Germans in that category hold that belief. Moreover, while the average expectation of gain drops by 37 per cent as one moves from the lowest to the second highest income category in the West, it drops by less than 22 per cent in the East.[20] Thus, at every income level, even the

---

19 Again, monthly net household income is employed. The income categories used are similar to those reported in Table 3.12, although because the coding scheme in the ISSP survey did not allow exactly the same operationalization, the higher categories are slightly different. Category 7 in this data set is for the income range from DM 5,500 to DM 5,999, 8 is for the range DM 6,000 through DM 7,999 and 9 is for the open-ended range extending from DM 8,000 upwards.

20 Since the highest (the 9th) income category is open-ended or unbounded, using this category for comparison is problematic and so I have chosen to use the 8th category that is a closed grouping.

highest ones, a large majority of East Germans anticipate financial gain from an egalitarian redistribution of income. From the fourth through the highest income grouping level in the West, only a minority anticipate such gains.

The general patterns in relationship between income and anticipated gain from redistribution in both regions are pretty well aligned with expectations. Further, the difference one observes in the proportions of the population anticipating gain from an egalitarian redistribution fit what one would broadly expect given the fact that in the East there is a far larger proportion of the population in the lower income categories.[21]

Still, there are a couple of peculiar features of the two regional relationships. First, why is it that such a relatively low number of people in the lowest income categories (where income is well below the average for the country as a whole) in the West do not anticipate to gain from a policy of egalitarian redistribution? This may be due to the widespread view in the West that even the poorest would be called upon to pay a cost to bring the standard of living in the East up to that of the West. And, indeed, as it turned out, those in the lower and medium categories were clearly bearing significant and perhaps disproportionate costs. This was particularly evident by the way in which the federal government managed to impose a great deal of the burden of reunification onto lower and middle income earners through increases in social security program contributions as well as indirect taxes (Rürup, 2000). This may have contributed to the peculiarly low proportion of poorer people in the region anticipating a financial gain through redistribution.

Second, why is it that East Germans in the highest income categories expect gain from an egalitarian redistribution while those in the same categories in the West do not? The very low proportion in the West accords with what one would expect, but the fact that majorities of the high-income earners in the East anticipate gain from such policy is inconsistent with the laws of mathematics and actual economic conditions. This perhaps shows a lack of information about unified Germany's economic reality on the part of Easterners in these categories. While it was generally the case that East Germans were clearly convinced that the economic situation was much better in the Federal Republic than in the GDR, perhaps their exposure to West German media may have given them a far brighter and rosier picture of the economic situation there than was actually the case.

Overall, the evidence presented in this section goes a long way in substantiating an alternative to the widespread view of the sources of ideological preferences. This

---

21 Note that in a parallel but open-ended question to the respondents, people were asked to name the exact amount of their households' net monthly income. Far fewer (59 per cent) answered this question than did the question where they were asked to choose which broad category their household's net income fit (84 per cent). Still, based on the open-ended question, the average household net income in the East was approximately DM 2,250; this is only 67 per cent of the corresponding West figure of approximately DM 3,350. These figures line up relatively well with information on household income in 1993 provided the Federal Ministry of Labor's report on living situations in Germany (BMA, 2000, Table 1.12).

widespread view emphasizes the effects of cultural socialization. Numerous scholars have adduced evidence in the German context that show large differences on ideological preferences between the two regions, particularly on the socialist-capitalism dimension and have concluded that this supports the socialization model. In turn, this finding lends support to pessimistic expectation that the divergence between the two regions will not be eliminated prior to the passage of generations.

The approach presented here argues that the rational self-interest of an individual is the principal source of ideological preferences. It has been shown that attributes of individuals that would lead a rational being to favor either socialism or capitalism have the effects attributed to them. And, importantly, the implications of this are far less pessimistic than those derived from the socialization approach. Improvements in income and enhancement of the labor market possibilities within the East German region would go a long way in eliminating the ideological gap between the two regions.

Conclusion

This chapter set out to examine two aspects of German political culture. The first relates to shared assumptions and meanings and the second to values. The primary aim of the chapter was to illuminate the differences and similarities between elites and citizens of the two regions as well as to assess the degree to which the two parts of Germany differ from other long-established as well as transitional democracies.

In dealing with the first matter, an undertaking was made to confirm an interesting finding developed by Robert Rohrschneider in his extensive study of politicians in East and West Berlin. Rohrschneider reports some remarkable differences in the way in which the elites from the two parts of the city define democracy. He concludes that the elites from the eastern part of the city were far more prone than their western colleagues to define democracy in terms of social equality and direct participation. Using the same instrument and coding scheme, this question was examined among the broader group of East and West German local elites included in this study. Unlike Rohrschneider's Berlin elites, these elites evidence no important differences in the ways in which they conceive of democracy. Indeed, on at least this level, the political cultures of the local elites of both regions seem very similar.

Attention then turned to the question of ideological values and the differences between the local political and administrative elites of the two regions. Here, relying upon a set of scales long used by the international project on Democracy and Local Governance, a portrait of East and West German elites was presented and a comparison with local elites in other democracies provided. While some interesting similarities and differences emerged, it was shown that there are good reasons to suspect the utility of these scales in providing a picture of political culture. This, in turn, led to an effort at developing a more robust portrayal of the main ideological dimensions within the German regions and the other countries included here for comparison purposes.

This effort resulted in the uncovering of two dimensions that capture significant ideological conflicts on political and economic order. These two dimensions, authoritarianism-libertarianism and socialism-capitalism are indeed the same axes of ideological division that Kitschelt has argued best characterizes the political culture of modern industrialized societies. It turns out that, on the whole, local elites in both East and West Germany have quite similar positions on the authoritarianism-libertarianism dimension while holding strikingly different positions on the socialism-capitalism dimension. This pattern is evident as well between the general populations of the two regions.

While others have noted this difference between the two regions' populations and elites on the ideological dimension of economic order, they have generally treated this as a residue of socialization effects associated with the two opposed regimes in existence prior to reunification. In this chapter, an alternative approach to the sources of this difference was presented. This approach, based on a model of rational self-interest turns out to be at least as adequate an explanation of the difference and one with far less pessimistic implications for the potential of convergence in the political cultures of the two regions.

Chapter 4

Problem-Ridden and Conflict-Riven

Introduction

The chapter provides a picture of the problems, responsibilities, capacities and successes of local government as seen through the eyes of the elites and, to an extent, the citizens within these communities. It adds to this picture by providing a view of the conflicts that exist within these towns and cities and the extent to which they hinder policy-making and community development. First, I describe the problem agendas of the local elites. Comparing these agendas with those defined by the citizens governed by these elites then complements this description. In addition, the problem agendas defined by the elites of the two German regions are contrasted with those formulated by local elites in other countries. Second, the beliefs the local elites have with respect to the responsibilities of local government as well as the powers and capacities of local government to act are presented. Following that, I describe the conflicts and divisions within the communities, as reported by these elites and examine the extent to which these are believed to hinder the success of local governance and development. Finally, I turn to the elites' assessments of their policy-making activities and the successes and failures that they report. This last is complemented by an examination of the extent to which the elites evaluate the overall performance of the local political system and, more importantly, the evaluations of the performances of different actors and institutions in the local system provided by citizens within the communities. This latter serves as a background to the focus in the succeeding chapter where an attempt is made to account for the success and failure of these local governments in the eyes of the citizens ruled by these governments.

Problems Confronting the Local Communities

At every level of the political system problems arise, that need to be dealt with by those engaged in governing. In this section, I provide an overview of the problems that the elites report as being on the agenda of their local governments.[1] This is supplemented by comparing aspects of this agenda with the reports on a similar question posed to citizens in a sub-sample of the communities in the study. In addition, com-

---

[1] An informative study that is annually carried out by the DIFU queries city planners in scores of German towns and cities on the major problems of these communities (see, e.g., Schmidt-Eichstaedt, 1991; Bretschneider, 1994).

parisons are provided with the problem agendas that confront local elites in other democracies, both in some of the more established in the West and in some that have recently begun to take root in Central Europe.

The questionnaire used in the elite study initially concentrates on the problem agenda of the local elites. It does this by first asking the respondents, in an open-ended form, to name the three most important problems confronting their communities. This is followed up by a menu of problem areas that substantially corresponds to the list of problem areas contained in the questionnaire employed in other national studies by members of the Democracy and Local Governance International Program. The list in the German elite survey is a slightly amended version of the International Program's list, with a number of other areas of potential relevance in the German context being added. Let me turn first to the open-ended question on the three most important problems confronting the community.

The question prompted a wide variety of answers. Nevertheless, it was possible to classify the answers by adopting a coding scheme that permits one to categorize the answers employing the fixed-list of problem areas used in the close-ended question and supplementing this list by adding a number of other categories. Even with all of these categories, it is still clear that there are only a limited number of areas where large numbers of the responses fit. The results of the classification of the responses are presented in Table 4.1. This table summarizes the responses based on the following procedure. First, the sum of all answers to these questions was calculated (note that some respondents did not answer the question and others supplied only one or two problems). Second, the total number of times an answer fit one of the categories was calculated and this figure was then used to calculate the percentage of times it appeared in the sum of all responses. Note that individuals sometimes listed a problem more than once that fell within the same general category. An example of this would be the mention of high unemployment in the community as the first response and then the mention of lack of jobs (or training positions) for young people in the community as the second or third response to this question. Each of these responses is counted as a mention of the general problem category of unemployment. Had none of the respondents answered so, the percentages mentioned here would be easily translated into a more interpretable form by multiplying by three. Thus, in the case of the financial capacity of local government in the West, approximately 76 per cent of all respondents would have mentioned this as a most important problem. While the observed tendency to provide multiple mentions of what can be considered the same problem area is not widespread, it was felt to be more legitimate to present the results on this question in the way it has been done.

As can be seen in the table, the problem category most frequently mentioned deals with the financial capacity of local governments.[2] Indeed, in the West, this problem

---

2 The results from some DIFU surveys (Bretschneider, 1994) on problems in town/city development correspond with this finding. While local transportation issues led the problem agenda in earlier years (cf., Schmidt-Eichstaedt, 1991), budgetary consolidation, especially in the Western communities, has come to the fore in recent times.

Table 4.1 Salience of problems in the eyes of the elites (percentage identifying area as one of the three most important facing the community)

	East Germany	West Germany	Difference East-West*
Unemployment	16.5	7.6	8.9
Poverty	0.4	0.6	−0.2
Economic development	13.4	6.6	6.9
City planning and development	6.4	5.1	1.3
Inherited burdens	1.3	0.2	1.1
Conversions	0.4	1.4	−1.0
Property-rights questions	1.6	0.4	1.2
Housing	6.2	5.3	0.9
Environment	1.1	3.0	−1.9
Waste disposal (and fees)	4.1	4.9	−0.8
Social services	1.0	1.1	0.0
Education	1.8	3.5	−1.8
Recreation and culture	2.1	0.7	1.5
Health services	0.0	0.2	−0.2
Youth policy	1.6	0.8	0.8
Improvements in public infrastructure	4.6	3.0	1.6
Financial capacity of local government	19.8	25.4	−5.6
Costs of local government administration	1.6	2.0	−0.4
Efficiency of local government administration	2.9	4.9	−2.0
Control of local government administration	0.3	0.7	−0.4
Local public transportation	0.2	3.2	−2.9
Traffic (and parking)	6.0	12.7	−6.7
Public safety	1.6	0.5	1.1
Conflict in local political system	1.0	1.1	0.0
Citizen participation	0.8	1.3	−0.5
Inter-governmental relations	2.4	0.9	1.5
Relations between Germans and foreigners	0.0	0.3	−0.3
Immigration	0.0	1.6	−1.6
Other	0.8	1.2	−0.4

* Positive difference implies problem more frequently mentioned as one of the three most important in the East, negative more frequently mentioned in West. As with Eldersveld et al. (1994), based on total number of problems mentioned.

Source: Democracy and Local Government in Germany, Elite Surveys.

area is cited twice as often as the next most frequently mentioned item. In the East, however, the financial situation of the local governments has only a slight lead over the second most frequently mentioned problem, unemployment. The whole domain related to the financial and management aspects of the local city government clearly stands out as a major area of concern for the elites. Adding across the four categories, financial capacity, costs, efficiency and control of the local government apparatus, one-third of all responses in the West fit into this area. In the East, nearly a fourth of all responses are found in this area.

Closely related, in both substantive terms and in its salience on the problem agendas of local government elites in both East and West is the economic situation within their communities. This is particularly prominent in the East. The dominant category among the seven that are loosely combined in this general area is unemployment. In the East, over 16 per cent of all responses to this question indicate that the labor market situation represents one of the three major problems in their communities. Another way of seeing this, assuming that there were no duplicate mentions of the problem category by any single individual, is that nearly half the respondents suggest that it is one of the three most important problems. Not as prominent in the West, still 7.6 per cent of the responses fall into this category. The category of economic development is almost as salient with 13.4 per cent of all the responses in the East and 6.6 per cent of all the responses in the West. Also relatively frequently mentioned in this broad area is the category of housing with 6.2 per cent of all responses in the East and 5.3 in the West falling into this category. In all, slightly more than 46 per cent of all responses to the question, what are the three most important problems confronting your local community, refer in the East to the economic situation in the community; in the West, slightly more than 27 per cent of the responses are to be found here.

The environment does not register very prominently on the two regional lists of most important problems. Only 1.1 per cent of the responses in the East and 3 per cent of those in the West mention this. The closely related category of waste disposal is more frequently mentioned, with 4.1 per cent of the elites in the East and 4.9 per cent in the West citing this. However, it should be noted that frequently this item was joined with the problem of the fees that are charged for this service by the local government.

Six categories of public services, which to varying degrees are in the sphere of responsibility of local government units, were mentioned. These range from social services and welfare to improvements in the local public infrastructure. However, none of the items received a great deal of attention.

The general area of transportation does seem to be on the agenda of these elites. This is particularly the case of traffic (and parking) problems in the local community. It is especially prominent in the West, nearly 13 per cent of all responses fall into this category; in the East, it constitutes 6 per cent of all of the responses. Far less frequently mentioned was local public transportation in both regions.

Public safety does not rank very high in either region for these elites in terms of its placement as one of the most important problems confronting the community. The same also extends to purely political problems and to the general problem area of the place of foreigners in the local community.

In the questionnaire survey of citizens within a sub-sample of the towns and cities included in the elite study, the respondents were asked the same question: '[W]hat are the three most important problems confronting your community?'. Table 4.2 presents the results on this item from the citizen survey as well as those to be found amongst the elites within the same communities. In neither region, the East nor the West, does one detect completely similar distributions in terms of the way in which elites and citizens construct the problem agendas they see confronting their community. There are some significant similarities in a few areas, but also important points where discrepancies clearly exist.

Economic issues, a broad area, are treated with great concern by elites and citizens alike in both areas, especially in the East. Overall, approximately 49 per cent of the problems mentioned by citizens in this region dealt with economic concerns, while 46 per cent of the elites' (in the sub-sample of 15 cities) responses fell into this general area. However, differences exist with respect to the specific problem that citizens and elites see as most important. Thus, while 26.5 per cent of all responses by the citizens focused on unemployment, only 14.9 per cent of the elites responses did so. In turn, while citizens cited economic development 5.6 per cent of the time, the frequency with which this was mentioned by elites is twice as high. Economic concerns are cited with less frequency in the West (approximately 28 per cent of the problems cited by both groups), but the divergence between citizens and elites in the specific type of economic problem mentioned is comparable to that in the East.

A general area where citizens and elites diverge greatly in terms of the problems confronting their communities that they see as most important is to be found in the resource and control area of local government. While a salient item on the problem agenda for elites in both regions, this area barely registers among the citizens of their communities as an important problem. For example, in the East, while approximately 19 per cent of all elite responses cite the financial capacity of local government as one of the three most important problems confronting their community, only 2 per cent of the citizens' responses refer to this issue. Similarly, in the West, this is by far the most frequently cited issue by elites; 25 per cent of all responses from elites in these communities mention this item, while only 6.5 per cent of the citizens' responses fall into this category. Other items in this general area, while of some concern to the elites, barely register as significant problems in the minds of the citizens.

One issue emerges across the entire range of problems that clearly divides the elites and citizens in terms of the importance they attribute to it: this is the problem of traffic and parking within their communities. This item dominates the list of concerns for the citizens in the West, indeed it is mentioned two times more frequently then the issue of unemployment, the second most frequently cited problem, but receives far less concern from the elites in these towns and cities. This difference holds in the East as well, although unemployment is clearly seen more often as a major problem in that region. Public safety and education, the first in the East and the latter in the

Table 4.2 Salience of problems in the eyes of the citizens and the elites compared (percentage identifying area as one of the three most important facing the community, based on sub-sample of 30 cities)

	East Germany			West Germany		
	Citizens	Elites	Diff. citizens-elites	Citizens	Elites	Diff. citizens-elites
Unemployment	26.5	14.9	11.7	12.5	8.3	4.2
Poverty	0.5	0.0	0.5	0.7	1.0	−0.3
Economic development	5.6	12.7	−7.1	3.2	6.5	−3.3
City planning and development	5.7	7.5	−1.8	5.9	6.5	−0.6
Inherited burdens	0.0	1.7	−1.7	0.0	0.2	−0.2
Conversions	0.0	0.0	0.0	0.0	0.3	−0.3
Property-rights questions	0.0	1.8	−1.8	0.0	0.3	−0.3
Housing	10.9	7.5	3.3	6.0	4.9	1.1
Environment	4.2	1.8	2.4	5.8	3.3	2.5
Waste disposal (and fees)	3.5	4.4	−0.9	6.9	5.2	1.7
Social services	0.0	1.1	−1.1	0.0	5.1	−5.1
Education	3.7	1.5	2.2	9.0	2.4	6.6
Recreation and culture	2.1	1.8	0.3	2.5	1.1	1.3
Health services	0.3	0.0	0.3	0.2	0.3	−0.2
Youth policy	5.0	1.8	3.2	3.1	0.3	2.8
Improvements in public infrastructure	1.2	3.7	−2.5	0.6	1.5	−0.9
Financial capacity of local government	2.0	19.3	−17.3	6.5	25.1	−18.6
Costs of local government administration	0.0	1.7	−1.7	0.0	2.0	−2.0
Efficiency of local government administration	0.0	0.5	−0.5	0.0	0.8	−0.8
Control of local government administration	0.7	3.3	−2.6	0.5	4.6	−4.1
Local public transportation	0.0	0.0	0.0	0.0	2.6	−2.6
Traffic (and parking)	15.9	6.1	9.9	24.0	10.6	13.4
Public safety	7.3	1.1	6.2	3.2	0.5	2.7
Conflict in local political system	1.1	1.7	−0.5	1.7	1.3	0.4
Citizen participation	0.2	0.5	−0.3	0.3	1.3	−1.1
Inter-governmental relations	0.9	2.9	−2.0	0.3	1.1	−0.8
Relations between Germans and foreigners	0.3	0.0	0.3	0.8	0.3	0.4
Immigration	0.4	0.0	0.4	3.7	1.0	2.7
Other	2.0	0.7	1.3	2.8	1.5	1.4

Source: Democracy and Local Government in Germany, Elite and Citizen Surveys.

West, are two other issue areas where the elites and citizens divide in terms of the priorities they attach. In the West, education constitutes 9 per cent of all the problems mentioned by citizens, while the elites cite this only 3 per cent of the time. A similar asymmetry holds in the East on the issue of public safety; constituting more than 7 per cent of all the problems mentioned by the citizens, it makes up only 1 per cent of the problems mentioned by the elites in the region.

In addition to the open-ended question on problems confronting the community, the elite respondents were presented with a list of items. They were asked if any of these posed a problem and if the problem was major. There were seventeen items on the list and a breakdown of the results by region is provided in Table 4.3. What comes through clearly here is that hardly any area mentioned was not considered a problem confronting the community in the eyes of the elites. Across all 17 areas, approximately 82 per cent of the elites, on average, in the East considered these areas problematic. The corresponding figure in the West is nearly 71 per cent. Six of the areas in the East are considered major problems by a majority of the elite respondents. These include unemployment (95 per cent), economic development (85 per cent) housing (slightly more than 50 per cent) improvements in public infrastructure (68 per cent), the financial capacity of local government (92 per cent) and the costs of local government administration (nearly 78 per cent). In addition, 46 per cent of the Eastern respondents see public safety as a major problem confronting their local communities. In the West, the list is slightly smaller. Here four areas are considered to be major problems by a majority of the respondents and these four are among those just mentioned for the East: unemployment (55 per cent), economic development (nearly 54 per cent), the financial capacity of local government (nearly 83 per cent) and the costs of local government administration (66 per cent). A similar profile emerges when one examines the problem list on a community-by-community basis in each region (see Table 4.4). In this table, I have listed the percentage of towns/cities in each region where a majority of the respondents in a community report that this is a major problem area. Elites held unemployment to be a major problem in every town/city in the East and in three out of every five communities in the West. Economic development poses a major problem in all but one of the localities in the East and in more than half the towns/cities in the West. In more than 85 per cent of the towns/cities in the East, improvement in public infrastructure is reported by a majority to be a major problem, though this is the case in only one quarter of the communities in the West. In all the localities in the East and nearly all in the West, majorities report that the financial capacity of the local government constitutes a major problem. Costs of local government are also seen by majorities in very large percentages of the communities in both regions (approximately 95 per cent in the East and more than three quarters of the communities in the West). Finally, while public safety is not reported to be a major problem by a majority in any of the localities of the West, nearly half of the towns/cities of the East have majorities where this area is reported to be a major problem.

How do the local elite problem agendas within the two German regions compare with those reported by local elites in other countries? In their own view, German

Table 4.3 Broad overview of types of problems confronting elites (per cent)

	East Germany		West Germany		Difference East-West
	(1)	(2)	(1)	(2)	(2)
Unemployment	99.6	95.0	59.7	55.1	39.9
Poverty	90.7	25.7	86.1	21.1	4.6
Economic development	98.1	88.3	63.4	53.6	34.7
Housing	89.6	50.3	75.1	35.8	14.5
Environmental pollution	92.5	32.8	87.0	27.3	5.5
Social services and welfare	63.1	9.3	69.1	15.3	−6.0
Education	60.1	9.2	54.9	4.0	5.2
Recreation and culture	86.7	30.0	61.3	4.6	25.4
Health services	36.2	2.4	34.3	0.5	1.9
Improvements in public infrastructure	98.7	68.4	65.9	35.6	32.8
Public safety	95.0	46.0	64.8	15.8	30.2
Financial capacity of local government	99.6	92.0	90.2	82.6	9.4
Costs of local government administration	99.4	77.8	87.8	66.2	11.6
Efficiency of local government administration	88.0	34.9	85.5	32.4	2.5
Control of local government administration	83.4	31.5	81.3	29.4	2.1
Relations between Germans and foreigners	65.8	9.9	62.8	6.9	3.0
Immigration	54.0	5.8	71.6	23.4	−17.6
Average	82.4	41.7	70.6	30.0	11.7

(1) = see as problem (per cent); (2) = see as major problem (per cent).

Source: Democracy and Local Government in Germany, Elite Surveys.

local elites in both regions seem to be confronting more challenges and more severe challenges than their colleagues in most other nations (see Table 4.5 and Figure 4.1). The information in Table 4.5 is summarized in Figure 4.1 and draws on data from recent national studies conducted in conjunction with the International Program (the Czech Republic, Hungary, Poland and Slovakia in the East and Austria, the Netherlands,

Table 4.4 Percentage of cities where at least 50 per cent of elites consider the area a major problem

	East Germany	West Germany	Difference East-West
Unemployment	100.0	60.0	40.0
Poverty	8.1	5.0	3.1
Economic development	97.3	52.5	44.8
Housing	54.1	20.0	34.1
Environmental pollution	18.9	12.5	6.4
Social services and welfare	0.0	0.0	0.0
Education	18.9	0.0	18.9
Recreation and culture	0.0	0.0	0.0
Health services	0.0	0.0	0.0
Improvements in public infrastructure	86.5	25.0	61.5
Financial capacity of local government	100.0	95.0	5.0
Costs of local government administration	94.6	77.5	17.1
Efficiency of local government administration	21.6	22.5	−0.9
Control of local government administration	10.8	15.0	−4.2
Public safety	45.9	0.0	45.9
Relations between Germans and foreigners	0.0	0.0	0.0
Immigration	0.0	10.0	−10.0
Average	38.6	23.2	15.4

Source: Democracy and Local Government in Germany, Elite Surveys.

Spain, Sweden, Switzerland and the United States in the West). The values in this figure represent averages across 14 problem areas that are common to both the German and the other national questionnaires (in the German case, the three items included but not to be found in other national studies include: 'the financial capacity of local government', 'the efficiency of local government' and 'the control of local government administration').[3] The values along the horizontal dimension represent the mean across the fourteen problem areas of the percentages of the respondents in each nation that indicated problems existed, while the values along the vertical dimen-

---

3 One other major difference across the different national questionnaires deals with the item on the German questionnaire focusing on 'relations between Germans and foreigners'. Here, appropriate variations have been used to fit the national context; an example of this is the use of 'relations between the races' in the American study.

Table 4.5a Broad overview of types of problems confronting elites in East Germany and four Central European countries

	East Germany		Czech Republic		Hungary		Poland		Slovakia	
	(1)	(2)	(1)	(2)	(1)	(2)	(1)	(2)	(1)	(2)
Unemployment	99.6	95.0	43.2	7.6	97.9	62.6	96.4	62.7	97.2	40.2
Poverty	90.7	25.7	32.0	2.9	98.7	55.6	91.4	33.9	81.6	7.5
Economic development	98.1	88.3	82.3	23.0	96.4	52.1	92.1	47.2	95.7	48.3
Housing	89.6	50.3	98.0	64.3	91.3	35.0	98.7	63.0	99.1	71.4
Environmental pollution	92.5	32.8	76.0	19.8	–	–	95.5	46.2	80.6	20.4
Social services and welfare	63.1	9.3	34.0	7.0	91.9	24.4	89.6	25.0	35.6	3.8
Education	60.1	9.2	29.1	4.6	53.4	4.7	95.1	48.0	51.0	5.7
Recreation and culture	86.7	30.0	53.7	11.6	72.4	15.0	82.3	16.2	64.6	9.9
Health services	36.2	2.4	67.7	15.5	76.7	9.8	97.1	52.8	89.6	38.4
Improvements in public infrastructure	98.7	68.4	79.5	17.6	87.8	32.0	97.1	40.7	88.6	23.2
Control of local government administration	99.4	77.8	68.5	14.0	96.3	61.3	66.0	9.0	86.8	33.2
Public safety	95.0	46.0	67.8	18.4	84.1	32.8	93.0	47.3	89.0	33.5
Intra-group relations	65.8	9.9	47.6	2.9	21.0	4.0	12.5	1.3	82.0	13.3
Immigration	54.0	5.8	19.7	4.0	61.7	23.7	14.9	3.4	32.6	5.2
Average	80.7	39.4	57.1	15.2	79.2	31.8	80.1	35.5	76.7	25.3

(1) = see as problem (per cent); (2) = see as major problem (per cent).

Source: Democracy and Local Government International Data Base.

Table 4.5b Broad overview of types of problems confronting elites in West Germany and six Western countries

	West Germany		Austria		Netherlands		Spain		Sweden		Switzerland		United States	
	(1)	(2)	(1)	(2)	(1)	(2)	(1)	(2)	(1)	(2)	(1)	(2)	(1)	(2)
Unemployment	97.0	55.1	54.5	16.5	84.0	32.6	98.5	71.4	81.0	18.4	98.9	69.0	75.0	17.9
Poverty	87.7	21.1	35.9	1.8	83.0	21.1	83.1	23.5	54.6	4.7	87.2	18.1	76.5	13.8
Economic development	92.8	53.6	66.7	17.7	61.3	20.0	85.3	48.2	73.4	18.4	88.2	48.9	84.2	31.7
Housing	85.8	35.8	97.0	58.9	61.3	15.1	81.9	32.3	56.6	7.4	85.8	40.6	74.8	19.5
Environmental pollution	89.3	27.3	83.5	30.4	48.6	4.8	57.7	15.1	76.1	7.9	85.9	39.7	69.3	9.1
Social services and welfare	62.7	15.3	48.1	7.0	34.4	1.2	62.5	9.7	64.9	5.8	93.3	45.2	63.3	9.5
Education	34.2	4.0	16.8	2.1	25.4	3.4	37.3	3.6	71.1	6.4	45.7	13.6	69.0	23.9
Recreation and culture	48.1	4.6	17.9	1.5	24.8	2.9	46.5	10.8	51.5	3.1	56.9	12.4	43.9	7.9
Health services	21.3	0.5	36.1	8.5	17.2	0.7	49.7	7.7	46.4	3.2	62.4	14.9	62.8	9.0
Improvements in public infrastructure	87.4	35.6	47.4	4.3	81.7	29.8	82.8	33.2	41.4	5.5	60.0	10.5	72.9	21.6
Control of local government administration	95.4	66.2	64.8	15.7	67.2	26.7	67.8	31.0	95.3	58.0	88.1	57.2	85.5	33.8
Public safety	69.8	15.8	33.9	7.1	70.4	14.7	50.2	5.9	79.9	8.7	66.4	15.8	78.5	39.6
Intra-group relations	64.8	6.9	29.7	3.5	–	–	–	–	49.4	3.4	76.8	15.5	66.5	14.4
Immigration	81.8	23.4	53.0	13.9	48.7	6.0	26.8	4.7	46.2	7.4	81.3	21.1	–	–
Average	72.7	26.1	49.0	13.5	54.5	13.8	63.9	22.9	63.4	11.3	76.9	30.2	70.9	19.4

(1) = see as problem (per cent); (2) = see as major problem (per cent).

Source: Democracy and Local Government International Data Base.

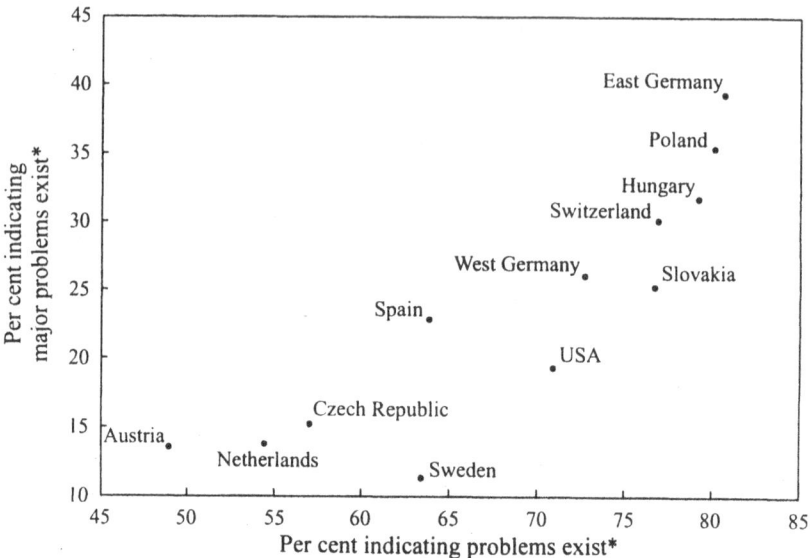

* Average across 14 policy areas.

Source: Democracy and Local Government International Data Base.

Figure 4.1 Elites' views of the extent and severity of local problems: an international problem comparison

sion show the national averages across the fourteen areas for the percentages of the respondents reporting that the problems being confronted were major.

For the Eastern part of Germany, perhaps the most appropriate countries to compare are Poland, Slovakia, Hungary and the Czech Republic. Here one sees that in only two of these four countries, i.e., Hungary and Poland, do local elites report problem agendas of the scope and severity that East German local elites suggest they confront. Comparing the West German elites with those of the six other Western countries one sees that only one of them, Switzerland, has local elites more frequently reporting both problems and severe problems. While the U.S. is comparable in terms of the extent to which the existence of problems is being reported, these seem to be severe in the eyes of a far smaller proportion of the American elites. Swedish and Austrian elites seem, by their own reports, to be confronting a smaller number of problems and far fewer of these elites report that the problems are of major importance.

Both East and West German local elites report that they are confronted with a wide range of important problems in their communities. Despite this diversity, a few problems stand out in terms of the frequency with which they are mentioned. In the main, these relate to economic difficulties, especially unemployment and economic development within the communities and the problem of the financial capacities of local governments. While citizens within these communities rank economic concerns high in their problem agendas, they are by far less concerned with the financial situation of their local governments. Their problem agendas give a very high ranking instead to the local traffic and parking problems. When asked to choose from among a large but fixed menu of potential problem areas, elites in both regions are prone to suggesting that nearly all of these areas constitute a problem for their communities. Furthermore, they hold that a significant number of issues, especially unemployment, economic development, the financial capacity as well as the costs of local government, pose major problems in the communities of both regions. In addition, in the East, housing and public safety seem to be major problems in the eyes of large numbers of the local elites. When compared with local elites in other countries, both East and West, the German local elites seem to be among those with the most crowded and severe problem agendas.

Responsibilities and Power of Local Government

Across nations, local governmental systems vary significantly in terms of the policy areas for which they are responsible (Norton, 1994; Page and Goldsmith, 1987; Baldersheim, 1996; Gunlicks, 1986; Linder, 1994). In some cases, local governments have wide-ranging formal responsibilities while in others local government either bear no responsibility for many areas or act as non-autonomous agents of higher-level government authorities. In turn, local government elites vary significantly in the degree to which they believe local governments should be responsible for problems within their communities (Eldersveld et al., 1995). Germany has a complicated federal system with a complex pattern of power sharing (Scharpf, 1988; Norton, 1994). Nevertheless, relative to many countries its local governments are granted widespread responsibilities and powers.

How do German local elites see the situation? Are they of the belief that their mandate is wide or narrow and, importantly, do they believe that the power and autonomy of local government is sufficient for the tasks at hand? Using the same list of 17 policy problem areas detailed in the last section, the elite respondents were asked to respond to two related questions. First, they were queried as to what level of government (local, state, federal) should have primary responsibility in each of the problem areas (note that non-governmental organizations and citizens themselves were also included as possible options for primary responsibility). Second, they were queried as to whether they felt local government indeed had sufficient power and autonomy to handle the problem areas. The results from these questions are summarized in Table 4.6.

There is a good deal of similarity in terms of the responses across the two regions. In twelve out of 17 policy fields, a majority in each region thought the primary responsibility should reside with local government. There is some disagreement as to which fields these should be. Thus, in the East, unemployment was seen by a slight

Table 4.6 Responsibility vs. power and autonomy of local government: inter-German comparisons

Local governments:	East Germany		West Germany	
	should have responsibility	have sufficient power & autonomy	should have responsibility	have sufficient power & autonomy
Unemployment	51.7	7.1	37.1	16.9
Poverty	39.6	27.2	31.5	25.0
Economic development	70.1	13.3	66.4	31.2
Housing	86.2	45.4	75.4	58.9
Environmental pollution	62.0	37.7	67.5	39.3
Social services and welfare	63.5	80.8	61.3	68.2
Education	54.9	67.3	60.2	74.1
Recreation and culture	87.7	62.0	80.5	90.2
Health services	46.4	84.2	35.2	72.6
Improvements in public infrastructure	79.8	31.5	82.1	55.9
Financial capacity of local government	65.5	10.9	70.5	21.9
Costs of local government administration	92.3	33.3	91.4	51.5
Efficiency of local government administration	90.1	55.0	89.7	67.6
Control of local government administration	44.8	60.3	62.3	67.4
Public safety	35.8	19.0	25.0	27.2
Relations between Germans and foreigners	52.3	73.7	61.2	70.7
Immigration	27.9	59.8	19.8	33.9

Source: Democracy and Local Government in Germany, Elite Surveys.

majority to be an area that should be of primary responsibility for local government. Only 37 per cent of the elites in the West agreed with this point of view. And, somewhat surprisingly, only a minority of Eastern elites sees the control of local government administration as a primary responsibility for local government itself. Alternatively, approximately 63 per cent of the elites in the West see this as a primary responsibility for local government.

One other difference is manifest. While Eastern elites, on average, have a slightly greater tendency to state that local governments should have primary responsibility for the 17 areas than Western elites do (average in East is 61.8 per cent while that in the West is 59.8 per cent), they are also less likely to agree that local governments have sufficient power and autonomy in these areas (Eastern average is 45.2 per cent while the Western average is 51.3 per cent).

What is critical in the comparison between the two items, responsibility on the one hand and power and autonomy on the other, is the degree to which there is concordance between the two. That is, if elites hold the belief that government at their level should have the primary responsibility for an area, do they also report that they have sufficient power and autonomy to cope with the area? Here the situation in both East and West, but particularly in the East, is such as to suggest there are severe misalignments. This can be seen readily in Figures 4.2 and 4.3 where I have charted

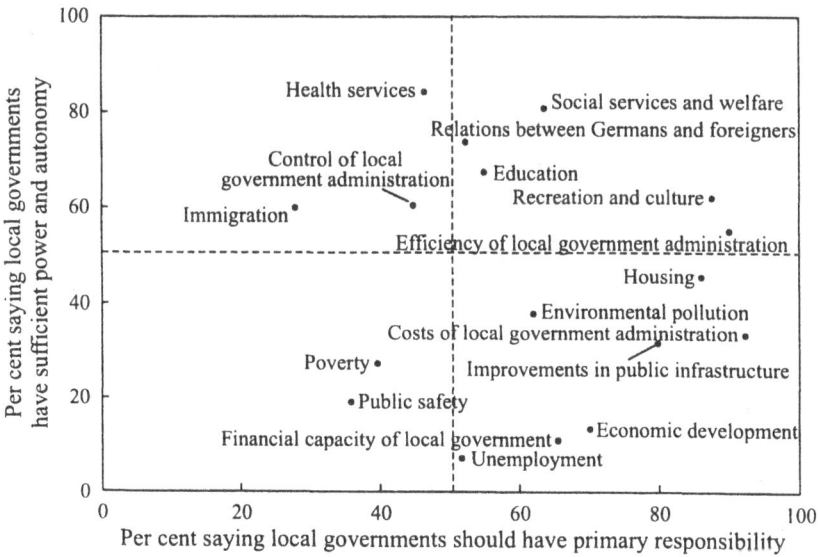

Source: Democracy and Local Government in Germany, Elite Surveys.

Figure 4.2 East German elites' views on the responsibility vs. power and autonomy of local government

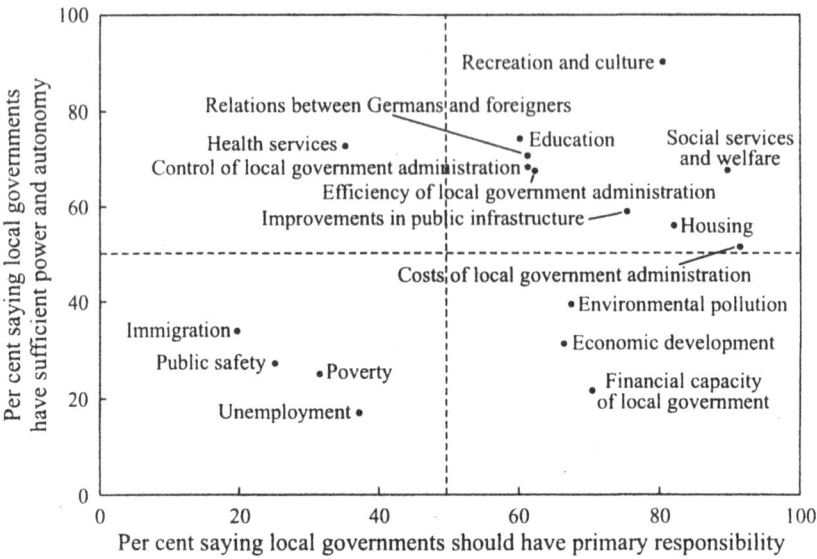

Source: Democracy and Local Government in Germany, Elite Surveys.

Figure 4.3   **West German elites' views on the responsibility vs. power and autonomy of local government**

the values presented above in Table 4.6. The vital region on these charts is in the lower-right hand quadrant. Here one sees functions where a majority (sometimes a very large majority) believes local government should have primary responsibility but where only a minority (and often a very small minority) believe that the power and autonomy of local government is sufficient.

In the East, there are seven policy areas where such a grave misalignment holds and these include the following: housing, the environment, the costs of local government, improvements in public infrastructure, economic development, the financial capacity of local government and unemployment.

In the West, the scope of misalignment based on the reports made by the local elites is clearly narrower. Here only three policy areas can be seen in the lower-right hand quadrant: the environment, economic development and the financial capacity of local government.

Some limited comparisons on this issue can be made with a number of other countries. Using a less extensive set of policy area items (13 areas are included in the International Program questionnaire; not included as in the German case are the policy areas of the financial capacity and costs of local government as well as the efficiency and control of local government administration), similar questions have been asked in four Central European countries and some of the Western democracies.[4] In addition, the question on primary responsibility by local government (but not the question on sufficient power and autonomy) has been asked in the Swedish study. Finally, using a much-reduced list (8 items only) both questions were also posed in the American study.

Tables 4.7a and 4.7b provide a perspective on the situation in other countries. If the four Central European countries are used as a basis of comparison with the situation in East Germany, one sees that, with the exception of Hungary, there is a tendency among the local elites of the new federal states to be moderately less willing to hold the view that local government should have primary responsibility for the policy areas listed. Further, the local elites in the new federal states and those in Hungary stand out for their belief that local government has less than sufficient power and autonomy to cope with the problems in these policy areas. While, on average, only a minority hold the view that local government is equipped to deal with these problems, clear majorities in three of the other four Central European Eastern nations are of the view that they have sufficient power and autonomy to cope.

The situation in the eyes of the local elites in the old federal states is not very different. Thus, while they are less willing than their colleagues in Sweden, Switzerland and the USA to accept that local government has primary responsibility for these policy areas, they are far more willing than their Austrian and Dutch colleagues to do so. And though they are less sanguine than their Swiss, Dutch and American colleagues on the question of whether local government has sufficient power and autonomy in these areas, they are as optimistic on this question as their Austrian colleagues and more optimistic than the Spanish elites.

It would seem that local elites in both the new and old federal states hold the view that local government has a wide range of areas for which it should bear primary responsibility. Nevertheless, these elites appear to be caught in a dilemma. They simultaneously believe that in many of these areas they have insufficient power and autonomy to cope with the problems they confront. Three deficit areas stand out because there is a consensus across both East and West; these include the policy areas of the environment, local economic development and, finally, the financial capacity of their local governments.

---

4   Note as well that there is some inconsistency across the different national studies in whether an item was included or excluded. Thus, while social services and immigration are included in the power and autonomy question in the Czech Republic, neither is part of the list in the responsibility question. The same holds for Poland. In Slovakia, only the immigration question was dropped. In Austria, the questions on social services and minority relations have been dropped from the list in the responsibility question, although they appear in the list on power and autonomy. In Sweden and Switzerland, the social services and immigration question are missing from the list in the responsibility question.

Table 4.7a Responsibility vs. power and autonomy of local government: comparison between East Germany and four Central European countries

	East Germany		Czech Republic		Hungary		Poland		Slovakia	
	(1)	(2)	(1)	(2)	(1)	(2)	(1)	(2)	(1)	(2)
Unemployment	51.7	7.1	41.1	30.5	19.0	9.0	60.9	32.0	55.6	43.1
Poverty	39.6	27.2	51.5	41.1	34.8	18.5	75.9	57.9	47.2	44.2
Economic development	70.1	13.3	66.4	60.7	16.5	16.6	69.2	60.7	–	64.0
Housing	86.2	45.4	81.8	87.0	43.4	10.5	82.4	70.0	81.3	80.2
Environmental pollution	62.0	37.7	79.1	75.9	57.9	29.7	68.1	68.5	77.9	66.2
Social services and welfare	63.5	80.8	–	86.1	–	31.1	–	82.9	76.2	68.6
Education	54.9	67.3	32.1	37.4	34.0	55.0	73.7	39.9	43.0	21.6
Recreation and culture	87.7	62.0	87.0	93.9	61.4	46.0	81.3	91.7	92.1	94.3
Health services	46.4	84.2	47.6	40.6	34.5	63.0	55.4	25.8	44.9	23.8
Improvements in public infrastructure	79.8	31.5	98.8	98.8	75.4	35.9	98.4	95.3	95.8	98.6
Public safety	35.8	19.0	74.2	60.9	33.0	19.6	45.8	31.0	72.9	60.1
'Minority relations'	52.3	73.7	42.0	44.7	–	52.2	23.0	26.4	37.4	46.2
Immigration	27.9	59.8	–	40.7	30.2	–	–	–	–	45.4
Average for all items available	58.3	46.8	63.8	61.4	40.0	32.3	66.7	56.8	65.8	58.2

(1) = local governments have responsibility (per cent); (2) = local governments have power and autonomy (per cent).

Table 4.7b Responsibility vs. power and autonomy of local government: comparison between West Germany and six Western countries

	West Germany (1)	West Germany (2)	Austria (1)	Austria (2)	Netherlands (1)	Netherlands (2)	Spain (1)	Spain (2)	Sweden (1)	Sweden (2)	Switzerland (1)	Switzerland (2)	United States (1)	United States (2)
Unemployment	37.1	16.9	18.0	21.9	33.6	26.4	58.6	20.5	61.8	—	46.7	21.0	—	—
Poverty	31.5	25.0	26.5	39.6	38.1	27.2	75.0	56.3	78.0	—	66.9	52.2	—	—
Economic development	66.4	31.2	70.1	44.5	44.4	57.0	70.0	31.6	78.6	—	46.5	35.1	71.2	80.2
Housing	75.4	58.9	63.5	30.9	75.4	71.6	79.3	48.6	88.0	—	65.4	54.3	55.0	62.1
Environmental pollution	67.5	39.3	51.9	32.9	38.1	66.9	82.7	59.0	91.8	—	68.4	48.1	97.3	39.2
Social services and welfare	61.3	68.2	—	72.1	—	94.7	—	69.1	—	—	—	79.3	33.4	41.2
Education	60.2	74.1	10.1	50.0	31.2	49.9	41.5	10.5	85.9	—	46.8	71.8	52.6	44.8
Recreation and culture	80.5	90.2	79.4	91.3	69.7	95.7	94.1	85.6	74.5	—	81.8	91.3	—	—
Health Services	35.2	72.6	27.0	64.3	17.3	46.3	41.9	15.4	65.0	—	43.4	65.1	—	—
Improvements in public infrastructure	82.1	55.9	70.1	75.9	52.5	63.5	79.5	56.3	93.6	—	87.4	88.2	—	—
Public safety	25.0	27.2	16.1	42.6	75.7	49.9	77.7	60.3	46.6	—	46.2	51.1	93.1	89.8
'Minority relations'	61.2	70.7	—	50.7	—	66.4	—	44.3	70.7	—	60.8	74.7	56.3	66.9
Immigration	19.8	33.9	39.7	44.1	52.7	53.4	83.3	13.0	—	—	—	42.9	—	—
Average for all items available	54.1	51.1	42.9	50.8	48.1	59.1	71.2	43.9	75.9	—	60.0	59.6	67.7	63.2

(1) = local governments have responsibility (per cent); (2) = local governments have power and autonomy (per cent).

Source: Democracy and Local Government International Data Base.

Divisions and Conflicts within the Community

Local government elites may be confronted with a large array of major problems and simultaneously faced with the dilemma of insufficient power to deal with their responsibilities. Nevertheless, in an atmosphere of cooperation and lack of conflict, where the community is not divided, it may still be possible to achieve success in governance through creative policy-making. The situation in Germany during the years after unification would appear to be one where local government elites are overburdened with problems and believe that the power and autonomy available to them is insufficient in an appreciable number of these areas to handle the problems. Is the broader situation within which they operate, in particular, their communities and conflicts and divisions that mark these communities such as to ameliorate or exacerbate this situation?

To deal with this query it is possible to draw upon the answers the elite respondents provided to a series of questions on conflicts and divisions within their communities that was posed in our questionnaire. Let me turn to examine the pattern of responses to these questions.

Table 4.8 provides data that help to answer the general question and it presents a rather bleak picture. In both East and West, two-thirds of the elites report that there are conflicts within their communities that interfere with problem-solving. Remarkably, this is the opinion of a majority of elites in nearly every city within both regions. In the opinion of the elites, as well, these conflicts pose severe difficulty in that they hinder the development of their communities. While not a majority view, it is one held

Table 4.8 Conflicts interfering with the solution to problems and the development of community: inter-German comparison (per cent)

	East Germany	West Germany
Reporting conflicts interfere (to varying degrees) with the solution of problems	66.6	66.3
Cities where majority report conflicts interfere with the solution of problems	89.2	87.5
Reporting conflicts interfere (to varying degrees) with the development of the community	44.0	43.9
Reporting conflicts interfere very much with the development of the community	43.2	40.0

Source: Democracy and Local Government in Germany, Elite Surveys.

Table 4.9 An international comparison of conflicts interfering with the solution to problems and the development of community (per cent)

	East Germany	Czech Rep.	Hungary	Poland	Slovakia
Reporting conflicts interfere (to varying degrees) with the solution of problems	66.6	30.8	52.1	67.9	29.9
Reporting conflicts interfere very much with the development of the community	44.0	13.6	15.2	15.2	10.3

	West Germany	Austria	Netherlands	Spain	Sweden	Switzerland	United States
Reporting conflicts interfere (to varying degrees) with the solution of problems	66.3	49.3	38.6	48.8	27.1	53.5	83.1
Reporting conflicts interfere very much with the development of the community	43.9	27.2	14.7	26.1	13.1	45.3	31.7

Source: Democracy and Local Government International Data Base.

by approximately 44 per cent of the elites in both regions. In addition, it is the opinion of majorities in 40 per cent or more of the cities in both regions.

Again, the German local elites stand out in a comparison with the elites in other countries. Table 4.9 provides an overview of how elites in both parts of Germany as well as in other countries responded to the two questions: '[A]re there conflicts within your community that hinder problem-solving?' and '[A]re there conflicts in your community that hinder its development?'. With respect to the first question, only the local elites in Poland and the United States respond positively to this question with as great or greater a frequency as the East and West Germans. Furthermore, only in Switzerland do we see such a large proportion of the local elites who respond that local conflicts hinder the development of their communities. In sum, local elites in both regions of Germany seem to confront more problems than those in other countries. They are more likely to be of the opinion that their powers and autonomy are insufficient relative to their responsibilities. Nevertheless, they also seem to be in a far worse situation than their colleagues in other countries when it comes to conflicts within their communities that both hinder problem-solving and hamper the development of their towns and cities.

What are the conflicts that prove so problematic for local German elites? Again, I rely upon both open-ended and close-ended questions to obtain the views of the elites. Table 4.10 provides an overview of the diversity of problems mentioned by the elite respondents in answering the open-ended question. While a wide variety of topics are mentioned, just as in the case of the open-ended question on the three most important problems confronting the community, there are nevertheless a few areas where most of the respondents concentrated their answers.[5]

In the East, the elites report that conflict within their local political systems represents the most frequent hindrance to problem-solving; this represents 22 per cent of all conflicts mentioned. Indeed, one can see that when this category is combined with other purely political problems and, in particular, conflicts over inter-governmental relations, it is clear that politics and not purely substantive issues represent more than a third of all reports on conflicts that hinder problem-solving within this region. The situation seems less severe in the West. Slightly more than 16 per cent of all reported conflicts that hinder problem-solving there deal with conflicts in the local political system. The total of politically-related conflicts comes to less than 21 per cent of all the conflicts that hinder problem-solving that were mentioned by the elites in the West.

A number of other sources of conflict stand out. In the West the traffic (and parking) situation seems to be the major source of conflict hampering problem-solving in the eyes of the elites; this leads all other categories with 22.3 per cent of all conflicts identified by the elites. Environmentally related issues are also major sources of conflict with the clash between 'environment and growth', the environment in general and the waste-disposal problem (along with associated fees) constituting nearly 17 per cent of all conflicts cited by the elites in this region. In both East and West economic issues constitute about 18 per cent of the conflicts. The financial and control aspects of local government seems to be particularly prone to producing conflict in the East with nearly 18 per cent of the items volunteered fitting into the four categories here; in the West this area may of course represent one of the most problematic but it seems to be less important as a source of conflict in the eyes of the elites.

---

5 The questionnaire was constructed in such a way that if a respondent indicated there were conflicts within the community that hindered problem-solving, she/he was prompted to name one or two. In terms of the way in which the data are presented in Table 4.11, the percentages refer to the frequency with which the respondent identified an area relative to the total number of conflict areas mentioned by all of the elites within the region. Again, I employ the basic list of problem areas described earlier and drawn from the close-ended question and added to this list those categories that captured the overwhelming residue of the responses.

Table 4.10 Types of conflicts hindering problem-solving in the communities as specified by the elites: inter-German comparison*

	East Germany	West Germany
Unemployment	0.9	0.0
Poverty	0.2	0.0
Economic development	7.6	6.2
City planning and development	3.2	7.4
Inherited burdens	0.5	0.0
Conversions	0.2	1.3
Property-rights questions	3.8	1.5
Housing	2.4	1.3
Environment vs. economic growth	2.4	7.4
Environment	3.8	5.1
Waste disposal (and fees)	4.8	4.3
Social services and welfare	1.6	2.0
Education	2.2	2.6
Recreation and culture	4.3	1.7
Health services	0.0	0.2
Youth policy	0.5	0.2
Improvements in public infrastructure	2.2	2.3
Financial capacity of local government	11.2	5.5
Costs of local government administration	0.7	0.0
Efficiency of local government administration	2.7	2.0
Control of local government administration	3.2	0.6
Local public transportation	0.5	3.6
Traffic (and parking)	5.1	22.3
Public safety	0.5	0.0
Relations between Germans and foreigners	0.0	0.0
Immigration	0.0	0.7
Conflict in local political system	21.9	16.4
Inter-governmental relations	7.6	1.2
Citizen participation	0.2	1.0
City administration vs. county council	2.1	2.5
Party internal conflict	1.8	0.7
Miscellaneous	2.1	1.0

* Percentage of all conflicts mentioned.

Source: Democracy and Local Government in Germany, Elite Surveys.

In addition to the open-ended question on conflicts that hinder problem-solving, the respondents were presented with a list of potential conflicts and divisions within their community and queried as to whether they existed and to what degree. The list is an amended version of that employed by the International Program. I excluded two items frequently used in other countries, namely divisions between those 'for and against change' and those based on 'education', and added to the list divisions between 'environmental advocates and growth advocates'. Further, in the new federal states two other potential divisions were added; these included divisions between 'alte Kader and the people' and 'Ossis and Wessis'. The results are summarized in Table 4.11.

Based on the reports of the local elites, there appears to be widespread divisions and conflicts within their communities. On average, over 80 per cent of the elites in both regions stated that the ten commonly listed potential divisions actually existed within their communities. In the East, an average of 31 per cent of the respondents suggested that these divisions were very severe; the figure is slightly lower on this in the West with approximately 27 per cent reporting severe divisions on average across

Table 4.11 **Degrees to which different types of conflict and divisions exist within local community: inter-German comparison (regional percentages)**

Types of conflicts	East Germany		West Germany	
	Somewhat	Very much	Somewhat	Very much
Between young and old	65.5	28.6	68.4	20.4
Based on income divisions	43.1	52.2	53.4	35.8
Between different religious views	35.8	2.8	33.3	1.3
Between different political views	30.3	67.5	43.4	52.4
Between managers and employees	65.5	30.7	70.9	21.6
Based on social origin divisions	69.9	17.5	71.1	21.9
Between Germans and foreigners	67.7	18.4	70.9	21.5
Between manual and non-manual workers	58.4	5.6	52.3	3.7
Between unemployed and employed	61.1	29.2	59.7	22.8
Between environmental advocates vs. growth advocates	41.8	55.2	32.1	66.6
Between 'Ossis' and 'Wessis'	59.6	32.9	–	–
Between 'Alte Kader' and 'The People'	53.4	36.5	–	–

Source: Democracy and Local Government in Germany, Elite Surveys.

Table 4.12a Degrees to which different types of conflict and divisions exist within local community: comparison between East Germany and four Central European countries (national percentages)

Type of conflict	East Germany (1)	East Germany (2)	Czech Republic (1)	Czech Republic (2)	Hungary (1)	Hungary (2)	Poland (1)	Poland (2)	Slovakia (1)	Slovakia (2)
Young-old	65.5	28.6	63.7	5.9	40.9	2.1	51.3	3.1	50.0	1.9
Education divisions	–	–	53.8	10.7	60.6	9.4	55.2	6.1	59.0	6.2
Income divisions	43.1	52.2	58.1	35.3	49.6	42.9	53.6	39.0	57.0	39.7
Religious views	35.8	2.8	25.4	5.9	27.9	2.7	41.7	8.5	50.2	7.6
Political views	30.3	67.5	62.8	28.1	62.6	13.7	58.6	31.3	50.9	41.1
Urban-rural	–	–	38.4	5.5	28.6	1.6	42.8	4.9	43.5	2.9
Manager-employee	65.5	30.7	70.1	7.7	55.7	5.4	69.5	7.4	69.5	9.9
Social origins divisions	69.9	17.5	46.8	4.3	32.1	2.7	31.1	2.5	48.8	5.2
Racial-ethnic origin divisions	67.7	18.4	48.3	17.9	45.7	14.0	16.8	1.6	51.4	7.6
For and against change	–	–	61.6	23.2	48.0	5.1	64.4	26.2	67.9	20.3
Manual and non-manual divisions	58.4	5.6	59.4	4.7	–	–	54.1	4.7	57.5	4.7

(1) = somewhat; (2) = very much.

Source: Democracy and Local Government International Data Base.

Table 4.12b Degrees to which different types of conflict and divisions exist within local community: comparison between West Germany and six Western countries (national percentages)

Type of conflict	West Germany (1)	West Germany (2)	Austria (1)	Austria (2)	Netherlands (1)	Netherlands (2)	Spain (1)	Spain (2)	Sweden (1)	Sweden (2)	Switzerland (1)	Switzerland (2)
Young-old	68.4	20.4	56.0	9.8	63.1	8.9	44.2	11.5	65.2	10.1	55.6	3.9
Education divisions	—	—	42.1	10.4	60.3	10.0	54.0	21.0	59.5	36.8	37.9	6.8
Income divisions	53.4	35.8	54.0	17.5	61.5	18.8	52.1	35.0	60.0	34.8	50.8	11.9
Religious views	33.3	1.3	14.0	1.6	37.1	9.4	32.5	9.9	42.3	9.9	22.8	2.8
Political views	43.4	52.4	61.4	34.8	55.9	18.0	54.9	28.4	56.7	9.9	56.1	32.2
Urban-rural	—	—	57.0	11.9	40.6	10.5	33.0	7.9	68.0	7.8	32.1	9.6
Manager-employee	70.9	21.6	34.3	3.1	55.4	6.2	56.3	14.8	61.8	10.3	43.9	4.8
Social origins divisions	71.1	21.9	57.6	11.3	67.2	19.6	50.1	14.2	71.3	14.8	53.6	7.0
Racial-ethnic origin divisions	70.9	21.5	33.7	14.1	59.0	12.5	41.9	8.4	54.7	21.2	59.3	13.2
For and against change	—	—	50.0	15.4	63.7	13.4	53.5	22.0	54.3	14.3	58.5	25.6
Manual and non-manual divisions	52.3	3.7	—	—	—	—	36.3	4.1	—	—	—	—

(1) = type of conflict: somewhat; (2) = type of conflict: very much.

Source: Democracy and Local Government International Data Base.

the ten items. Three divisions appear to be particularly significant in the East; these include divisions based on income differences, those based on political views and the discord between environmental advocates and those favoring economic growth. More than half of the elites in this region report that the income and environment vs. growth divisions are very severe. Leading the list in the East, though, are divisions based on political views. Here two-thirds of the elites report that these represent major fault lines within their communities. In the West, the divisions based on income appear to be less severe. Only a third of the respondents mention this. However, political disputes and divisions between environmentalists and growth advocates seem particularly strong; more than half report that the political divisions are very great and two-thirds characterize the division between environmentalists and growth advocates in this way.

Tables 4.12a and 4.12b provide information that allows one to compare the situations in the two parts of Germany with those reported by local elites in other countries. Once again, the two parts of Germany stand out. While in other countries elites report that many divisions exist within their communities, the general tendency is one that suggests that these divisions are not major. Only in East Germany does one find a majority of local elites reporting that divisions based on income differences represents a major fault line within their communities. Moreover, while majorities of elites in both East and West Germany report that differing political views significantly divide their communities, the local elites in no other country, in either East or West, seem to be confronted with such conflict-riven situations.

More so than in the other countries examined here, local government elites in Germany report that they are not only faced with a large array of major problems, but also are often weakened by a situation where they have insufficient power to deal with their responsibilities. In addition, they also report that they are confronted with much divided communities where conflict frequently obstructs problem-solving and stands in the way of community development. Under such circumstances, the latitude for successful policy-making and execution would appear to be very narrow and limited. In the next section, we will turn to this issue.

Policy Action and Its Effectiveness

In attempting to assess the success of policy-making in these communities I concentrate again on the fixed list of 17 policy areas used to query the elites regarding the problem agendas, responsibilities and capacities of local government. In the present case, respondents were queried as to whether their local government had recently undertaken action in each of these areas. In addition, they were asked to characterize the outcomes of these actions, viz., whether they were effective or ineffective. An overview of the results on this topic of policy action and effectiveness is presented in Table 4.13; the results also are presented in graphic form in Figures 4.4 and 4.5.

In both regions, large percentages of the elites report activity across the wide range of policy areas. Indeed, in every policy area, a majority of elites in the East

Table 4.13 Overview of elites' reports on policy action and effectiveness: inter-German comparison

	East		West		Difference: East–West	
	(1)	(2)	(1)	(2)	(1)	(2)
Unemployment	94.4	11.4	72.6	22.7	21.8	−11.3
Poverty	60.1	25.1	44.4	24.1	15.7	1.0
Economic development	96.8	25.2	89.6	42.9	7.2	−17.7
Housing	91.7	56.1	96.5	74.1	−4.8	−18.0
Environmental pollution	85.0	55.4	81.8	52.1	3.2	3.3
Social services and welfare	93.6	85.5	74.2	71.6	19.4	13.9
Education	89.8	78.5	75.3	86.7	14.5	−8.2
Recreation and culture	94.7	61.7	74.6	79.6	20.1	−18.0
Health services	86.2	90.0	49.6	82.1	36.5	8.0
Improvements in public infrastructure	93.1	48.2	86.6	51.6	6.5	−3.4
Financial capacity of local government	91.9	23.7	81.0	29.8	10.9	−6.0
Costs of local government administration	92.2	40.8	88.7	38.8	3.5	2.0
Efficiency of local government administration	92.6	51.8	81.3	40.3	11.3	11.5
Control of local government administration	80.9	52.5	48.7	40.2	32.2	12.3
Public safety	80.3	31.0	49.2	42.1	31.1	−11.1
Relations between Germans and foreigners	64.8	65.3	70.7	64.6	−5.9	0.6
Immigration	52.6	65.2	51.2	50.8	1.4	14.4
Average	84.7	51.0	71.5	52.6	13.2	−1.6

(1) Percentage saying action has been taken; (2) share (per cent) of those describing action taken as effective.

Source: Democracy and Local Government in Germany, Elite Surveys.

Problem-Ridden and Conflict-Riven 139

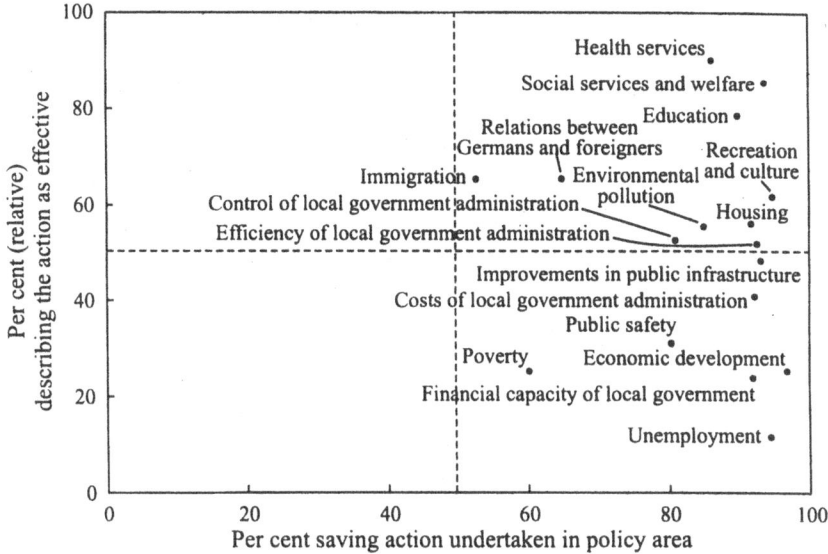

Source: Democracy and Local Government in Germany, Elite Surveys.

Figure 4.4   **East German local elites' views on policy action and effectiveness**

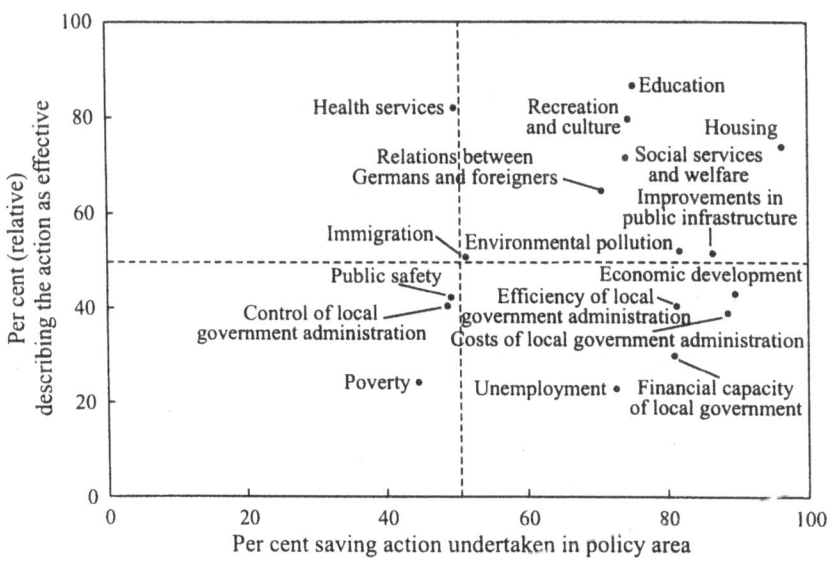

Source: Democracy and Local Government in Germany, Elite Surveys.

Figure 4.5   **West German local elites' views on policy action and effectiveness**

states that action has been undertaken. In the West there are only a few areas, viz., public safety, the control of local government administration, health services and poverty, where only a minority of elites report activity on the part of local government. However, there exist a large number of areas in both regions where these actions have not proven successful or effective in the eyes of the local elites (this can best be seen by examining the lower-right hand quadrant of Figures 4.4 and 4.5). Unemployment and economic development are seen in both regions as areas where the policy actions were ineffective. In the economic sphere poverty is an area where a majority of elites in the East also report that actions have been undertaken but also qualify these actions as ineffective. The elites are split on whether actions taken to improve the public infrastructure have met with success. Elites in both regions widely share the view that the actions that have been undertaken to deal with the financial capacities and costs of their governments have not proven successful. There is a mixed perspective on whether actions to improve the efficiency and control over the local government administration have worked or not. In the East, while a large percentage of the respondents report that actions have been taken to improve public safety, only a small minority of these report that the actions have been effective.

Tables 14a and 14b summarize information on policy action and effectiveness from an international perspective. Here, a restricted list of policy areas are included with fourteen items common to the questionnaires used in most of the countries. Note as well that in the U.S. study only seven of the policy areas were dealt with. Briefly summarized, in comparison with the reports available from a limited number of other nations, it turns out that the local elites in both East and West Germany, despite confronting heavy problem agendas, often working with insufficient power and autonomy and faced with very factious and conflictual environments, appear to be doing relatively well in taking effective action across at least a limited number of policy areas. It can be noted that on the list of fourteen policy areas, majorities of elites in the new federal states report success in eight of the areas; the corresponding figure in the old federal states is nine. By contrast, in the Czech Republic and Slovakia, majorities in only two of these areas report effective action and in Hungary none; while in Poland the figure is six. In the West, only the Dutch elites report greater success with majorities stating that the actions taken in ten areas had been effective. In the case of both Spain and the United States, the elites are quite pessimistic in their assessments. In not one area does a majority report that actions taken had been effective.

In sum, while doing relatively well by comparative standards in taking effective action across a wide number of policy areas, majorities of German local elites still report that ineffectiveness has marked action in a number of significant areas on their problem agendas. In particular, both actions in dealing with the local economic situation as well as gaining a handle on the financial situation of local government stand out as troublesome in both regions. In addition, the area of public safety appears to be a challenging item for local governments in the new federal states.

Table 4.14a International comparison of elites' reports on policy action and effectiveness: comparison between East Germany and four Central European countries

	East Germany		Czech Republic		Hungary		Poland		Slovakia	
	(1)	(2)	(1)	(2)	(1)	(2)	(1)	(2)	(1)	(2)
Unemployment	94.4	11.4	72.0	36.0	68.8	22.1	83.6	40.6	78.8	22.2
Poverty	60.1	25.1	42.1	38.0	54.5	9.2	77.1	44.0	43.1	25.5
Economic development	96.8	25.2	77.8	33.3	62.2	22.8	84.3	44.0	82.4	22.6
Housing	91.7	56.1	48.2	18.5	45.2	17.9	76.3	38.9	57.8	24.4
Environmental pollution	85.0	55.4	79.6	41.6	–	–	88.5	66.8	71.2	37.1
Social services and welfare	93.6	85.5	35.7	36.1	78.8	24.6	89.5	65.9	42.1	29.7
Education	89.8	78.5	79.1	54.7	78.1	41.6	87.0	70.3	76.0	63.9
Recreation and culture	94.7	61.7	81.1	44.6	65.4	32.7	77.8	65.0	86.8	48.4
Health services	86.1	90.0	86.1	29.0	77.8	36.2	81.6	42.4	69.7	28.6
Improvements in public infrastructure	93.1	48.2	95.1	49.5	84.9	52.9	93.7	67.8	97.1	59.0
Public safety	80.3	31.0	91.0	37.8	77.8	26.2	83.7	44.1	92.0	39.8
Costs of local government administration	92.2	40.8	75.4	39.3	79.9	37.2	59.5	64.5	75.9	31.6
'Minority relations'	64.8	65.3	88.7	57.0	71.1	26.2	9.5	54.7	76.3	36.7
Immigration	52.6	65.2	25.2	44.4	21.1	29.4	6.0	26.7	26.6	35.7
Average	83.9	52.8	69.8	40.0	66.6	29.2	71.3	52.6	69.7	36.8

(1) Percentage saying action has been taken; (2) share (per cent) of those describing action taken as effective.

Source: Democracy and Local Government International Data Base.

Table 4.14b International comparison of elites' reports on policy action and effectiveness: comparison between West Germany and three Western countries

	West Germany (1)	West Germany (2)	Netherlands (1)	Netherlands (2)	Spain (1)	Spain (2)	United States (1)	United States (2)
Unemployment	72.6	22.7	89.0	38.1	48.4	14.9	–	–
Poverty	44.4	24.1	77.5	41.2	58.4	17.6	–	–
Economic development	89.6	42.9	88.4	54.3	53.4	18.0	95.4	29.4
Housing	96.5	74.1	96.7	67.1	71.8	32.0	92.1	26.1
Environmental pollution	81.8	52.1	91.2	71.1	58.0	26.7	87.1	32.1
Social services and welfare	74.2	71.6	87.3	63.8	85.2	31.1	86.7	19.8
Education	75.3	86.7	79.0	70.3	75.5	38.9	89.7	31.8
Recreation and culture	74.6	79.6	82.2	73.6	82.9	38.2	–	–
Health services	49.6	82.1	48.5	58.8	82.2	37.7	–	–
Improvements in public infrastructure	86.6	51.6	92.3	46.7	77.0	38.7	–	–
Public safety	49.2	42.1	93.2	50.1	71.0	27.5	95.0	35.1
Costs of local government administration	88.7	38.8	95.9	69.7	52.0	22.9	–	–
'Minority relations'	70.7	64.4	65.4	57.0	50.9	22.3	84.5	18.9
Immigration	51.2	50.8	40.7	48.6	40.8	20.1	–	–
Average	71.8	56.0	80.5	57.9	64.8	24.9	90.1	27.6

(1) Percentage saying action has been taken; (2) share (per cent) of those describing action taken as effective.

Source: Democracy and Local Government International Data Base.

Performance: Elites and Citizens

In this section, I briefly examine a few evaluative aspects of the performance of local government. While presenting some information on how the local elites judge the performance of local government, the primary focus here is on how the citizens within these towns and cities appraise the workings of their local governments.

In Figure 4.6, one can observe that there is a fair amount of satisfaction on the part of the elites with respect to how democracy works at the national level as well as within their own communities. This is true across both parts of Germany although levels of satisfaction in the East are a bit lower than in the West. Nevertheless, as can be seen by comparing the data presented in Figure 4.7, where I have plotted the degree to which citizens express satisfaction with German democracy, the elites clearly take a far more favorable view – at least of national politics – than do their fellow citizens. While 63 per cent of the elites in the East express satisfaction with democracy at the national level (the corresponding figure for their satisfaction with communal democracy is 70 per cent), only 38 per cent of the citizens in this region indicate that they are satisfied. Although higher levels of satisfaction are registered in the West, there is still a large difference between elites and citizens. Approximately 87 per cent of the elites express satisfaction with the way democracy works in Germany (the corre-

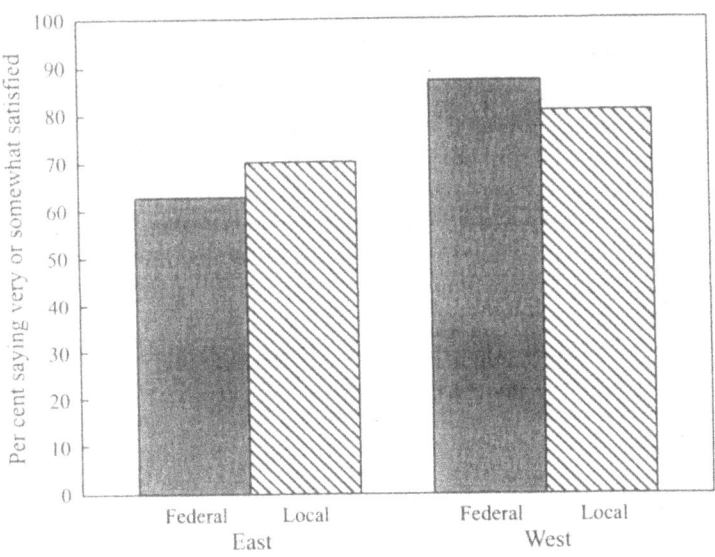

Source: Democracy and Local Government in Germany, Elite Surveys.

Figure 4.6   Elites' satisfaction with the way democracy works at the federal and local levels

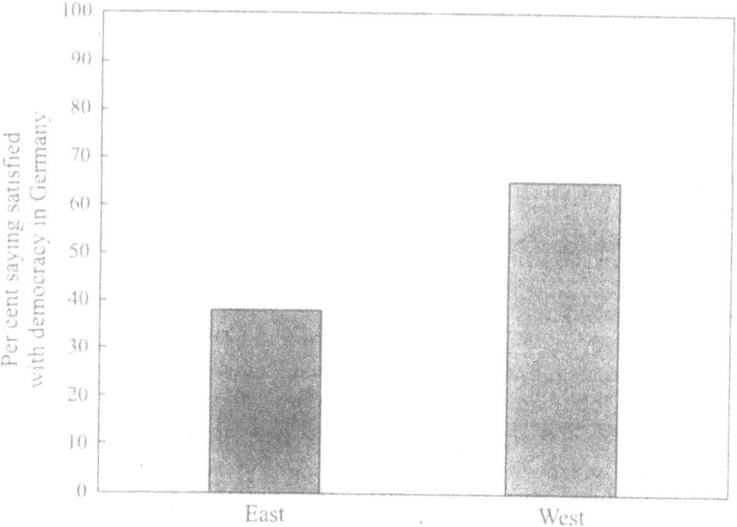

Sources: Politbarometer Ost 1994 (Trenduntersuchung), Z. A. Nr. 2559; Politbarometer West 1994 (Trenduntersuchung), Z. A. Nr. 2546.

Figure 4.7 Citizens' satisfaction with democracy in Germany

sponding figure for communal democracy is 81 per cent); only 65 per cent of the citizens express such a favorable view.

Citizen interest in communal politics in both regions is relatively strong. In the East, 70 per cent of the citizens express interest in communal politics, a figure slightly higher than interest in politics in general (68 per cent) within the region (see Figure 4.8). In the West, however, there is less interest in communal politics on the part of citizens (64 per cent) and it is lower than the interest citizens express in politics in general (71 per cent).

Citizens in both regions do not seem particularly trustful of their local politicians (see Figure 4.9). Indeed, only about 31 per cent of the citizens in the East and approximately 26 per cent of those in the West indicate that they had a lot of trust in the politicians within their own communities. Relative to the degrees of trust that they express for people in general (in the East 46.3 per cent and in the West 53.5 per cent), these are very low figures. Nevertheless, the region-wide figures mask the marked variation that exists across the communities in terms of the levels of trust citizens have for their own local politicians. Thus, in the West the communities range between 16 per cent and 53 per cent. In the East, the lowest figure is 8 per cent while the highest is approximately 56 per cent.

In the survey of citizens, respondents were asked how satisfied they were with the performance of a number of actors and organizations within their local govern-

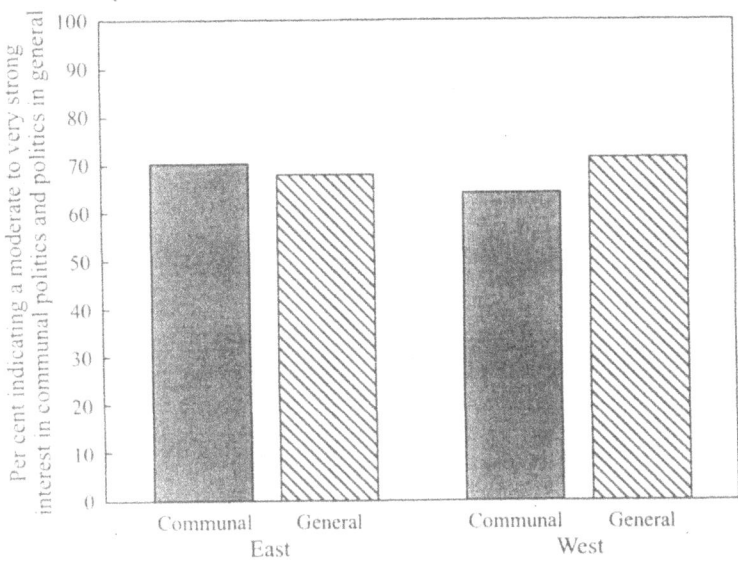

Source: for interest in politics in general: ALLBUS Survey (1994), Z. A. Nr. 2400.

Figure 4.8 Citizens' interest in communal politics and politics in general

mental and political systems. Questions about the performance of the local political parties, the city bureaucracy, the city council and the city executive were posed. The results are summarized on a regional basis in Figure 4.10.

The performance of the political parties inside the communities received the worst overall ratings from the citizens there of all of the actors and organizations operating in these towns and communities. Only 46 per cent of the citizens in the East rated their performance as satisfactory. In the West, the parties did a bit better, with 52.6 per cent rating their performance as satisfactory. Again, there is significant variation on this dimension across the different communities. The lowest level in the East is 27.3 per cent while the highest is 64.1 per cent. The range in the West is from 35 per cent to nearly 75 per cent.

In both regions, citizens generally rate the performance of their local government bureaucracies very favorably. Ranging from 46 per cent to 81 per cent across the 15 communities in the East, the average level is slightly above 64 per cent. In every community in the West, the town/city bureaucracy receives a favorable rating from a majority of the citizens. Thus, the lowest approval rating is 54 per cent and the highest is 85 per cent. The average across the region is nearly 72 per cent. It should be noted that none of the other organs of local government receive as high an overall approval rating as this in the region.

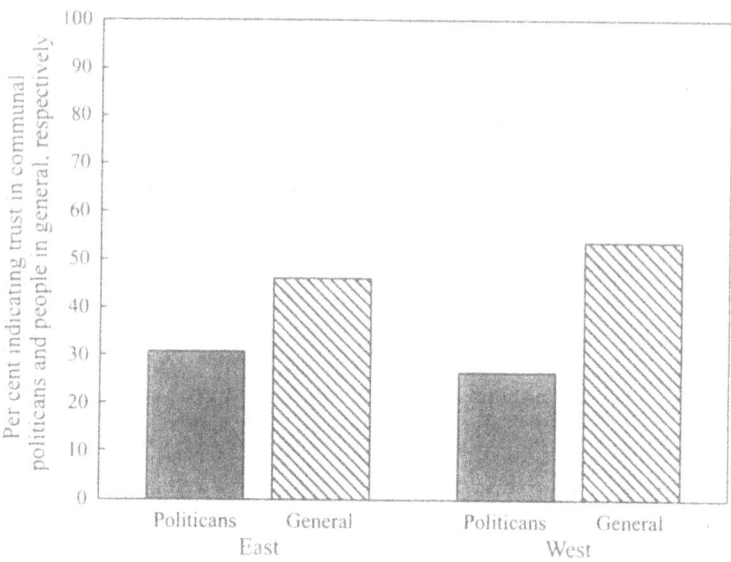

Source: Democracy and Local Government in Germany, Citizen Surveys.

Figure 4.9   Citizens' trust in communal politicians and general trust

The average levels of satisfaction with the performance of the town/city council are reasonably high in both East and West. The lowest level in the East is about 40 per cent, while the highest is 73 per cent, and the average is 53 per cent. In the West, the values range from a low of 26 per cent to a high of 75 per cent with the average being 52 per cent.

The local government chief executives in both regions generally receive high approval ratings for their performance. The regional average in both East and West is 60 per cent. The range in the East extends from approximately 45 per cent to 83 per cent; the comparable figures in the West are 47 per cent and 81 per cent.

In Figure 4.10, I have also presented regional averages for an index that shows the approval ratings for the entire town/city government. In this index, approval for the performance of the entire local government is based on simultaneous approval for the performance of all three local governmental organizations and actors, i.e., the bureaucracy, the council and the executive. The average level in the East for this measure of approval of the overall performance of local government is approximately 47 per cent with a low of 30 and a high of 67 per cent. In the West, the average is slightly higher, 51 per cent, and the community values range from a low of 29 per cent to a high of 75 per cent.

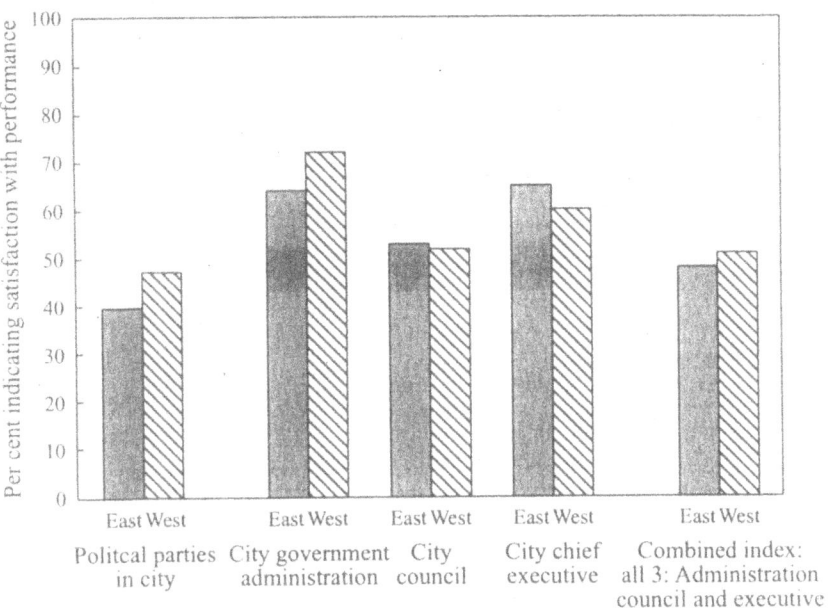

Source: Democracy and Local Government in Germany, Citizen Surveys.

Figure 4.10 Citizens' satisfaction with local political and government institutions

Conclusion

The problem agenda of local governments in Germany appears to be especially crowded and filled with difficulties that local elites see as important. At the same time, many of the more severe problems on this agenda are policy areas where elites report that there is insufficient power and autonomy on the part of local government to cope with these problems. Furthermore, the exceptionally high levels of conflicts and divisions within the local communities exacerbate this situation. Local elites report, here more than in most of the other countries examined in this study, that these conflicts and divisions hamper policy-making and community development. Nevertheless, German local elites report far more successful policy actions in quite a number of areas than do their colleagues in other countries. Admittedly, though, this success is not to be found in such vital areas as local government finances and the economic conditions prevailing within the local communities.

Among the citizens of these communities, satisfaction with the performance of local government in both East and West is generally high. However, there is a great deal of variation across the communities in both these regions with respect to the level of satisfaction and in some communities there are only very small minorities that rank the performance of their local government as being satisfactory, while in other communities one finds nearly universal satisfaction with the performance of these governments.

Chapter 5

Social Capital, Institutional Structures and Democratic Performance*

Introduction

This chapter explores the sources of citizens' satisfaction with the performance of their local governments. Why do some municipal governments perform well in the evaluations provided by their constituents and why do others perform poorly? In attempting to answer this question, I draw upon two research traditions, the cultural and the institutional, which have endeavored to illuminate the sources of governmental performance. As with the earlier chapters I rely principally upon data collected in two surveys conducted across a large number of municipalities in the Eastern and Western regions of Germany during 1995, five years after German reunification.

The political culture approach to explaining governmental performance has a long and checkered history. The central notion is that a set of internalized norm structure political behavior and that the widespread presence or absence of one or another of these norms dictates the chances for a society having a successful or unsuccessful governmental regime. These norms arise out of the socialization process and are reinforced or reproduced in the normal conduct of social life. The political culture approach, in the eyes of one critic, has long been in a moribund state (Laitin, 1995). One advocate of this approach has recently suggested that it is enjoying a renaissance (Inglehart, 1988). While that claim was perhaps premature when made, certainly the publication of Putnam's (1993) research on Italian regional government and much of the initial reaction to it suggest that the political culture approach is resurgent (see La Palombara, 1993; Laitin, 1995). The research reported here attempts to evaluate the utility of Putnam's concept of social capital in accounting for variation in local government performance within Germany.

The long tradition that has attached importance to the differences in institutional features of government is another approach to explaining variations in the success of governments. There is a significant amount of work on differences in institutional structures at the national level (see, e.g., Lijphart, 1984; Baylis, 1989; Weaver and Rockman, 1993; Schmidt, 1995). Moreover, while, particularly in the United States and Germany, similar efforts have been made using rather gross distinctions in insti-

---

* This chapter is a revised version of my paper that appeared in the *European Journal of Political Research*, Vol. 35, 1999, pp. 1–34. I gratefully acknowledge Blackwell Publishing Ltd. for permission to use this material.

tutional features to account for variations in local government performance, little consensus has developed on the importance of such differences.[1] In its most advanced form, this general approach has paid particular attention to formalizing arguments about how structure shapes incentives and strategies and thereby influences the performance of government (Shepsle, 1989). Drawing on a model in this tradition, a model focused on veto players in a decision-making system (Tsebelis, 1995), an effort is made to illuminate the possible effects of institutional differences on local government performance in Germany.

The next section outlines the social capital and institutional approaches to democratic performance. The central elements of Putnam's argument and findings are described. It then goes on to describe the way scholars have traditionally approached the question of institutional differences (and their importance for performance) across German local governments. A critique of this approach is provided and an alternative thesis is presented along with the empirical basis for evaluating this thesis. The third section presents an empirical analysis of the social capital and institutional theses. Focusing on citizens' satisfaction with the performance of their local governments, it embeds both of these arguments within a broader model intended to explain variation in performance levels. The last section provides some concluding comments.

Explaining Democratic Governmental Performance

Political Culture or Political Institutions?

Robert Putnam's (1993) claims about the centrality of cultural factors in determining institutional performance have received a great deal of attention (see, for example, Tarrow, 1996). On the basis of an elaborate theoretical argument and extensive evidence drawn from a decades-long study of regional governments in Italy, the major claim made by Putnam is that communities marked by high stocks of social capital will have better performing governments than those in which these stocks are low. Putnam is, to my mind, somewhat ambiguous as to the meaning this has for institutional reform and engineering. On the one hand, the work can be read as suggesting that culture, with its deep historical roots, can hinder government performance regardless of the institutional arrangements one adopts to govern with. Laitin (1995, p. 172), for example, sees this as the principal lesson to be drawn from the Putnam study: '[t]he deeper conclusion is that democratic institutions cannot be built from the top down (or at least not easily). They must be built up in everyday traditions of trust and civic virtue among its citizens.' On the other hand, he suggests, 'changing formal institutions can change political practice' (1993, p. 184). Indeed, in a much earlier

---

[1] Examples in the American context are Morgan and Wilson (1995); Stoker and Wolman (1992); Svara (1990); Wolmann (1995) those in the German context include Shimanke (1989).

study (where a good deal of the same evidence was presented but where the conclusions were far less sweeping in their claims with respect to the primacy of political culture), he and his collaborators suggested that

> [e]ndogeous theories [which] seek to explain institutional success or failure in terms of internal characteristics and processes of the institution itself, ... and ... ecological theories [which] emphasize characteristics of the environment of the ... institution ... are complementary [approaches] (Putnam et al., 1983, p. 55).

This approach, one of complementarity, is taken here. Thus, it posits that the more balanced view, viz., both institutions and culture matter that one can take away from Putnam's work is correct. It is based on two assumptions: neither the 'institutional' nor the 'cultural' approach is sufficiently well developed theoretically nor are the empirical claims made by advocates of either approach sufficiently well validated. Furthermore, even if the claims that Putnam and his colleagues have made about Italy and the United States hold there, it is not at all clear that they have any relevance to other contexts. Certainly, the case of the Federal Republic of Germany, in the mid-1990s, with the presence of the old and the new federal states, can serve as an appropriate setting for examining both Putnam's claims about culture and the claims made by the 'institutionalists'. As will be pointed out below, significant differences exist in terms of local government institutional structures both within and between the two regions. Further, there is evidence in both the Allensbach and Forschungsgruppe Wahlen Politbarometer surveys (Cusack, 1997) that stocks of social capital differ across localities both within and between the two regions.

Social Capital and the Civic Community

In Robert Putnam's view, the effectiveness of democratic regimes critically depends on the social environment within which they exist. This 'exogenous' theory of democratic performance, variously called 'republican' or 'civic republicanism', makes the major claim that the 'civic virtue' of citizens strongly shapes the performance potential of democratic government. In 'civic communities', i.e., communities where civic virtues are widespread among the citizenry, democratic governments perform well. In non-civic communities, there is little civic virtue to be found and, consequently, democratic governments therein perform poorly.

Civic virtue is a mix of traits. A citizen with civic virtue is interested in public affairs, is tied to the community through membership in civic associations whose principal defining characteristic is equality and is a person who through such participation learns to be trusting of others and tolerant of diverging views. A hallmark of the civic community is therefore a dense network of civic associations. Such an environment promotes 'habits of cooperation, solidarity and public spiritedness'. This internal effect is conducive to producing citizens capable of working effectively in a democratic political system. It further helps the democratic political process through its external effects, especially, its facilitation of interest 'aggregation' and 'articulation'.

Civic virtue is an individual-level manifestation of what Putnam describes as social capital. Social capital is defined as a feature of society that promotes social efficiency by way of 'facilitating coordinated actions' (Putnam, 1993, p. 167). There are a number of facets of social capital and these are themselves interdependent. Putnam stresses three. First, there is trust, which is held to be an 'essential component of social capital' because it facilitates the cooperation necessary for coordination within society (Putnam, 1993, p. 170). Second, there is the norm of generalized reciprocity, which facilitates 'the resolution of dilemmas of collective action'. It is described as a 'highly productive component of social capital' (Putnam, 1993, p. 172). Third, there are networks of civic engagement that are also said to constitute 'an essential component of social capital' (Putnam, 1993, p. 173). Represented by secondary associations, such as sports clubs and choral societies, they provide venues for 'intense horizontal interaction' that fosters 'social trust and cooperation' (Putnam, 1993, pp. 173–4). Ultimately, then, the value of social capital is to be seen in its facilitation of cooperation among citizens within a community.

What impact does social capital have on governmental performance? In addition, what are the mechanisms by which this impact is transmitted? Since social capital promotes civic virtue in citizens, it is expected then to create civic communities with well performing democratic governments (Putnam, 1993, pp. 175–6). Putnam suggests two channels through which this effect comes about. In one, because citizens with civic virtue are heavily engaged in their communities, they are more effective in demanding and acting to get good government. Through their dense organization networks, they can act to pressure government to perform well. In the other channel, by providing a strong social infrastructure for the community and inculcating democratic values within elites and masses, social capital facilitates the kind of cooperation and collaboration needed to identify, adopt and implement effective policies for the community (Putnam, 1993, p.182).

The consequence of this for democratic theory can be seen as either pessimistic or optimistic. Pessimistically viewed, it suggests that no amount of institutional engineering will allow a democratic government to perform successfully if the culture within which it is embedded is not replete with social capital. Optimistically viewed, it implies that while performance is degraded in environments marked by a dearth of social capital, institutional effects can still work an independent effect. Nevertheless, whatever positive effects an institutional design might have, it would still work better if the social environment within which it existed were more favorable.

Putnam's argument can be summarized in the following five points. First, social capital promotes cooperation and cooperation facilitates problem-solving within the community and polity. Second, the components of social capital reinforce each other, they are mutually related and their use facilitates greater stocks while their disuse diminishes the stocks. Third, unless undergoing some dramatic change, either high levels of social capital or low levels of social capital mark communities. Fourth, the stock of social capital in a community's mass political culture is reflected in the stock within the community's elite political culture. Fifth, and finally, in democratic communities with high levels of social capital, government's performance will be good; in such communities where the levels of social capital are low, this performance will be poor.

The findings provided in Putnam's two major reports (Putnam et al., 1983; Putnam, 1993) on Italian regional government performance are extensive and in characterizing them here, I will concentrate only on those that have greatest relevance and importance for this chapter. First, Putnam found that while there were clear differences in citizen and elite satisfaction with their regional governments, nevertheless, there had been an appreciable improvement in the levels of satisfaction over time. Still, many, particularly those directly involved in these governments, grew less optimistic about the capacities of these institutions to solve the problems of their regions.

Second, using a composite measure based on 'objective' indicators of regional government output, Putnam demonstrated that there were major differences across the regions in terms of governmental performance. Importantly for the question of democratic performance, this composite measure is strongly correlated with both citizens' and elites' expressions of satisfaction with the performance of their governments across these regions.

Third, it was found that the degree of civic community strongly correlated with the performance index and its components. Initial theoretical and empirical work (Putnam et al., 1983) argued and found that the performance effect of political culture was contingent upon the level of socio-economic modernization. At low levels of modernity, culture plays little if any role and economic conditions dominate the determination of performance; at higher levels of modernity, culture becomes very important and replaces socio-economic conditions in terms of their importance in shaping performance.

Later theoretical and empirical work (Putnam, 1993) casts these two factors as independent and theoretically competing elements in the explanation of governmental performance. And, indeed, while socio-economic modernization is statistically strongly correlated with governmental performance, it is clear that the pattern that one finds in the relationship between these two variables is not so convincing that one can conclude that performance really depends on modernization in an independent or an interactive manner. When, however, one examines the relationship between Putnam's index of civic community and the performance measure, the results are far more compelling. This is the case not only across all of the regions within Italy, but also across the regions within both South and North. And when other potential causes of governmental performance were examined (for example, the ideological polarization and the fragmentation of the party systems, or the degree of conflicts within the regions), none of these indicators of social and political strife was found to be related to regional government performance.

Institutional Structures

The Conventional Categories

Traditionally scholars have held that four distinct categories of local government structures exist within the Federal Republic.[2] These four categories are rooted in the historical development of Germany and reflect the unique contributions of different German regional powers as well as external influences, especially French (in the 19th century) and Britain (in the occupation period after World War II).

The South German Council *(Süddeutsche Ratsverfassung)* form's origins were influenced by the 19th century Prussian Magistrat system and French local government practices. Further development of this model occurred in Bavaria after World War I and spread to Baden-Württemberg. These two states now have fairly similar government structures and this is to be seen especially with respect to the position of the mayor in the power structure. The mayor is directly elected and chairs the city council. Further, the mayor has direct control of the city government administration. This system of government is quite analogous to the strong mayor council governmental systems found in some municipalities in the United States. Differences do exist between the Baden-Württemberg and Bavarian models. In the former case, mayoral elections are putatively non-partisan and the mayor and the city council are elected at different times (in addition, the mayor serves for a longer period of time than the council). In the Bavarian case, the mayoral elections are held at the same time as the council elections and the format of the elections is such as to allow for partisan affiliation of the mayor.

It is notable that in the period since Unification all of the new federal states have adopted variants of the South German Council form of local government. However, each of the states made modifications to the system when it was adopted and some have been slow in bringing into existence all of the planned features.[3]

The North German Council *(Norddeutsche Ratsverfassung)* form was introduced by the British occupation forces in the period after World War II. It embodied an

---

2 This set of categories refers to those states, *Länder*, that are not city-states (Berlin, Bremen and Hamburg); it also ignores some of the different structures to be found in very small municipalities not included in this study. For a useful overview of the differences that exist across these categories, see Derlien et al. (1976). More detailed discussions can be found in Püttner (1982), Gunlicks (1986), Norton (1994) and the municipal constitution documents compiled in Schmidt-Eichstädt's (1994) volume.

3 See, for example, Wollmann (1994, 1995, 1996 and 1998) and Osterland (1994). Note that Derlien (1994, 1995) argues that this tendency, found to an extent as well in the West, was prompted more by partisan political considerations (especially in the state parliaments which define the constitutional frameworks for local government) and has not been based on arguments that have any solid scientific evidence supporting them. Furthermore, the climate of opinion and putative (and empty) claims of efficiency by advocates of particular models are seen as playing an important role in this development.

effort to de-politicize governmental administration in response to the abuses during the Nazi era. Modeled on the British 'town manager' system, this form is very similar to the city manager council form introduced by the 'Progressive' movement at the beginning of the 20th century in the United States. Here the city council is theoretically the only legitimate source of authority within the government structure. The mayor is not directly elected by the voters but rather is elected by the council itself. The administration is headed by a city manager *(Stadtdirektor)*, appointed by the council and is charged with carrying out the wishes of the council. Originally, three states had this form, North-Rhine Westphalia, Lower Saxony and Schleswig-Holstein. In the early 1950s, however, Schleswig-Holstein abandoned this system and adopted two different forms of local government, one for larger municipalities and another for the smaller communities. Across the two states that have retained this system of government, differences exist. One of the most important relates to the city manager's term of office and the ability of the council to remove the city manager from office (possible in the North-Rhine Westphalia system, not possible in the case of Lower Saxony). A special feature of the Lower Saxony system is the role and power of the 'executive committee' *(Verwaltungsausschuss)*. An organ separate from the council, it has broad powers to shape the agenda of the council and has veto powers over council decisions. This committee, headed by the mayor, is reputed to afford this latter office with greater powers over the city manager than those found in the North-Rhine Westphalia system.

The Magistrat *([Unechte] Magistratsverfassung)* form is a derivative of the reforms introduced in the early 19th century by Prussia. It departs from this model in that the Magistrat, an executive committee responsible for overseeing the city administration, does not have the right to reject decisions made by the city council. The mayor, the chairperson of the Magistrat, and the other members of this organ are selected by the city council but may not be members of the council. Additionally, there is a fixed ratio of 'professional' to 'non-professional' members of the Magistrat. Each member of the Magistrat is responsible for a specific administrative area and the Magistrat itself makes decisions in a collective fashion. Found in Schleswig-Holstein and Hesse, this form underwent a significant change during the early 1990s within Hesse. Now the mayor is elected directly by the citizens. At the same time, the collegial character of the Magistrat and other aspects of this system designed to minimize concentrated executive power have not been altered.

The strong mayor *(Bürgermeisterverfassung)* form is the last category.[4] Its origins can be traced back to the period of French occupation during the Napoleonic era. Unlike in the French form that served as the model for this system, the chief executive is an elected official and not appointed by a higher level of government.

---

4   It is interesting to note that this form is somewhat similar to that characterized as weak mayor council form where the chief executive officer, the mayor, has to share power with a committee selected by the council and is quite constrained in the autonomous exercise of power.

However, the electoral body is the city council and not the citizenry.[5] Developments over time have moved this system in the direction of lessening the concentration of power in the hands of this chief executive. While chair of the council as well as chair of the major committee within this council, i.e., the city executive committee or *Stadtvorstand*, the mayor can only make executive decisions if a majority of the members of this committee agrees. The mayor shares authority over the city administration with the other members of the committee. This system is found in the two Western states of Rhineland-Palatinate and Saarland.

Operationally, scholars have used four principal characteristics in distinguishing among these forms of local government (see Table 5.1). Included are (1) whether primary competence for decisions (or sovereignty) is divided or not; (2) the form which executive leadership takes; (3) the role of the chief executive in the legislative branch, the municipal council; and (4) the mode of electing the chief executive.

On the first dimension, three distinct patterns are observable. In one, found in the North German Council form, primary competence is not divided but rather confined to one ('Monistic') governmental organ, in this case, the council. In the ('Dualistic') South German Council and strong mayor forms, primary competence constitutionally is split between two elements of the governmental structure, the mayor and the council. The third pattern is to be found in the ('Trialistic') Magistrat system where primary competence is divided among three elements of the government including the council, the Magistrat and the mayor.

There are two principal forms of executive leadership. In the more common one, executive leadership is concentrated in the hands of the ('Monocratic') chief executive officer, who is the mayor in the South German Council and strong mayor systems, or the city director in the North German Council form. In the Magistrat system, the chief executive officer and the other members of a collegial body, the Magistrat, share executive leadership.

The third dimension deals with the relationship between the head of the administration and the council. The role of the chief executive with respect to the council is seen to shape the possibility for sensible cooperation between the elected representatives of the people and the administration. Two general patterns hold. In both the South German Council form and the strong mayor form, the chief executive officer (in this case, the mayor) both chairs the council and has voting powers. In the other two constitutional types, the chief executive officer, whether the city director (North German Council form) or the mayor (in the Magistrat form), neither chairs the council nor has voting powers.

---

5   Note, however, that since 1994, direct election of the mayor has been introduced in a large number of municipalities in the Rhineland-Palatinate. The timing of its introduction in individual municipalities has been keyed to the end of the term of the indirectly elected incumbent mayor.

Table 5.1 Standard classification of local government forms generally found in the literature

Constitutional tpye

	South German Council – SGC (*Süddeutsche Ratsverfassung*)	North German Council – NGC (*Norddeutsche Ratsverfassung*)	Magistrat – M (*Unechte Magistratsverfassung*)	Strong mayor – SM (*Bürgermeisterverfassung*)
Principal characteristics	'dualistic'	'monistic'	'trialistic'	'dualistic'
Division of competence (sovereignity)	'monocratic'	'monocratic'	'monocratic' and 'collegial'	'monocratic'
Form of executive leadership	vote and chair	neither vote nor chair	neither vote nor chair	vote and chair
Mode of electing chief executive	direct	indirect	indirect	indirect
Classification of old federal states	Bayern Baden-Württemberg	Nordrhein-Westfalen Niedersachsen*	Hessen* Schleswig-Holstein (large)*	Rheinland-Pfalz Saarland Schleswig-Holstein (small)*
Classification of new federal states	Brandenburg Sachsen Sachsen-Anhalt Thüringen (Mecklenburg-Vorpommern)*			

* Recently adopted and/or employed direct forms of election for mayor.

Finally, as to the way in which the chief executive is elected, two general modes are also prevalent. In the West, the most common form has been indirect election, with the council electing the executive. Until recently, direct election of the mayor was confined to the two states using the South German Council form. Most of the new federal states in the East have implemented this mechanism, and in the West it was adopted by Hesse (with its Magistrat constitutional form) and Rhineland-Palatinate in the early 1990s. This election modus will become more widespread in the other Western states over the next few years.

What importance do these differences in governmental institutional structures have for the performance of government? This has been something of an issue for administrative and political scientists in recent times and has also played itself out in political debates in both the old federal states and the new ones. In the old federal states the question has centered on the need some believe exists to alter one or another specific model and adopt attributes found in others. In the new federal states, both the need to create systems of local government that fit within the German federal system and the desire to preserve the special democratic climate associated with the revolution that brought about the collapse of the old regime have played a role (Wollmann, 1995).

The two most prominent positions on the importance of these categories are those held by Banner (1984) and Derlien et al. (1976). Banner contends that there are important differences across these categories in terms of their ability to provide effective government performance. In particular, because the South German Council form provides strong powers for a directly elected chief executive, it assures that a coherent and rational policy-making and implementation process takes place. By contrast, power is diffused in the other systems, particularly in the North German Council form, and thereby coherence is lost and collectively irrational policies are adopted and implemented.

In contrast, Derlien, et al. (1976) contend that while differences on the formal level exist, they have no impact on the effectiveness of government performance. When one looks at the inner workings of different types of city government forms, ultimately the same sort of decision process is at work with a certain city council committees and particular elements of the city government bureaucracy effectively dominating this process. Derlien (1994) is himself still convinced of this position and is critical of both the theoretical quality of Banner's argument and what he describes as the lack of empirical support found for the argument.[6]

Does the traditional classification scheme outlining institutional variations in local government forms in Germany help us? The answer to this is that its weaknesses undermine its utility and another approach is needed.[7] Before turning to that ap-

---

6 See the volume edited by Shimanke (1989) for a number of empirical studies related to the 'Banner Thesis'.
7 See Derlien (1994) and Schmidt-Eichstaedt (1985).

proach, let me outline two major problems with the traditional scheme. First, per the discussion above, the assumed (and permanent) homogeneity within categories does not hold.[8] There are notable differences; these differences have existed since the outset or have come into being through the course of modern German history. One is left in the awkward situation of using a scheme where different things are treated as being the same (and at times, the same things are being treated as different). Ultimately, then, one needs a more fine-grained assessment of the differences and similarities that hold across the various systems. Second, the theoretical status of these categories is at best uncertain. Analogous to an approach commonly found in dealing with institutional differences at the national level, some examples being contrasts between 'presidential' vs. 'parliamentary' systems, 'majoritarian' vs. 'consensual' systems, the import of these traits and the mechanisms by which they putatively shape performance is not at all clear (Lijphart, 1984, 1989; Linz, 1990). This has implications for the way in which one should go about measuring the differences and similarities between systems. The scheme that one uses needs to be tied to the theoretical argument that one is making. Below, then, I will outline such an argument and then proceed to describe the measurement effort and the results that follow from it.

An Alternative Approach

In attempting to account for the relevance of institutional differences for governmental performance I draw upon an approach developed by Tsebelis (1995). At the core of this formulation are the notions of veto players and their influence on policy-making. In the formulation, the object of explanation is policy stability or what also can be described as policy ineffectiveness (which in turn is connected to the performance of government).[9] Vital to policy stability in any governmental system are the number of veto players, their coherence and the distances between veto players in policy space.

A veto player is an actor, institutional or partisan, whose agreement is necessary for a policy change decision. As noted above, Tsebelis' model of policy stability centers on three attributes of veto players in a decision system. First, the sheer number of veto players in a system is critical to the ability of the system to alter policies. In the general case, the greater the number of veto players, the greater the policy stability, that is, the smaller the ability of the system to adopt policies congruent with any

---

8 See the commentaries by Derlien (1994, 1995) on changes that have taken place or are in the process of being implemented and how structurally incompatible configurations are being forged together. For a detailed discussion, from a legal perspective, of structural changes in local government institutional forms, see Schefold and Neumann (1996).

9 What it is being assumed here is that governmental performance is intimately connected to the possibility for policy innovation. Policy stability, that is a policy of the status quo, in an environment subject to change, certainly will diminish the performance of a government by nearly any subjective or objective standard.

policy outcome other than the status quo. This follows from the tendency for the size of the area of agreement that is possible to reach between players not to increase in size with the addition of one or more actors whose agreement is needed to bring about a change in policy. At best, the addition of such an actor does not decrease that area.

Second, policy differences between veto players shape the area of potential agreement among the players. The more distant the policy positions are, the lower the ability to find agreement and therefore the greater the policy stability. This is a straightforward proposition regarding the difficulties that arise in reaching agreement when the preferred policies of actors differ in significant ways from one another.

Finally, collective players, say, for example, a party caucus in a legislature, can induce greater policy instability to the extent that the positions of the individual members in the collective differ from one another. In other words, the presence of one or more veto players with incoherent policy positions lessens the difficulty with which agreement on policy change can be brought about within the system.

How does this approach relate to the question of local government structures in Germany? From the perspective of Tsebelis' veto player model, I see the key to handling institutional structure in the German local government context as existing within the role and powers of the chief executive officer of the local government.[10] I am assuming that in the situation where the role and power of this office are minimal, then other institutional elements, particularly the town/city council (and the party caucuses, or other groupings, therein) become of major importance. In this case, where party discipline is generally less developed, where fractionalization is quite high (hence increasing the number of 'effective parties'), where politics is ultimately a part-time job, then the local government may be characterized as having a large number of veto players, and the policy differences among these players will be significant. In addition, it is likely as well that in governmental systems where the role and powers of the chief executive are limited, than elements of the administration will more easily achieve the status of veto players as well. This situation detracts further from the possibility of providing superior performance.

Alternatively, systems that confer institutionally strong powers to the chief executive officer have the effect of greatly reducing the number of veto players. With strong control over the administrative apparatus of the local government, the chief executive can ward off 'Balkanization', the development of strong centers of power therein where these centers have competing and contradictory interests. Further, a strong position for the chief executive officer vis-à-vis the council can effectively eliminate or at least weaken the factions that potentially might achieve veto player status. By effectively dominating the 'pre-decision' phase of legislation (with centralized control over the administration and dominance inside legislative committees) and by having powers of agenda setting within the council itself, a strong chief exec-

---

10 In this, the basic point the argument is similar to that of Banner's (1984).

utive greatly reduces the number of players who can act to veto policy. In addition, excessive fractionalization within the council as a whole and within council caucuses expands the possibility of an institutionally strong chief executive finding the legislative support needed to carry out the program that officer has settled on.

In sum, within the German local government systems where the role and powers of the chief executive are very great, I argue that the council and its constituent parts lose (or are significantly weakened in) their status as veto players. This is especially so because of the agenda setting capacities of a constitutionally defined strong chief executive, the veto powers of that officer, and the executive's ability to hinder elements of the council and the administration from forging strong localized centers of power in coalition with one another. I also argue that this situation further minimizes the chances that the administration or parts of it can achieve veto player status. Furthermore, exclusive control and oversight over the administration enhances the chief executive officer's ability to assure that policy innovations are effectively carried out. The effects of this, particularly in light of the strong but not complete correlation within the German local government systems between direct election of the chief executive and the strength of that officer's powers, is to heighten citizen satisfaction with government performance in that directly elected chief executives are more likely to reflect the preferences of the median voter.

In order to apply this theoretical approach one needs some sort of encompassing measure that reflects the 'veto player' situation in the different governmental systems across the various states. While Tsebelis suggests that there are rules one can use to identify veto players and their attributes, the present research problem does not really lend itself to a straightforward accounting of numbers and attributes. The solution used here is to adopt a measure that reflects the prevailing general decision-making situation in the different local government constitutional orders.

In what follows, I have brought together a set of constitutionally defined structural elements of the twelve local government systems that have been the focus of the larger project.[11] These elements are central to illuminating the power position of the chief executive officer and facilitate identifying, in an admittedly crude fashion, the veto player situation that prevails within these systems.[12] Two general indices are constructed from sets of characters that have been coded using some simple rules; these two indices are then combined (in an unweighted fashion) to produce an overall index of power centralization in the office of the chief executive of the local government.

There are two general areas that give shape to the scope of powers available to the chief executive officer within German local government. The first of these is the autonomy and power granted to that officer in directing the execution of government

---

11 Note that no municipalities in Saarland are included in either sample and so no coding of institutional form is provided.
12 For a similar effort at assessing the relative powers of presidents in national political systems, see Shugart and Carey (1992).

administrative matters. The second is that officer's broad political position vis-à-vis the legislative branch, the city council. The scoring for each of the 15 characteristics used here is generally based on a three point system. The weakest situation for a chief executive is scored as 0. An intermediate situation is coded as 1. The strongest situation for the executive is coded as 2. In terms of some characteristics, it was deemed appropriate to use only the two extreme scores and to drop the intermediate score. The reasoning behind the use of each trait as well as the coding rules is presented in Table 5.2. For each of the two aggregate measures, the sum of the scores across the attributes was calculated and this sum then taken as a proportion of the maximum possible scores (in the administrative area the maximum is 12 and in the political area the maximum is 18). The joint index is the unweighted average of these two proportions.[13] The scorings for each local government system are presented in Table 5.3, as are the two aggregate measures and the overall index of power centralization. Note that the sources used in constructing the information needed for the various measures are listed at the end of Table 5.3.

Figure 5.1 allows one to visualize the differences that exist among all of these systems as well as the heterogeneous character of the traditional classification scheme. The placement of each system with respect to the political position of the chief executive vis-à-vis the council and the administrative autonomy of the chief executive are shown on the horizontal and vertical scales, respectively. Three features of this graph stand out. First, there is significant variation within the traditional categories at least along the horizontal or political dimension. Second, the fairly widespread view of the South German Council constitutional form as the one providing the maximum political and administrative power to the chief executive is largely confirmed here; still, there are notable differences among the systems employing this form and this can be seen especially among the new federal states. Third, while the North German Council constitutional form seems to provide the chief executive officer with the weakest political position (and even this is not uniformly so – compare North Rhine-Westphalia with Schleswig-Holstein and its Magistrat form), administrative autonomy is clearly greater for the chief executive officer in this type of system than it is in the Magistrat form.

Furthermore, it is interesting to note that even though one would have to conclude that based on the characteristics traditionally held to be important in distinguishing the South German Council form from the strong mayor form, no differences can be said to continue to exist between the Baden-Württemberg and Bavaria, on the one hand, and the Rhineland-Palatinate, on the other. The latter has recently instituted

---

13 Obviously, the small number of independent cases (12, the number of state-determined local government constitutional orders) and the large number of variables or traits (15) prohibit anything like factor analysis to validate the scales. It can be reported, though, that both the administrative and political scales meet the standard cut-offs for summated scales (with Cronbach's of .84 and .88, respectively). In turn, the two summated scales are highly correlated with a Pearson r of .74.

Social Capital, Institutional Structures and Democratic Performance   163

Table 5.2 Institutional characteristics of the office of the chief executive (CEO)

Features	Effects	Capacity to reduce number of veto players*
1. Leadership of administration	Reduces the power of higher-level administrators thereby lowering number of potential veto players. Inhibits council factions from developing blocking alliances with administration, lowers numbers of potential veto players in council and increases strength of CEO.	0 = Assigned to a collegial body (2) 2 = Assigned to CEO (10)
2. Autonomy of CEO in routine administrative business	Enhances strength of CEO over both council and administrators. Facilitates execution of policy.	0 = Only in those areas where council delegates this power (2) 1 = Can occur automatically if certain conditions are fulfilled (3) 2 = Unconditional autonomy for CEO (7)
3. Role of CEO in personnel decisions	CEO's role weakens both administrators and council and thereby lowers number of potential veto players. This facilitates the execution of policy by eliminating (or threatening to remove) any recalcitrant administrative officer.	0 = Role assigned to a collegial body (1) 1 = Delegated to CEO but can be withdrawn by council (8) 2 = Council's decisions hold only if these decisions accord with wishes of the CEO (3)

Table 5.2 (continued)

Features	Effects	Capacity to reduce number of veto players*
4. 'Intermediary organ' or 'main committee'	Presence of these types of bodies adds to the number of effective veto players. Its presence also weakens the CEO. This thereby reduces CEO's ability to bring about an efficient and focused operation of administration. Note: The powers of a 'main committee' are less intrusive than an 'intermediary organ', nevertheless these features weaken CEO and add potential veto players.	0 = Exits either in a form of a *Magistrat* or a community board (*Gemeindevorstand*) (4) 1 = 'Main committee' of city council (3) 2 = None of the above exists (5)
5. Chair of 'intermediary organ'	Given 4 above, the absence of such an institution strengthens CEO and reduces veto players in system. If chairperson is other than CEO, veto players increased and CEO weakended.	0 = 'Intermediary organ' exists but CEO does not chair it (1) 1 = 'Intermediary organ' exists and CEO chairs it (3) 2 = No 'intermediary organ' exists (8)
6. Legal authority of council to withdraw a competence	The grant of this authority to the council increases the number of veto players and weakens CEO. Restricting this authority lessen both impacts. Its absence reduces veto players and increases strength of CEO.	0 = Council has unrestricted-authority (4) 1 = Council's ability to do so restricted to certain areas (6) 2 = Authority not available to council (2)

Social Capital, Institutional Structures and Democratic Performance   165

Table 5.2 (continued)

Features	Effects	Capacity to reduce number of veto players*
7. Formal veto power of CEO	If denied or restricted, this increases potential number of veto players and weakens CEO. Expansive formal veto power of CEO can effectively eliminate many potential veto players.	0 = No such power (0) 1 = Veto power only over council actions/decisions contrary to law (5) 2 = Veto power as in 1, but expanded to council actions/decisions that are contrary to the 'well-being of the community' (7)
8. CEO's right to make urgent decisions	If denied or restricted, this has the same impact as 7 above.	0 = No such right exists (0) 1 = Available if other specified office holders are in agreement with decision (4) 2 = Unrestricted right (8)
9. Possibility to recall CEO	Weakens CEO. If power granted to council, this enhances number of potential of veto players inside decision-making system. Less intrusive (and productive in terms of generating veto players) when power not in council but in electorate where mobilization are costs greater. Its absence lowers number of potential veto players and increases power of CEO.	0 = Council has the prerogative (4) 1 = Recall available but right allocated to the electorate (6) 2 = No recall possibility (2)

Table 5.2 (continued)

Features	Effects	Capacity to reduce number of veto players*
10. Council chair	Chair has agenda setting rights as well as powers to steer deliberations and votes. Granting this to someone other than the CEO increases number of veto players and weakens CEO.	0 = CEO may not chair council (5) 1 = Possible for CEO to be elected to council chair (2) 2 = CEO is ex-officio council chair (5)
11. Chair of council committees	Similar to 10. Much of the 'pre-decision' work of the council occurs in such bodies. Granting this power to council members enhances number of veto players (both council members and higher administrative officers on whom council committees' chairs would rely). When reserved for CEO reduces number of veto players and enhances power of CEO.	0 = CEO prohibited from chairing council committees (4) 1 = Possible for CEO to chair committees (or at least certain committees) (6) 2 = CEO is ex-officio chair of committees (2)
12. Composition of 'intermediary organ'	Where composition mixed, i.e. where council persons may be members, enhances the potential for these persons (or the factions they represent) to become veto players. Where council persons denied membership, less intrusive, but still that potential that non-council members may develop into veto players.	0 = Mixed, with some council members included in mix (2) 1 = CEO members and council members excluded (2)

Table 5.2 (continued)

Features	Effects	Capacity to reduce number of veto players*
12. Composition of 'intermediary organ' (continued)	Absence of such an entity lowers number of veto players and decreases strength of potential veto players other than CEO.	2 = No 'intermediary organ' exists (8)
13. Flexibility in mode of electing council members	Two general considerations hold here: First, either indirect elections of the CEO occurs or a party list rule governs council elections. The indirect election effect is described immediately above. Party list procedures decrease fracionalization within the council; they thereby reinforce discipline within council fractions. This increases number of potential veto players. Second, if multiple votes for single candidates (*Kumulierung*) or division of votes across party lists (*Panaschierung*) is permitted, fractionalization within council is promoted and party caucus discipline is diminished or weakened. This decreases the number of potential veto players.	0 = Strict party list (or mayor is elected by council and not by citizens) (5) 2 = A voter can give more than one of her/his votes to a single candidate (*Kumulierung*) or her/his votes to candidates from different party lists (*Panaschierung*) (7)

Table 5.2 (continued)

Features	Effects	Capacity to reduce number of veto players*
14. Mode of electing chief executive	Election by council weakens CEO and enhances power of potential veto players in council. Direct election by voters enhances legitimacy of CEO, increasing power of that office and reducing potential number of veto players within council.	0 = CEO indirectly elected, i.e., elected by council and not by voters (4) 2 = CEO directly elected by voters (8)
15. Timing of CEO election	Veto player enhancing situation (where CEO is also weakened) is when CEO is elected by council. Power and legitimacy of CEO and potential for reducing number of veto players enhanced when council and CEO direct elections occur at different times. Intermediate situation is where these two elections occur at the same time.	0 = CEO indirectly elected, i.e. elected by council and not by voters (4) 1 = Both CEO and council elected by voters at the same time (1) 2 = CEO elected by voters at a time different from council (7)

* 0 = low or nil; 1 = moderate; 2 = high. Number of systems with this feature in parentheses.

Table 5.3 Institutional characteristics and the centralization in the office of the chief executive

State:* Traditional category:**	BW SGC	BA SGC	HE M	NS NGC	NW NGC	RP SM	SH M	BR SGC	MV SGC	S SGC	SA SGC	TH SGC
I Administrative autonomy of chief executive												
1 Leadership of administration	2	2	0	2	2	2	0	2	2	2	2	2
2 Autonomy of chief executive, routine business	2	2	1	1	0	2	0	1	2	2	2	2
3 Role of chief executive in personnel decisions	2	1	0	1	1	1	1	1	2	1	2	1
4 'Intermediary organ' or 'main committee'	2	2	0	0	1	0	0	2	1	2	2	1
5 Chair of 'intermediary organ'	2	2	1	0	2	1	1	2	2	2	2	2
6 Legal authority of council to withdraw a competence	1	2	0	1	0	1	0	1	0	1	1	2
Total administration	11 0.92	11 0.92	2 0.17	5 0.42	6 0.50	7 0.58	2 0.17	9 0.75	9 0.75	10 0.83	11 0.92	10 0.83

Table 5.3 (continued)

State:* Traditional category:**	BW SGC	BA SGC	HE M	NS NGC	NW NGC	RP SM	SH M	BR SGC	MV SGC	S SGC	SA SGC	TH SGC
II *Political position of chief executive*												
7 Veto power of chief executive	2	1	2	1	2	1	2	1	2	2	2	1
8 Chief executive's right to make urgent decisions	2	2	2	1	1	1	2	1	2	2	2	2
9 Possibility to recall chief executive	2	2	1	0	0	1	0	1	0	1	1	1
10 Council chair	2	2	0	0	0	2	0	0	0	2	1	2
11 Chair of council committees	2	1	0	0	1	2	0	1	1	1	1	1
12 Composition of 'intermediary organ'	2	2	1	0	2	1	0	2	2	2	2	2
13 Flexibility in mode of electing council members	2	2	0	0	0	2	0	2	0	2	2	2
14 Mode of electing chief executive	2	2	2	0	0	2	0	2	0	2	2	2
15 Timing of electing chief executive	2	1	2	0	0	2	0	2	0	2	2	2
Total political	18	15	10	2	6	14	4	12	7	16	15	15
	1.00	0.83	0.56	0.11	0.33	0.78	0.22	0.67	0.39	0.89	0.83	0.83
Joint index (adm. & pol. equal weights)	0.96	0.88	0.36	0.26	0.42	0.68	0.19	0.71	0.57	0.86	0.88	0.83

*   Key: BW = Baden-Württemberg; BA = Bayern; HE = Hessen; NS = Niedersachsen; NW = Nordrhein-Westfalen; RP = Rheinland-Pfalz; SH = Schleswig-Holstein; BR = Brandenburg; MV = Mecklenburg-Vorpommern; S = Sachsen; SA = Saarland; TH = Thüringen.

** For the acronyms of the categories, cf. Table 5.1

Table 5.3 (continued)

Sources for information on constitutional structures:

- Schmitt-Eichstaedt, Gerd (1994), *Die Gemeindeordnungen in der Bundesrepublik Deutschland* (Loseblatt-Ausgabe), Kohlhammer, Stuttgart;
- Gemeindeordnung für Baden-Württemberg i. d. F. vom 3.10.1983, geändert durch das Gesetz vom 8.11.1993;
- Gemeindeordnung für den Freistaat Bayern i. d. F. der Bekanntmachung vom 11.9.1989;
- Hessische Gemeindeordnung i. d. F. vom 1.4.1993;
- Niedersächsische Gemeindeordnung in der Fassung vom 22.6.1982;
- Gemeindeordnung für das Land Nordrhein-Westfalen i.d.F. der Bekanntmachung vom 14.7.1994;
- Gemeindeordnung für das Land Rheinland-Pfalz i.d.F. der Bekanntmachung vom 31.1.1994;
- Gemeindeordnung für Schleswig-Holstein i. d. F. vom 2.4.1990;
- Kommunalverfassung des Landes Brandenburg vom 15.10.1993, zuletzt geändert durch Gesetz vom 30.6.1994;
- Kommunalverfassung für das Land Mecklenburg-Vorpommern vom 18.2.1994;
- Gemeindeordnung für den Freistaat Sachsen vom 21.4.1993;
- Gemeindeordnung für das Land Sachsen-Anhalt vom 5.10.1990;
- Thüringer Gemeinde- und Landkreisordnung vom 16.8.1993.

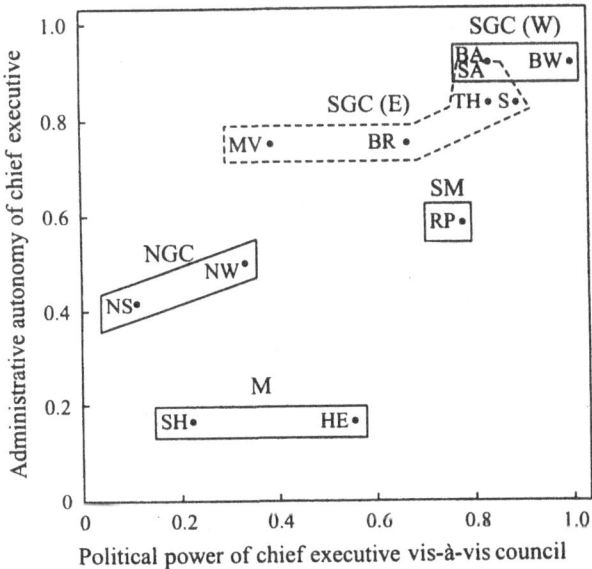

Source: Based on information in Table 5.3.

Figure 5.1 Centralization of power in the chief executive's office

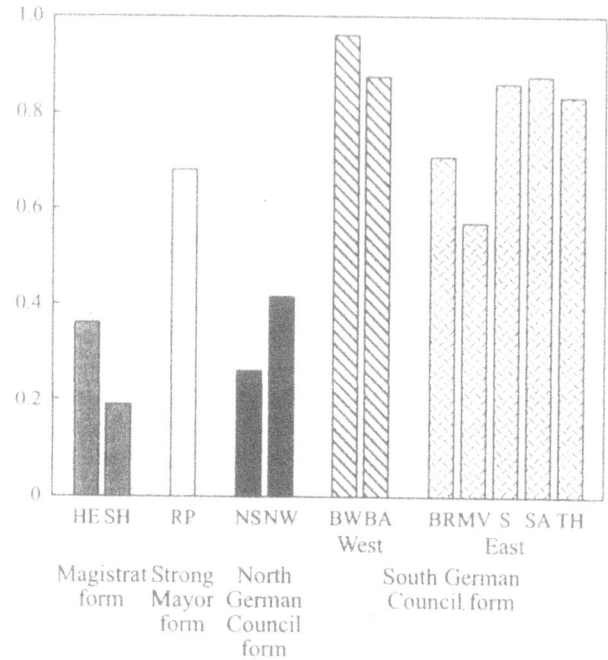

Source: Based on information in Table 5.3.

Figure 5.2   Joint power centralization index

direct elections of the mayor – the only difference that held across the four characteristics that mark the traditional scheme presented in Table 5.1. Yet, based on the more refined scheme being proposed here, appreciable differences, in terms of both the administrative autonomy of the chief executive as well as this officer's political power vis-à-vis the council, still prevail.

Figure 5.2 provides a graphic portrayal of the joint index power centralization. Each state's system is grouped together with the other state systems to which they are traditionally joined in the four-fold scheme. Again, while one notes significant variation between the groupings, a large amount of variance is contained within the groupings for which there is more than one example. On average, the South German Council group has the highest score, but there is large variation between the old federal states on the one hand and the new federal states on the other. In addition, significant variation exists within the grouping of the new federal states. Further, one can see that with this index the Rhineland-Palatinate system centralizes power in the chief executive officer to a greater extent than does one of the new federal state systems (Mecklenburg-Vorpommern).

Analysis

As shown immediately below, there is a wide amount of variation in government performance levels across German municipalities. What accounts for this significant variation? Concentrating solely on citizens' evaluations of their local governments' performance (and using a joint index described below), I employ a relatively parsimonious model that (a) seeks to control for some obvious factors that would influence performance, and (b) attempts to evaluate the social capital and institutional hypotheses. Let me turn first to the dependent variable in this analysis.

The measure of local government performance used here derives from a survey of citizens in a set of 30 cities chosen to maximize variation on both an indicator of social capital and the index of local government institutional structures developed in the last section.[14] In that survey, citizens were asked how satisfied they were with the performance of a number of actors and organizations within their local governmental and political systems.[15] Questions about the performance of the city bureaucracy, the city council and the city executive (as well as the local political parties) were posed.[16]

---

14 A description of the elite and citizen surveys that form the core of the empirical base for this study is provided in the Appendix to this book. The rules used for the selection of municipalities included are also provided there.

15 The approach taken here obviously employs what some characterize as subjective measures of democratic government performance. I do not share the view that such measures are inherently inferior to so-called 'objective measures', such as fiscal deficits or the timeliness of budget implementations. Indeed, citizens' evaluations of government performance are at the core of democratic theory. Ultimately, the purpose of a democratic system is to satisfy the preferences of its citizens. The example of fiscal deficits is instructive here. If an overwhelming majority of citizens thinks deficit spending may be an appropriate response to prevailing economic conditions, then for an analyst to assume these deficits are a sign of democratic failure can be described, at best, as misguided.

16 There are three questions in the citizen survey (translated from German) on government performance. The questions on satisfaction with government performance took the following general form:
(14–17) All in all, how satisfied are you with the performance of the _____ here in your town or city?
___ Very satisfied
___ Pretty satisfied
___ Somewhat satisfied
___ Somewhat dissatisfied
___ Pretty dissatisfied
___ Very dissatisfied
___ Don't know

Question 14 dealt with the city government administration, 16 dealt with the town or city council, and 17 dealt with the mayor, the chief mayor or the city manager as appropriate for the municipality. In addition, a fourth question (No. 15) dealt with citizen satisfaction with local political party performance.

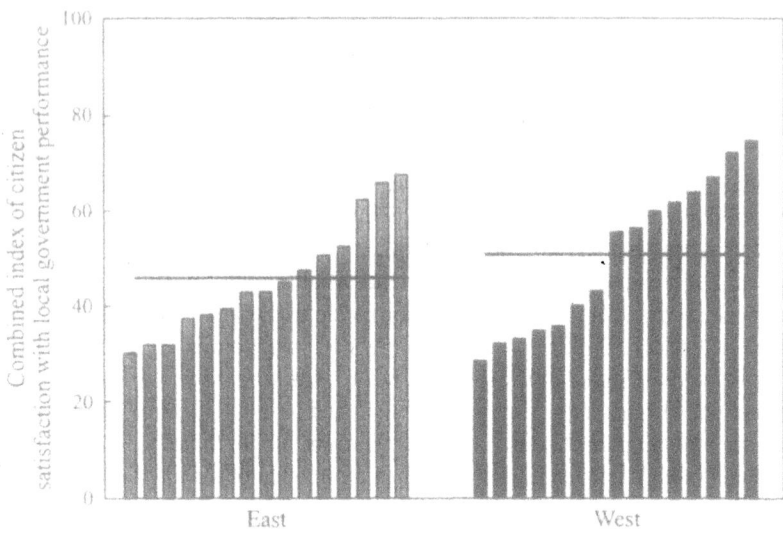

Source: Democracy and Local Government in Germany, Citizen Survey.

Figure 5.3 Distribution of citizens' satisfaction with local government performance across the communities in East and West Germany

Figure 5.3 portrays the situation across the cities within each region. Recall from the discussion in chapter 4 that the data on the three governmental elements are combined to produce the joint index of performance satisfaction with this index set equal to the percentage of the population expressing satisfaction with all three elements of the local government. As pointed out before, the two regions have an average level that is relatively similar. At the same time there is tremendous variation in these levels across the cities within each region. Note the relatively equal regional averages stands in sharp contrast with the large difference that has held persistently between East and West in terms of citizens' satisfaction with the national political system. Since the time of reunification, Eastern levels of citizen satisfaction with the national political system have been consistently far below those prevailing in the West (Cusack, 1999).[17]

Three control variables have been introduced into the model meant to capture the cross-sectional variation in the levels of citizens' satisfaction with their local governments' performance. The first of these variables is simply the population size of the community. In other national settings, it has been demonstrated that the size of the community plays a key role in democratic performance. While there may be increasing returns to scale in terms of the variety and efficiency of government services

---

17 The average Eastern level of citizen satisfaction has remained at a level equal to only two-thirds that prevailing in the West.

delivery, there are also grounds to believe that size itself will undermine the democratic workings of the local political system: A large sized political unit may make it difficult for the local government authorities to provide the performance that satisfies citizens within the communities (Dahl and Tufte, 1973; Mouritzen, 1989; Nielsen, 1981).[18] Heterogeneity generally increases with size, thus producing a greater diversity of interests and thereby lowering the possibility for coherent policy-making with a chance of finding strong popular support.

The second term included simply distinguishes between the communities in the East and those in the West. There are ample grounds to believe that the experience of the citizens in the East with the workings of political system in the Federal Republic has been disappointing, at least relative to the expectations they had at the time of reunification, and that lower satisfaction levels might also be apparent with respect to their local political systems. Even though little differences show up in the average evaluations of their local governments (see Figure 5.3), all indications suggest that there should be a significant difference, with the Easterners being less satisfied.[19] The contention here is that the gap is not significant at this level because of differences that hold between local conditions in the East and those in the West.

The third control factor introduced into the model is meant to capture the effects of conflict within the community. This can only be measured indirectly and here I rely on reports by the respondents in the elite surveys.[20] The inclusion of the conflict term is warranted to the extent that the elites' reports on this matter, if accurate, would reflect difficulties in formulating and executing policy at the local government level and thereby undermine the satisfaction felt by the citizens within the community (Eldersveld et al., 1995).

The other two terms included in the model are meant to capture the effects of social capital and institutional differences. Following the lead of Putnam (1993) and

---

18 For an opposing view on this question, see Newton (1982).
19 See Cusack (1997) for extensive documentation on the development of public opinion in both East and West Germany since reunification. Another (and not necessarily contradictory) argument would be that the relatively lower level of economic well-being in the East produces a generalized discontent that manifests itself not only with national governmental institutions but also with those in the local community (see Cusack, 1999).
20 The question wording in the elite surveys about community conflict was as follows:
(11) In many communities there are conflicts that interfere with effective action to meet community problems. Are there some major conflicts in your community that interfere with solving problems?
____ Yes
____ No (If no, please go to question 14)
(12) If yes (to question 11), would you please name one or two of these conflicts?

In terms of the entire sample of cities, conflict levels by this measure appear to be similar in both regions.

his discussion of the contribution that social capital makes to successful democratic performance, I have introduced a term that attempts to measure the degree of trust to be found among the elites within each community.[21] The wording of the question is the same as the generally employed question on social trust.[22] As above, the basic expectation is that trust facilitates cooperation and that cooperation, particularly within the political elite, smoothes the way for effective policy-making. The latter should result in good public policy that, in a democratic system, enhances the level of satisfaction citizens have with respect to their government's performance.

Finally, a measure of institutional characteristics is included. In the present context, I employ the index of power centralization constructed earlier in this chapter. Following the line of argument developed, the expectation here is that the greater the degree of concentration of power within the hands of the executive, the more efficient and effective is the policy-making and, in turn, the greater the level of satisfaction the citizens will express for their local government's performance.

The complete model estimated using data from the thirty municipalities included in this study takes the following form:

$$CitSat_i = \alpha + \beta_1 Size_i + \beta_2 East_i + \beta_3 CommConf_i + \beta_4 EliteTrust_i + \beta_5 Cntrlz_i + e_i$$

where:

- *CitSat* is the percentage of citizens within the community expressing satisfaction with the local government's performance (this is the overall index of satisfaction described above); source is the citizen survey;
- *Size* is the population of the community (expressed in thousands); source is Deutscher Städtetag (1994);
- *East* is a dummy variable taking on a value of 1 if the community is located in the new federal states; it takes on a value of 0 if the community is in one of the old federal states;
- *CommConf* is a measure of the scope of conflict in the community. It is operationalized here as the percentage of the elite respondents reporting that conflicts exist within the community that hinder problem-solving; based on elite surveys;

---

21 The assumption here is in keeping with Putnam's arguments. First, trust is one of three components of social capital – all of which are highly interrelated. Second, the stock of social capital within a community's elite corresponds to the stock within a community's citizenry.
22 The trust question employed in both the elite and citizen surveys takes the following form:
(17) Generally speaking, would you say that most people can be trusted or that one cannot be too careful dealing with people?
____ Most people can be trusted
____ One cannot be too careful
____ Don't know

- *EliteTrust* is a measure of the social capital amongst the elites within the local government system. Here it is the percentage of elites indicating that they have trust in other people; source is the elite survey;
- *Cntrlz* is a measure of the centralization of power (vis-à-vis the town council and the town government administration) in the hands of the local government executive. It ranges from 0 to 1.0 and weights equally the relative strength of the executive in both areas. Higher values are indicative of greater centralization of power. For coding and sources see Tables 5.2 and 5.3.

The results for the estimation of this model are reported in the Table 5.4. Note that examination of residuals from the OLS estimates (reported in the first column) suggested that four cases were marginally problematic in terms of their undue influence and so Welch's bounded influence technique (results reported in the second column) was also employed. The results from both estimation techniques are very close to one another.[23] The overall fit of the equation to the data is good. Note as well that the three control variables take on the expected signs and are statistically significant. Larger size municipalities have governments that achieve lower performance levels, with each increment of 10,000 lowering satisfaction levels by about one per cent. Thus, a community with 250,000 people (the maximum value for the sample frame) would have, on average and controlling for other variables, satisfaction levels approximately 25 per cent lower than a community with a population of only 25,000 (the minimum value for the sample frame). The regional term's parameter implies that on average and other things being equal, communities within the new federal states have citizen satisfaction levels about 11 per cent lower than those to be found in communities in the old federal states.[24] And, once again, communities with high levels of conflict that hinder problem-solving as reported by the elites also achieve lower levels of performance in the estimation of their citizens.

Importantly, both the social capital and institutional terms demonstrate substantive and statistical importance. Thus, the parameter for the trust term, meant to capture the effects of social capital on government performance, takes on the expected posi-

---

23 In addition, various robust regression as well as bootstrap estimations were undertaken and all provided essentially the same results as those reported in Table 5.4.
24 In an alternative specification of the model, an economic well-being term was substituted for the East regional dummy. The economic well-being index used is based on the average of two standardized measures: (1) an index of unemployment and (2) an index of income per capita.

Needless to say, this standardized measure, while picking up intra-regional differences, is still dominated by inter-regional disparities. Indeed, the correlation between this index (where low values indicate poor economic conditions and high values good economic conditions) and the regional dummy is −.91. Regression results from the estimation with this index are similar to those with the dummy variable. All the coefficients are statistically significant and their values are approximately equal to those reported in Table 5.4, with, of course, the parameter on the economic index being positive.

Table 5.4 Determinants of citizens' satisfaction with local government performance: regression results*

Variables	OLS b (t-statistic)	Bounded influence** b (t-statistic)
Population size of city (in thousands)	−.11 (2.29)	−.11 (2.17)
East Germany (1 = East, 0 = West)	−10.96 (3.10)	−10.55 (3.08)
Conflicts in community (percentage of elite reporting conflict)	−.30 (2.82)	−.31 (2.99)
Trust amongst elites (percentage of elite trusting others)	.23 (1.92)	.22 (1.88)
Institutional centralization of power (ranges from 0 to 1.0)	22.63 (2.71)	23.53 (2.76)
Constant	57.39 (4.60)	51.99 (5.26)
Summary statistics:		
$\overline{R^2}$	.57	.59
F-statistic	8.7	9.5
Significance of F-statistic	.01	.01
Number of cases	30	30

*   Dependent variable: average of percentage satisfied with performance of all three local government institutions.

** Bounded influence technique based on Welch (1980). Weighting of individual cases determined by the size-adjusted cut-off (Fox, 1991, p. 31) for influential points as revealed by the DFFITS measures. The cut-off is equal to

$$2 \times \sqrt{\frac{(k+1)}{(n-k-1)}} \ .$$

Four cases surpassed this value as did the same four cases exceed the cut-off point for Cook's D.

tive sign and is significant (at least at the .10 level by a conservative two-tailed test). This finding accords with that of Putnam who has demonstrated that regions where the culture is marked by trust have more effective governments that produce satisfaction on the part of their citizens. Note that in both regions the average level of trust amongst elites is 45 per cent. In the East, the lowest level is 25 per cent and the highest is 86 per cent. In the West, the lowest level is 20 per cent and the highest is 71 per cent. Other being equal, the impact of moving from one observable extreme to another in the East, given the estimated coefficient for the trust term, would be to increase citizen satisfaction by approximately 13.5 per cent. In the West, it is slightly more than 11 per cent. In sum, trust among government and political elites in a local community makes an appreciable difference in the levels of citizens' satisfaction with their local governments' performance. Thus, governments in communities with high social capital do a better job in satisfying their citizens than do those in communities where the stock of social capital is low.

The coefficient on the executive power centralization term is also positive and significant. It takes a value of approximately 23. Recall that the system with the lowest power centralization score has a value of .19, while the highest has a .96. Comparing these two observable examples suggests that, other things being equal, moving from a very decentralized system to a highly centralized one would increase citizen satisfaction by approximately 18 per cent. This is, again, an appreciable substantive effect. Figure 5.4, with the results from a large set of simulations based on a set of counter-factuals, illustrates this. Based on the assumption that all other variables in the model are fixed at their sample average values, a 1,000 expected values of the levels of satisfaction with local government under the most decentralized and most centralized institutional forms observed have been generated using the CLARIFY simulation routine (King et al., 2000; Tomz et al., 1999).[25] With the most decentralized form, one would expect an average level of satisfaction equal to 36.05. With the centralized form, the average level expected would be 54.16. This large difference is in accordance with the institutionalist argument that concentrated power leads to more effective governmental decision-making that is reflected in performance as evaluated by citizens.

Taken together these results support Putnam et al.'s (1983) thesis that endogenous and exogenous theories of institutional success are complementary. In other words, both the internal characteristics of an institution as well as its environment matter; and they matter independently of each other. While one should not make too much of the point, the German data suggest that the effects of both are relatively equal. Given the estimated parameters on both terms, it turns out that moving from a situation of

---

25 Figure 5.4 plots the smoothed density estimates of the expected levels of satisfaction under the most extreme versions of power centralization observed in the sample of communities included in the study. These estimates were generated using the univariate kernel density estimation routine (kdensity) in STATA and are based on the expected values simulated with CLARIFY.

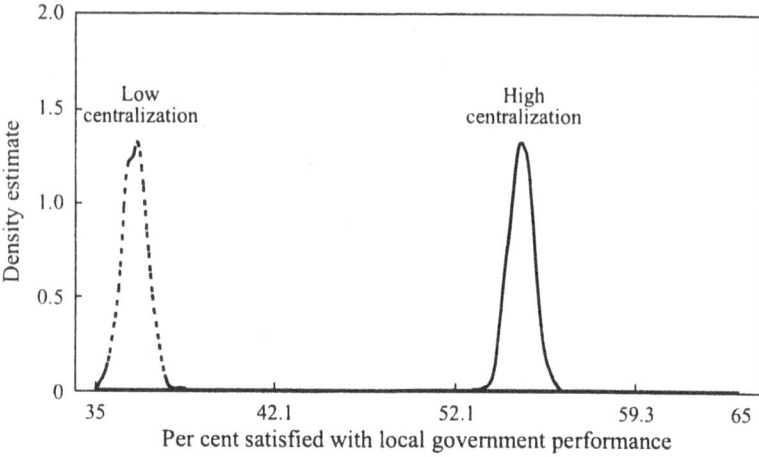

Source: Simulation results based on estimates presented in Table 5.4.

Figure 5.4 Simulated levels of citizens' satisfaction with local government performance in Germany based on low and high levels of institutionalized power centralization

complete distrust to one where trust is universal has about the same impact as changing from an institutional design where power is most diffuse (centralization index equals 0) to that where it is most concentrated (index equals 1).

In sum, the evidence suggests that the appropriate institutional design need not fail in the context of low stocks of social capital. In the German case, this is particularly important. Note that, other things being equal, the estimation results suggest that satisfaction levels should be about 11 per cent lower in Eastern communities relative to those that hold in the West. Given that many of the states in the East have adopted local government forms with more highly concentrated executive power than those most frequently found in the West, the estimation results on the parameter for the institutional term suggest that a lot of this deficit has been diminished if not eliminated through institutional engineering.

Conclusion

In a period when many countries are struggling with the problem of forging effective democratic institutions, Robert Putnam has drawn our attention to an important but often overlooked obstacle, the social context within which these institutions need to function. If there is a precept that can be drawn from his work, it is that institutions work best when enmeshed in a culture of cooperation. The design of his Italian study is such as to eliminate any variation in institutional structures among the objects being compared and thus to highlight the impact of his variable of central concern, social capital. While such a design cannot of itself be faulted, the conclusions one can draw from such a study necessarily are limited. Such a design does not answer the question of what impact institutional differences have in isolation or in conjunction with variation in such things as social capital. The more pessimistic interpretation one might give to Putnam's findings is that it is futile to engage in institutional engineering if the community's culture is one marked by low social capital. Given the results reported here, such a conclusion does not seem warranted.

The results here on German local governments show that institutional differences matter to democratic performance regardless of the stock of social capital within a community. Indeed, they appear to have the same magnitude of impact as social capital. The institutional structures of German local governments vary in numerous of ways. Stipulated by constitutions provided them by their state parliaments, there is marked variation in the extent to which power is centralized within local governments. The thesis presented here argues that power diffusion within governmental institutions can block or hinder effective public policy and thereby undermine the democratic performance of a local government. Empirical analysis supports this position. Where administrative authority and legislative control is concentrated in the hands of a directly elected chief executive, performance (as reflected in citizens' satisfaction with the performance of their local government institutions) is significantly higher than where power is diffuse and the chief executive is administratively weak and dominated by legislative actors. In sum, institutions do matter. Even in political cultures where one might expect poor performance, an appropriate institutional arrangement can make a significant difference in terms of democratic performance.

Furthermore, the great dissatisfaction one finds in East Germany across a wide spectrum of issues has been avoided at least in the area of local government. Ironically, this is the one area where East Germans (or more precisely, their elected representatives) have had a say about the form and shape of the institutions that govern their lives. Given the federal structure of the German system, as well as the clear unwillingness of West Germans to alter the institutions that had proven so successful for them since the founding of the Federal Republic, there were no choices to be made regarding the national government or the structure of state governments in the East (Wiesenthal, 1995). And while constrained to some extent by the notion that the local government institutions that they put in place would need to bear some resemblance to those in the West so as to facilitate integration into the complex federally based legal, regulative and public finance systems, East German politicians at least had a menu of choices from which to select. Some would hold that the institutions adopted are insufficient to the tasks confronting local governments (Osterland, 1994), while others suggest that they were chosen for reasons other than the objective value they have (Derlien, 1995). However, from all appearances, many chose wisely and adopted institutional features that enhance performance.

Chapter 6

Conclusion

With the fall of the Berlin Wall in 1989, the dissolution of the German Democratic Republic and its entry into the Federal Republic, Germany underwent a tremendous transformation accompanied by high economic, social and political costs. Both the transformation and the costs have been particularly great in the East, as this society has tried to cope with its integration into a completely different economic and political system. East Germans have seen a tremendous decline in employment and this has had not only economic, but also social and political effects as well. Nevertheless, through large transfers from the West, particularly through the public sector, the general economic situation has at least been stabilized.

However, this huge financial effort combined with stringent monetary policy on the part of the *Bundesbank* and a very restrictive fiscal policy followed in order to meet the Maastricht criteria have placed the entire German economy under tremendous strain and set in train a dramatic increase in unemployment throughout the country. The effects of this and related factors have been multi-fold and have intruded extensively into the political arena. For example, not only have East Germans become more and more skeptical of the Federal Republic's political-economic regime, but this has spilled-over into the West where once quite high levels of satisfaction with and acceptance of that regime have declined markedly (Cusack, 1999). At the local level, because of the responsibilities and restrictions local governments in the German federal system face, the economic disruption has resulted in rising costs (particularly social transfers) and declining revenues to cover those costs.

Local governments within Germany are embedded in a relatively more integrated political system than found in other federal polities such as the United States (Gunlicks, 1985). While the right to local government is constitutionally guaranteed, the individual state governments dictate the structures of these local governments. These structures range, for example, from their spatial scope, the extent of their responsibilities and competences, up to and including, most importantly, the form of their decision-making institutions. Furthermore, local governments' financial resources are drawn principally from various federal revenue-sharing schemes, some of which promote a degree of equality across localities. The range and returns on other, purely local, tax bases are quite narrow. In addition, local governments are often burdened with federal and state mandated responsibilities, which often strain their resource and administrative capacities. In recent years, lagging revenues, heightened expenditures, and efforts to limit fiscal deficits, have led federal authorities to delegate greater costs to lower levels of government and this has added to the fiscal pressures felt at the local level.

Most scholarly and journalistic writing on Germany after reunification has focused on what might be described as 'big picture' problems. They have concentrated attention on how the federal government, the party system, the national economy and the general public have responded to the various society-wide challenges that have arisen. At the same time, very little attention has be accorded to an area of governance and politics that plays an undeniably important role in the daily life of the German public, namely local government.[1] This work has focused attention on that area. It has dealt with issues such as who it is that governs at this level, the extent to which their views about basic political questions align with those of the citizens they serve, the problems and challenges that those who govern confront, their assessments of how well they have mastered these challenges and the extent to which these assessments are share by the governed. In addressing the last issue, particular attention has been given to dealing with the institutional and cultural bases of popular satisfaction with government performance.

What sorts of people occupy positions of power and responsibility at the local level in Germany? It was shown that local political/administrative elites are dissimilar to officials at higher levels of government in Germany in that they are less likely to come from privileged backgrounds. Still, they conform to the 'law of increasing disproportion' that characterizes the hierarchy of elites in Germany and elsewhere. At least in terms of class origin, they are less privileged and more representative than those holding positions at higher levels of government. Nevertheless, the backgrounds of local elites do not conform to the populist image of a democratic governing elite.

Particularly so in the new federal states, they are much more likely than ordinary citizens to have had a university education. Another distinguishing trait, though less marked than elites at the federal level, is that local elites are far more prone than ordinary citizens to come from families where the parents were involved in politics or official life. These characteristics aside, it is clear these elites do not conform to an image of a local governing class where dominance of the local scene passes from one generation to the next. In a country where geographic mobility is not very high, it turns out that a very large share of the local political/administrative elites in both

---

[1] For example, in an Allensbach survey conducted in 1993 (cf. Noelle-Neumann and Köcher, 1997, p. 790), citizens ranked the three levels of government within Germany in terms of their influence on their personal lives in the following way:

	Level:		
	Federal	State	Local
Effects:			
Strong	29	17	24
Moderate	43	48	41
Little or none	23	29	29
No answer	5	6	6

parts of Germany actually come from places outside of the communities in which they now serve in public office. And despite this distinguishing characteristic, it is also clear that, at least at this level of government, there is no evidence to support the notion that the East has been 'colonized' by the West.

Most members of the local elites in the West have long years of experiences in politics and/or public administration. Indeed, a very large number have served for extensive periods in the offices that they held at the time the survey was conducted. For the most part, the picture in the East is starkly different. Outside of the PDS and to some extent the two former block parties of the GDR, the CDU and the FDP, the elite members are quite new to official life: they have held both party membership and political/administrative office for only a short period of time.

All in all, the local elites in both parts of Germany are not especially representative of the socio-economic patterns that characterize their communities. Still, they are very well integrated within their communities. They are typically long-time residents who have a wide range of associational ties, though in the West these frequently reflect the political orientations of the parties of which they are members. In addition, they uniformly rely on a broad spectrum of individuals and groups within the community.

If local elites and citizens differ in their socio-economic background, are they nevertheless linked by common political values and ideologies? And to what extent has there been convergence or a lack of convergence in fundamental values since reunification? In addition, how do the local elites in Germany's two regions compare to local elites in other more established as well as transitional democracies?

German local elites, in both East and West, are divided principally along those two dimensions Kitschelt (1993) has identified as the primary conflict axes in post-industrial democracies, namely, socialism-capitalism and authoritarianism-libertarianism. West German elites, when compared with their East German colleagues, lean further toward the capitalist end of the first dimension but are no more libertarian than their Eastern colleagues. In terms of international comparisons, West German local elites look similar to those in a number of other Western democracies. On the other hand, the East German local elites are far more socialistic in their orientation than are most of the local elites one finds in four other recently democratized Central European states and indeed share some traits suggestive of an affinity with the 'third way' one finds in Sweden.

The differences between the two elites, particularly on the socialism-capitalism dimension, however, pale in comparison to the differences between the average citizens in East and West. East German citizens lean very much in the direction of socialist principles while their fellow citizens in the West are far more supportive of capitalistic principles. Furthermore, the citizens in both West and East Germany are markedly similar in their position along the authoritarian-libertarian dimension and at the same time much more authoritarian than the local elites in their respective regions. Relatively speaking, then, while Eastern local elites are clearly distinguishable from their Western colleagues, the gap between the two elites is far and away narrower than that between the masses of citizens in the two regions.

In the literature on the experience of reunification in Germany, there is a fair amount of agreement as to the sources of the differences in ideological positions between the two regions' populations, particularly with respect to socialism-capitalism. In a nutshell, they are seen as arising out of the effects of cultural socialization. This position lends weight to pessimistic conclusion that a convergence in mass (and elite) ideology between East and West will only come to pass through a lengthy process of generational replacement.

The approach taken in this book takes a different perspective. It holds that the rational self-interest of an individual is the principal source of ideological preferences. It follows that the differences one sees between ideological propensities across the regions are attributable to the differences in the interests of the people in the two regions. I have been able to demonstrate that the attributes of individuals that would lead a rational being to favor either socialism or capitalism have the effects (and they are substantial) one would expect using this theoretical approach. The implications of this are far more optimistic than those drawn from the socialization approach. Active efforts to improve in income and enhance labor market possibilities within East Germany would help immensely to eliminate the ideological gap between the citizens of two regions.

I also examined the problems confronting city governments within Germany and attempted to evaluate how successful these governments have been in solving these problems. These city goverments are embedded in a complicated federal system. Their elites are beset with many of the problems confronting the local elites in other advanced industrialized states. In addition, the local elites in East Germany are faced with the special problems of the transition to democracy and the conversion to the market system. One might then expect that these elites are having a difficult time. What are the problems they face and do these differ significantly between the two parts of Germany? In addition, a similar assessment is made at the mass level. Do elites and masses define the problem agendas of their communities in similar ways or differently?

Recognition of something as a problem does not necessarily mean that an actor sees it as her or his responsibility to deal with the problem. To what extent do local elites see these problems as the responsibility of local government? In addition, how competent are local governments in dealing with these problems – do these elites believe they have sufficient power and autonomy to cope with the problems confronting them? What success, in their own assessment, have they had in coping with these problems and does political-economic conflict within the community hinder problem-solving?

In both East and West Germany, local elites report that they are confronted with a wide range of important problems in their communities. Despite this diversity, a few problems stand out in terms of the frequency with which they are mentioned. In the main, these relate to economic difficulties, especially unemployment and economic development within the communities and the problem of the financial capabilities of the local governments. While citizens within these communities rank economic concerns high in their problem agendas, they are by far less concerned with the financial situation of their local governments. Their problem agendas give a very high ranking instead to the local traffic and parking conditions. When asked to choose from among a large but fixed menu of potential problem areas, elites in both regions are prone to suggesting that nearly all of these areas constitute a problem for their communities and that a not insignificant number, especially unemployment, economic development, the financial capacity as well as the costs of local government, pose major problems in the communities of both regions. In addition, in the East, housing and public safety seem to be major problems in the eyes of large numbers of the local elites. When compared with local elites in other countries, both East and West, the German local elites seem to be among those with the most crowded and severe problem agendas.

It would appear that local elites in both the new and old federal states hold the view that local government has a wide range of areas for which it should bear primary responsibility. Nevertheless, these elites are caught in a dilemma. They simultaneously believe that in many of these areas they have insufficient power and autonomy to cope with the problems they confront. Three deficit areas stand out because there is a consensus across both East and West; these include the policy areas of the environment, local economic development and, finally, the financial capacity of their local governments.

More so than in most of the other countries examined here, local government elites in Germany report that they are faced with a large array of major problems and are often weakened by a situation where they have insufficient power to deal with their responsibilities. In addition, they also report that they are confronted with very divided communities where conflict frequently obstructs problem-solving and stands in the way of community development. Under such circumstances, the latitude for successful policy-making and execution would appear to be very narrow and limited.

A principal aim of this study was to illuminate the basis of successful performance on the part of local governments. The results can shed light on the broader question of the roots of successful governance that has animated so much research in political science. The approach taken here gives particular emphasis to the roles of institutions and political culture in shaping government performance. The key question is: do either or both of these things matter?

While the elites in both parts of Germany are somewhat negative in their assessments of the success of the efforts by local government in dealing with the various challenges facing them, these elites are generally quite positive about the way in which the democratic process operates inside these communities. However, their optimism in this regard does not correspond very well with what the citizens of their communities express in terms of the views they express about the performance of the various central elements of the local government system. Regardless of how elites rate the operations of their local governments, in a democratic system a major concern is the extent to which the citizenry evaluates this performance positively. The question of the sources of citizen satisfaction with their governments was explored extensively with data collected from the citizen survey.

The role of institutional structures in shaping government performance is a contested issue, both generally and especially within the context of local government in Germany. There is marked variation in the institutional forms of local government across Germany. I reviewed the way in which scholars have traditionally attempted to describe these differences and to relate them to the performance capacity of local government. The common conception is that there are four distinctly different types of local government structures to be found within Germany. These include the North-German Council system, similar to a city manager type system, the Magistrat system, similar to a commissioner system, the strong mayor system, which is really close to the weak mayor system in the United States and the South German Council system, which is actually similar to a strong mayor system in the United States. However, these categories traditionally have been somewhat heterogeneous and, indeed, post-War (and post-reunification) developments have seen some significant changes in particular cases. Simultaneously, the debate on why any particular type of system might be more or less superior has rested on the putative powers of the chief executive within each system. However, these differences do not rest on very strong theoretical reasoning and empirical work has failed to sustain this reasoning. In sum, the review demonstrates that the traditional approach is plagued by problems on both the theoretical and empirical levels.

An alternative theoretical approach to institutions, based on Tsebelis' model of 'veto players', and a way of representing this empirically was presented. The core argument here is that centralization of power within a decision-making system enhances policy flexibility, which is necessary for effective policy output in an environment subject to change. The local government constitutions, created by each state legislature for the municipalities within the state, were examined and coded to reflect the degree to which power is concentrated in the hands of the chief executive relative to the two other principal potential institutional power bases, the municipal legislature and the administration. While this new approach does lend some support to the traditional scheme in showing that there is a fair amount of homogeneity within the four categories and a fair amount of heterogeneity between categories with respect to the administrative side, the legislative measure belies the utility of the traditional scheme because of the large amount of diversity one finds inside systems of supposedly the same type.

Culturalists have traditionally given primacy in importance to value and attitudinal attributes of the masses and elites in shaping government performance. This approach has received widespread renewed interest as a result of Putnam's work in demonstrating the critical role of social capital in promoting government performance in Italy. Indeed, one of the principal conclusions Putnam reached is that 'institutional engineering' is futile in the face of recalcitrant political culture. Changing the way in which government operates will do nothing to enhance its performance when the political culture is lacking in social capital. Institutionalists, on the other hand, have given short shrift to culture's role; instead, they have emphasized the importance of the structural features of government in shaping performance. This approach has become particularly central to political science, as the use of rational choice models has found more and more favor.

Both approaches have strengths and weaknesses. Much of the cultural work has been rightly criticized for the lack of compelling rigor in the logic of the arguments. Putnam's work certainly redresses this weakness but suffers from a fundamental defect in design. While arguing that his results contradict the institutional approach, his own research actually fails to deal with the question of institutional differences. On the other hand, the institutional approach, particularly of the rational choice form, often provides persuasive logical arguments but fails to deliver much in the way of systematic empirical evidence to evaluate these arguments (Green and Shapiro, 1995).

The strength of the research reported in this book is that it remedies these deficiencies. First, it provides systematic arguments about why culture and institutions should affect performance. Second, the collection of a large-scale data set has been guided by a design that allows one to test the implications of both these arguments. And, third, the results it provides are based on a theoretically guided systematic analysis of these data.

I have been able to show that institutional differences matter to democratic performance regardless of the stock of social capital within a community. The thesis presented here argues that power diffusion within governmental institutions can block or hinder effective public policy and thereby undermines the democratic performance of a local government. Empirical analysis supports this position. Where administrative authority and legislative control is concentrated in the hands of a directly elected chief executive, performance (as reflected in citizen's satisfaction with the performance of their local government institutions) is significantly higher than where power is diffused and the chief executive is administratively weak and dominated by legislative actors.

The results with respect to social capital that have been reported here are also encouraging. There is evidence that high social capital (at least in the form based on elite trust) leads to better democratic government performance in that in communities where such trust is low also have populations expressing little satisfaction with their local governments' performance and those where such trust is high have populations expressing high levels of such satisfaction.

There are three important implications that derive from this research. First, a trait of social capital does seem to improve democratic performance. Second, institutions do matter. Even in political cultures where one might expect poor performance, an appropriate institutional arrangement can make a significant difference in terms of democratic performance. Third, the great dissatisfaction one finds in East Germany across a wide spectrum of issues has been avoided at least in the area of local government.

Ironically, this is the one area where East Germans have had a say about the form and shape of the institutions that would govern their lives. While constrained to some extent by the requirement that the local government institutions that they would put in place would need to bear some resemblance to those in the West so as to facilitate integration into the complex federally based legal, regulative and public finance systems, East German politicians at least had a menu of choices from which to select. Some hold that the institutions adopted are insufficient to the tasks being confronted. Others suggest that they were chosen for reasons other than the objective value they have. However, from all appearances, many chose wisely and adopted institutional features that enhance performance.

This has important consequences for those who believe that many democratic systems today are being undermined by a growing dissatisfaction on the part of the governed. Rather than bemoan the lack of civic culture and pessimistically conclude that only a long-term project to change the values of the citizenry can work to secure the stability of these systems, one can take the alternative, speedier and possibly easier route of restructuring the institutional forms of democratic governments. Such a strategy would improve their performance while simultaneously bolstering the satisfaction of the citizens they serve.

Appendix

The German Local Elite and Citizen Surveys

Introduction

This appendix describes a number of technical issues related to carrying out a large-scale survey project dealing with local government within Germany. In collaboration with an international network of scholars that has conducted similar studies in nearly a score of countries, this project has executed two parallel surveys of political and administrative elites in the Eastern and Western sections of Germany.[1] In addition, follow-up surveys of citizens were conducted in sub-samples of the communities included in the elite surveys, one in the new federal states and one in the old federal states.

Focused on medium size communities (with populations in the range between 25,000 and 250,000), 30 political and administrative elites in each of 40 cities in the West and 37 cities in the East were contacted and asked to complete and return the Project's questionnaire. The overall response rate was a fairly high 53 per cent. A number of months later the follow-up telephone survey of citizens was conducted in 15 communities in the West and 15 in the East. The average sample size in each community for the citizen survey was 80 adults.

Analysis of the patterns of completed and returned questionnaires used in the elite surveys indicates that there are no significant biases in the response rates for different groups and that the rates of response fairly closely resemble the quotas in the carefully designed targeted samples. Results from the telephone surveys also appear to possess no major bias in terms of the socio-economic characteristics of the respondents.

This report proceeds as follows. Sampling techniques recommended by the International Project and those actually employed by some of the other national groups involved in the Democracy and Local Governance Study are first described. Following that an overview of the German samples is given. The sample frames of cities and the actual samples of these cities within the two German regions are described. Next, the sample frames, sampling technique and actual samples of local political elites are presented. Information on the samples having been presented, I then move on to describe the way in which the survey was undertaken. This is followed by a description of the response patterns to the survey. After that, the procedure for selecting the

---

[1] International Project on Democracy and Local Governance.

samples of cities wherein the survey of citizens was conducted is described. Finally, both the method by which this citizen survey was conducted is described and response patterns are presented.

Sampling Techniques Used in Previous Country Studies

The sampling guidelines provided by the International Group include the following:

- the local government units included within the sample frame should have population sizes ranging from 25,000 to 250,000 people;
- the preferred sample construction technique is that of random selection;
- regional coverage should be as encompassing as possible.

Of course, nation-specific conditions need to be taken into account in constructing the sample of local governments. One problem often encountered is that a country has relatively few municipal governments that fit within the sample frame. National investigators are obviously free to adjust the size criteria in light of such a problem. More often than not, this has meant extending downward the lower limit of the range so as to include smaller cities.

According to the International Project's guidelines, the elites that constitute the target populations in a national study are the following:

- local government elected officials (both executive and legislative);
- senior public administrators within local government units;
- leaders of local political party organizations.

However, the International Project provided no guidance as to the proportions of the total sample that should be taken from each of these three major groupings. In terms of special characteristics within each of the different groups, preference was only expressed with respect to the need to have samples of local legislative officials that are representative of the party composition of the individual municipal government councils.

In light of the International Project's expectation that the response rates for a mail survey across the communities would average around 33 per cent, it recommended that the minimum sample size for each community should be 30 individuals. This conservative assumption would imply that one could expect ten individual elites to be respondents in any community. While not a very large number, this was considered a reasonable sample from which one might construct an image of some of the important features of a community's elite political culture. Of course, all of this is predicated on at least two conditions: first, that the response rates are relatively uniform across communities and, second, that the individuals who do respond are not a particularly biased sub-sample of the local elites.

Appendix: The German Local Elite and Citizen Surveys 193

Ten individual country-studies were conducted during 1991 and 1992. In addition, a study was also carried out in Switzerland during 1994. Table A.1 summarizes the sample frames and sampling techniques used in these different studies. As can be seen in the table, local conditions would appear to have dictated the use of some rules that are significantly different from those meant to serve as uniform international guidelines. Often, however, the documentation available makes it difficulty to say precisely just what sample selection procedures were used in some of the country studies.

One can observe that the sample frames for communities are often different. In many instances, this has arisen because the specific national situation is such that very few local government units fit within the frame. A straightforward random sample, the preferred method of the international coordinating group, was rarely employed. Sometimes certain criteria (e.g., economic conditions) were used to categorize the local government units within the frame and then a random selection from within each category was undertaken. Still other country-studies relied on non-conventional sampling techniques in terms of the towns and cities included within the final samples.

Elite sample frames differed markedly – in part because of real cross-national differences in the forms of local governance and in part for reasons not made clear in the documentation available. There was also very large variation in the ways in which the samples of local political elites were drawn. At times, stratified random sampling was used – a reasonable approach in such a situation. At other times, selection appears to have occurred in a fairly casual way.

The German Study employed sample frame construction and sample creation procedures that are in conformity with the expressed international standards. Let me turn now to describe how the samples were constructed.

Outline of the German Elite Samples

The German project undertook two parallel studies, one dealing with the new federal states and one with the old federal states. In each regional study, the goal was to gather information from 30 local political/administrative elites within each of 40 selected communities. The preliminary phase of the project included an effort to draw a random sample of these 80 communities, the collection of relevant information on local elites (i.e., names, functions, addresses, party affiliations of all political and administrative elites within the sample communities), the construction of a data bank with this sample frame information and the construction of a complex stratified sample within each community of the individuals that constitute the local elites as conceived and defined by the International Project. In each community, the goal was to draw a representative sample of individuals; five groups are included:

1. Higher elected/public management officials (*Oberbürgermeister* = chief mayor, *Bürgermeister* = mayor, *Stadtdirektor* = city manager, *Beigeordneter* = deputy

Table A.1 Sample selection procedures in previous Democracy and Local Governance studies

Country	Date of study	Communities: sample frame	Communities: sampling techniques and results	Individuals: sample frame	Individuals: sample technique and results	Totals: communities/ individuals
Austria	1992	Since so few municipalities fit within in the 25k to 250k population category, the frame extended downward to include municipalities with as few as 10k population.	Municipalities were categorized 'on the basis of a socio-cultural standardization combined with a regional partition'. From these 31 were chosen.	Four major categories of individuals included: 1. municipal administrative officials; 2. leaders of special interest groups; 3. municipal council members; 4. leading local party officials.	Members of certain categories were always included in sample. Council members chosen to provide a representative sample of the party composition within the municipal council. Of the 899 local elites asked to participate, 42 per did so.	31 / 440
Belarus	1991	No information provided on sample or frame for communities.	Random selection of 30 communities.	Only description of sample frame of leaders is that it includes 'officials at all levels of local legislative and executive power'.	Apparently a random selection procedure used to generate 449 respondents.	30 / 449
Hungary	1992	Only 166 'towns' in Hungary, of which more than half have less than 20k population.	Used as set of size categories for those towns with 20k or more population. Matched relative	No detailed information on sample frame. Indicates that three groups were included:	No information on sampling procedure. 450 respondents.	30 / 450

Appendix: The German Local Elite and Citizen Surveys 195

Table A.1 (continued)

Country	Date of study	Communities: sample frame	Communities: sampling techniques and results	Individuals: sample frame	Individuals: sample technique and results	Totals: communities/ individuals
Hungary (continued)			frequency in sample to proportion in sample frame. Selection also took into account 'regional considerations'. A total of 28 towns for the sample from this procedure. Note that the two parts of the capital city were also included.	1. 'appointed leaders of the administration'; 2. 'representatives of local government'; 3. other local 'influentials'. Sample of 15 of these leaders for each town.		
Kazakhstan	1992	Six regions included within framework wherein all communes within the population size range from 50k to 250k were included.	Used random selection procedure in each of the six regions to select five communes therein. 30 communes in total.	Sample frame of local leaders included deputies of local Soviets, administrators and 'political activists'.	Random selection procedure used to select between 10 and 15 leaders from the three groups. No details on stratification of other selection criteria.	30 / 448
Lithuania	1991	Cities and regional authorities with populations between 25k and 200k.	Selection of units based on the criteria of size, urban/rural characteristics and ethnic composition.	Local elites composed of administrators, deputies and political, economic and social leaders.	No information given on selection, sampling criteria.	18 / 289

Table A.1 (continued)

Country	Date of study	Communities: sample frame	Communities: sampling techniques and results	Individuals: sample frame	Individuals: sample technique and results	Totals: communities/ individuals
Lithuania (continued)			Four cities and 14 regions were included in sample.			
Poland	1991	All local administrative units with a population between 25k and 200k.	Random selection of sample of 30 units.	Leaders in three categories: 1. administrators; 2. elected council members; 3. leaders of political parties and movements.	No information on sampling technique. A total of 440 leaders interviewed.	30 / 440
Russia	1992	No information on sample frame.	Non information on sampling technique.	No information on sample frame.	No information on sampling technique.	36 / 548
Slovenia	1991	54 communes within sample frame.	A representative sample of 15 communes (details on sampling procedure are apparently available in other documentation).	Sample frame included member of four different functional councils and the executive council made up of the leading members of the functional councils.	Sample included the top two executives in these five bodies and a sample (procedure not described) of the normal members of these councils. Of the 300 planned interviews, 275 actually took place.	15 / 275

Table A.1 (continued)

Country	Date of study	Communities: sample frame	Communities: sampling techniques and results	Individuals: sample frame	Individuals: sample technique and results	Totals: communities/ individuals
Sweden	1991	Four groupings based on population size. Only three used for basic study, the fourth is a control group with population less than 25k. Three basic groups consist of: 1. those between 25k and 49k; 2. those between 50k and 99k; and 3. those between 100k and 250k.	Apparently selection criterion for the five communes in each group based upon level of economic development. No specifics provided.	Composed of leading administrative, executive and legislative officials within the commune.	No complete set of rules on sampling procedures used is provided although occupants of certain leading offices in both political and administrative spheres were apparently always included within sample. 470 political officials and 196 administrative officials included in basic and control samples.	30 / 440
Switzerland	1994	Given the paucity of communes (19) that fit within the international framework of 25k to 250k, frame was extended to bring in communes in the size category of 5k to 24k.	Used random selection procedure to create sample of 40 communes in the 5k to 24k frame, included all 19 in the 25k to 250 frame and added in the larger city of Zurich.	Four local leadership target groups: 1. member of the executive body; 2. the legislative body; 3. civil servants; and 4. chairpersons of political parties.	No specifics on sampling procedure. Using a 'top to bottom' principle, selected four members of executive, four of the legislative, six administrator and seven party chairpersons in each commune. Response rate: 64 per cent.	61 / 1,281

Table A.1 (continued)

Country	Date of study	Communities: sample frame	Communities: sampling techniques and results	Individuals: sample frame	Individuals: sample technique and results	Totals: communities/ individuals
Ukraine	1991	Local government districts.	30 local government districts in 19 separate regions selected for purposes of balanced coverage. Apparently rejected preliminary samples based on random selection because of regional imbalances.	Sample frame is described as including 'representatives of all structural levels of local legislative and executive power'.	No description of sampling technique is provided; an average of 15 local leaders drawn from each of the units.	30 /450

Sources: Based on Jacob, Ostrowski and Teune (1993); Linder and Nabholz (1994).

mayors, *Dezernent* = major administrative chief), maximum of four per community: stratified, random sub-sample;
2. party chairpersons *(Parteivorsitzender)*, maximum of five per community: random sub-sample;
3. party caucus chairpersons *(Fraktionsvorsitzender)*, maximum of five per community: random sub-sample;
4. council members *(Ratsmitglieder)*, minimum of ten, stratification based on party strength, random selection within each party; and
5. administrative department heads *(Amtsleiter)*, maximum of six; stratified, based on six groupings of the 15 most important local government administrative departments, random within groupings.

Selection of City Samples

Sample Frame

In 1991, there were 79.75 million people resident in Germany. Of these, the overwhelming majority, around 65 million, lived in the old federal states and only 14.7 million lived in the new federal states. According to the Deutsche Städtetag, there were 16,121 *Gemeinden* (towns and cities). 8505 were in the old federal states, while 7616 were in the new federal states. As might be expected, the typical population sizes of cities in the two regions of Germany are dramatically different with small communities being something of the norm in the new federal states. This is depicted graphically in Figure A.1, which provides an overview of the numbers of towns in different size categories for both regions of Germany. Nearly half of all the towns in the East have fewer than 500 residents.

Figure A.1 also highlights an important aspect of the study that needs to be kept in mind. Namely, adherence to the international sample frame guidelines for the types of municipalities that are to be employed serves to restrict the scope of the study. This obviously entails limitations with regard to the kinds of inferences one might draw from results generated by the study. Thus, the sample frame for the old federal states incorporates towns and cities that have only 31.2 per cent of the population in this region. 24.5 per cent live in cities with population sizes greater than the maximum in the study, while 44.3 per cent live in towns with population sizes smaller than the minimum. The situation in the East is even more restrictive. Only 28.5 per cent of the population in this region lives in cities that fall within the sample frame. 12.8 per cent live in towns larger than those that fall within the guidelines, while 58.7 per cent live in communities too small to fit within the framework.

Table A.2 provides an overview of the sample frames in both the old and the new federal states. In the West, there are 357 local government units (cities independent of county level governments and cities subordinate to county level governments) that fit within the frame; in the East, there are only 80 such units. Given the objective of

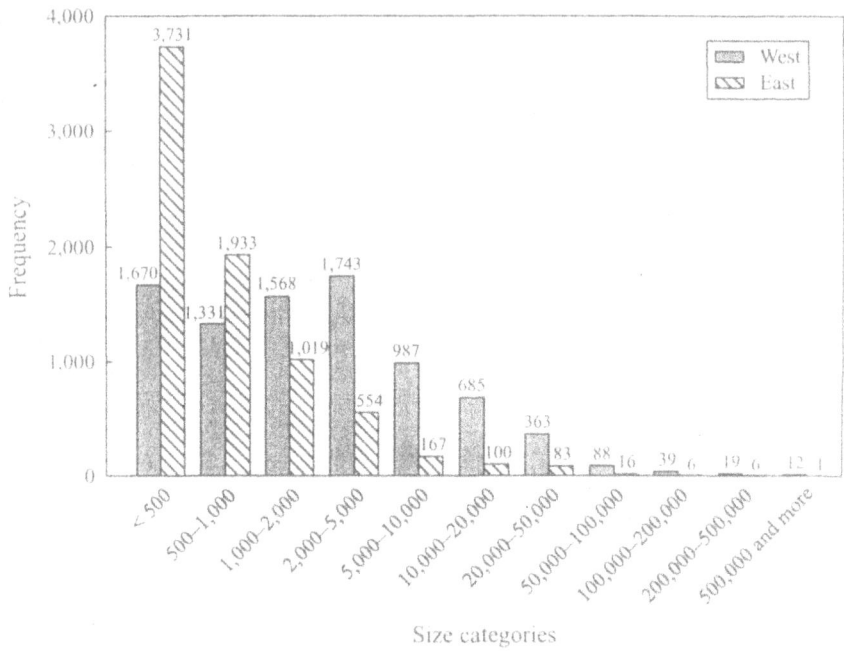

Situation as of 1 January 1991

Source: Statistisches Jahrbuch Deutscher Gemeinden, Vol. 79, 1992.

Figure A.1   An overview of East and West German local government units (towns and cities) by population size

securing a sample of 40 communities in each part of Germany, this means that 11 per cent of the relevant communities in the West could be included within the sample while a much larger share, i.e., 50 per cent, could be included in the Eastern sample.

In terms of the different size categories, the relative frequencies are rather similar across the two parts of Germany. Approximately 63 per cent of the cities in the West fit within the category of small towns and cities (population between 25,000 and 50,000) while 70 per cent in the East belong to this grouping. Most of the other size categories described are similar in their relative frequencies across the regions.

The distribution of local governments within the sample frame does differ dramatically across the states in the West. Berlin and Hamburg have been excluded because these two city-states have population sizes well beyond the maximum of the size range defining the frame. Only one of two cities in the Federal State of Bremen fits into the frame. At the other extreme is North Rhine-Westphalia that clearly dominates the distribution in the West. With more than a quarter of the total population in the region, it has about 40 per cent of the Western communities that are encom-

Table A.2 Sample frames of communities in West and East Germany

West Germany

Population size	SH	NS	HB	NW	HE	RP	BW	BA	SL	Total frequency	(Per cent)
25,000 – 49,999	8	39	0	84	19	9	37	22	6	224	(62.7)
50,000 – 74,999	1	7	0	27	6	2	8	9	1	61	(17.1)
75,000 – 99,999	2	2	0	14	1	3	5	0	0	27	(7.6)
100,000 – 149,999	0	5	1	9	2	1	5	5	0	28	(7.8)
150,000 – 250,000	2	1	0	9	1	2	1	0	1	17	(4.8)
Total frequency	13	54	1	143	29	17	56	36	8	357	
(Per cent)	(3.6)	(15.1)	(0.3)	(40.1)	(8.1)	(4.8)	(15.7)	(10.1)	(2.2)		

Key to state names: SH = Schleswig-Holstein; NS = Niedersachsen; HB = Bremen; NW = Nordrhein-Westfalen; HE = Hessen; RP = Rheinland-Pfalz; BW = Baden-Württemberg; BA = Bayern; SL = Saarland.

East Germany

Population size	BR	MV	S	SA	TH	Total frequency	(Per cent)
25,000 – 49,999	10	2	15	17	12	56	(70.0)
50,000 – 74,999	3	3	3	0	3	12	(15.0)
75,000 – 99,999	2	1	0	1	0	4	(5.0)
100,000 – 149,999	2	1	1	0	2	6	(7.5)
150,000 – 250,000	0	1	0	0	1	2	(2.5)
Total frequency	17	8	19	18	18	80	
(Per cent)	(21.3)	(10.0)	(23.8)	(22.5)	(22.5)		

Key to state names: BR = Brandenburg; MV = Mecklenburg-Vorpommern; S = Sachsen; SA = Sachsen-Anhalt; TH = Thüringen.

passed by the sample frame. The distribution of communities across the five federal states in the East is far more uniform.

Samples Chosen

The two regional local government unit samples were constructed on the basis of a straightforward random selection process (cf. Kalton, 1983). The cities within each sample frame were assigned random numbers blindly and then each list of cities was ordered on the basis of the random numbers. The first 40 cities on each regional list were taken into the sample and the remaining cities in the frames were dropped from further consideration.

Comparisons of the sample frames and the drawn samples can be seen in Table A.3. In the West, there is some incongruence between the frame and the sample when seen from the perspective of the distributions across the states in the region. In particular, while North Rhine-Westphalia has a relatively large share of the sample (20 per cent), this is only half the size of its relative presence in the frame. The other outlier is Baden-Württemberg, a state with a relatively large share of the frame (15 per cent), which has nearly 30 per cent of the cities in the sample selected. In terms of the size of cities, the distribution and sample frames match quite closely (note that details both at the state and regional levels on the frequency distribution on this dimension have been suppressed for purposes of privacy protection). In the East, the match of distributions both in terms of geographical as well as size considerations is quite close. All in all, while there are a couple of misalignments between the frames and samples drawn, the results of the random selection process for the construction of the samples of local government units in both regions appear to be satisfactory.

Selection of Local Elites

Having drawn the city samples for both regions of Germany, the next task was to obtain detailed information on the identity of the project-relevant political and administrative elites within the sets of cities in the samples. Only very limited information regarding these people can be found in widely accessible documents. Efforts to ascertain whether one might obtain this information from state-level ministries charged with responsibility for local government political affairs within their states proved futile. The experience of other projects on German politics also suggested that approaches to political party organizations might not prove to be universally effective. In light of all of this, it was decided that the most feasible solution to the problem would be a direct approach to local government offices where requests could be made for the needed information.

Contacts were made by mail, phone and in person with various governmental and political party offices in each of the 80 cities selected for this study. Requests were made for information on the identity (name, office held), address and, where appropriate, political party affiliation for all of the relevant individuals within each city.

Table A.3 Information on the sample frames and samples of communities in West and East Germany

West Germany:	SH	NS	HB	NW	HE	RP	BW	BA	SL	Total
Sample frame frequency	13	54	1	143	29	17	56	36	8	357
(Per cent)	(3.6)	(15.1)	(0.3)	(40.1)	(8.1)	(4.8)	(15.7)	(10.1)	(2.2)	
Sample frequency	2	5	0	8	5	1	12	7	0	40
(Per cent)	(5.0)	(12.5)	(0.0)	(20.0)	(12.5)	(2.5)	(30.0)	(17.5)	(0.0)	
Population size	Sample frame by size frequency				(Per cent)		Sample by size frequency		(Per cent)	
25,000 – 49,999	224				(62.7)		25		(62.5)	
50,000 – 250,000	133				(37.3)		15		(37.5)	

Key to state names: SH = Schleswig-Holstein; NS = Niedersachsen; HB = Bremen; NW = Nordrhein-Westfalen; HE = Hessen; RP = Rheinland-Pfalz; BW = Baden-Württemberg; BA = Bayern; SL = Saarland.

East Germany:	BR	MV	S	SA	TH	Total
Sample frame frequency	17	8	19	18	18	80
(Per cent)	(21.3)	(10.0)	(23.8)	(22.5)	(22.5)	
Sample frequency	10	3	9	10	8	40
(Per cent)	(25.0)	(7.5)	(22.5)	(25.0)	(20.0)	
Population size	Sample frame by size frequency			(Per cent)	Sample by size frequency	(Per cent)
25,000 – 49,999	56			(70.0)	27	(67.6)
50,000 – 250,000	24			(30.0)	13	(32.8)

Key to state names: BR = Brandenburg; MV = Mecklenburg-Vorpommern; S = Sachsen; SA = Sachsen-Anhalt; TH = Thüringen.

Very positive and helpful responses came from a large number of these offices that led to the successful acquisition of much of the required information.

In some cases, however, there were difficulties and the requests met resistance. Often, though not always, the assurances that the information was needed for a legitimate social scientific research project and that any information obtained would be handled properly and in accordance with privacy protection regulations helped to overcome this resistance. In a few cities, the authorities indicated that they would not provide names of administrative department heads. Although this information is publicly available, the course of not offending the sensibilities of these authorities was chosen. In this limited number of cases, the name of the department and its office address was entered into the data bank but a blank was left in the field that would normally contain the department head's name.

Three cities in the new federal states proved unwilling to cooperate. Numerous efforts to assure the officials in these cities of the seriousness of the project and the commitment to preserving the anonymity of respondents failed to overcome their resistance. Rather than persist in a futile effort, these three cities were dropped from the sample. Since the efforts at collecting the required data involved a significant amount of time and because of the pressure to move on to the next phase of the project, it was not possible to substitute another three cities for those that had to be eliminated from the sample.

Data Base: Description of Sample Frame for Individuals

As Table A.4 shows, there were 5,085 individuals within the 77 cities in the samples that fit into the sample frame of political elites used in this study. This averages out to slightly more than 68 individuals per city. The range in terms of the numbers in these local elites extends across all of the cities from a low of 43 to a high of 115. Between East and West the city-level averages differ with the former region having 64.4 while the latter has 72.3 More than ten per cent of the individuals in these elites hold multiple offices at the local level, with most of these having two roles, while a few have as many as three or four. In terms of sheer numbers, men are clearly the dominant group within the local elites; in the West, there is a 4:1 male/female ratio while in the East there is a slightly less imbalanced ratio of 3:1.

Somewhat more than 60 per cent of the individuals within the sample frame of local elites are members of city councils. This averages out to about 41 per city although there is a wide range here with the smallest council containing 25 members and the largest having 70. Approximately ten per cent of the council members head up a party or elector group caucus within their respective councils. Based on the figures on party membership of the councils (see Tables A.8–A.10 below), the partisan landscape is rather diverse. In both regions, the CDU/CSU and the SPD are the two leading partisan factions but the degree of dominance is far less in the new federal states where the PDS, with 22.8 per cent of the council members, stands out as a relatively strong third force. The Bündnis 90/Die Grünen and the FDP trail behind

Table A.4 Respondent sample frame based on data from 77 communities in Germany*

	RMG	FrakV	PV	OBM	BM	SD	Dez	BeiG	Sonst	AL
Germany										
Total	3,174	346	385	46	103	15	201	73	62	1,557
Average	41.2	4.5	5.0	0.6	1.3	0.2	2.6	0.9	0.8	20.2
Range	25–70	2–10	2–8	0–1	0–5	0–2	0–11	0–7	0–11	(0)1–50
West Germany										
Total	1,756	165	188	27	66	15	103	16	47	872
Average	43.9	4.1	4.7	0.7	1.6	0.4	2.6	0.4	1.2	21.8
Range	26–70	2–6	3–7	0–1	0–3	0–2	0–11	0–3	0–11	(0)9–46
East Germany										
Total	1,414	181	197	19	37	0	98	57	15	695
Average	38.3	4.9	5.3	0.5	1.0	–	2.6	1.5	0.4	18.8
Range	25–53	3–10	2–8	0–1	0–5	–	0–6	0–7	0–6	1–50

Key to positions: RMG = Ratsmitglied; FrakV = Fraktionsvorsitzender; PV = Parteivorsitzender; OBM = Oberbürgermeister; BM = Burgermeister; SD = Stadtdirektor; Dez = Dezernent; BeiG = Beigeordneter; Sonst = Sonstige; AL = Amtsleiter.

* The total number of individuals in the sample frame came to 5,085, of which 2,891 were in West Germany and 2,384 were in East Germany. Of these there were 1,180 females in total, 557 located in the West and 623 in the East. A significant number of individuals in both regions held more than one office. In the West, 268 held two offices, 42 held three offices, and four held four offices. In the East, 275 held two offices, while 29 held three offices.

but the former has a significant presence in the Western councils. The Republikaner have an extremely small presence, particularly in the East. One should note the not insignificant number of council members classified as belonging to 'other' party and elector groupings. In some cities, these parties/groupings constitute a very large portion of the council; with 11.4 per cent in the West and 8.9 per cent in the East, they represent an important cluster within the local political elites of the regions. Very few individuals could be identified as being strictly non-partisan (which in this context generally comes down to being a completely independent and single candidate for office) in either region.

Another important group within the local political elites is composed of individuals who chair local party organizations or act as their spokespersons. The sample frame is composed of 188 such individuals within the West and 197 in the East.

There is a wide range of offices that constitute important executive functions within the local governments. Data has been gathered on five such groups as well as a miscellaneous category of such office holders. Altogether there are 274 executives within the 40 cities of the West sample and 226 in the 37 cities of the East sample. Differences in local government structures account for the diverse distributions one sees in the regions. The two categories, *Oberbürgermeister* and *Stadtdirektor*, having leading executive roles in city government together constitute a relatively small part of the sample frames. There are 42 such individuals in the West frame and 19 in the East (note the absence of the *Stadtdirektor* category within the new federal states).

The *Bürgermeister* category includes officers that may be either the leading executives within a city government or ones that are subordinate to officials at a higher level (e.g., an *Oberbürgermeister*). There are about 100 such individuals altogether with about two-thirds of these in the West. *Beigeordnete* are more common in the East sample frame (57) than in the West (16). *Dezernenten*, officials generally responsible for overseeing the work of a wide range of city government departments, constitute the largest category of executives within the sample frame with approximately 100 in each of the two regions. A miscellaneous category of executives also contains 62 individuals with the great majority of these in the West.

The last general category of local political-administrative elites for which data have been collected contains heads of administrative departments. People carrying out this administrative function constitute the second largest grouping within both sample frames. There are 872 department heads in the Western sample of cities, i.e., approximately 30 per cent of the sample frame of individuals. A similar figure exists in the Eastern sample of cities with approximately 29 per cent of the sample frame composed of department heads.

Sampling Algorithm

In order to go about the selection of individuals for inclusion in the survey a procedure based on a set of sample selection principles needed to be settled upon. Four principles were employed; these included (1) giving priority to important categories of elites but not at the cost of distortion, (2) using a hierarchical or stratified design, (3) taking into account the importance of particular characteristics within categories, and (4) employing random procedures within categories and subcategories (cf., Kalton, 1983).

Obviously there are office-holders within the local political-administrative elite, as defined by the broad rules of the International Project, whose importance in the shaping of decisions at the local level are greater than others. Rather than treat all of the individuals within a community's sample frame as equally important, greater weight was given to these 'important' categories but not at the cost of developing a sample with a distorted view of the local political culture. In the main, this was not too difficult given the commitment to having a sample size of 30 individuals per city. Recall from Table A.4 that across the two regions the average number of people within a local elite is only 68.5, with the range extending from 43 up to 115. This means that one can expect to include an average of nearly 44 per cent of the elites within each community. In the smallest community, indeed, the sample of potential respondents is nearly 70 per cent, while in the city with the largest elite the potential respondents would include approximately 26 per cent of the sample frame. Such broad coverage should, with a reasonable response rate, assure a fairly accurate portrayal of the local elite political culture.

As noted previously, the target sample distribution of office holders by category is as follows: four members of the group of higher elected/public management officials, six department heads, five party chairpersons, five council party caucus chairpersons and a minimum of ten council members (outside of those selected through the party caucus chairperson procedure or individuals from the other three categories who are also members of the city council). Given the numbers available within the sample frame and these specifications, one could be certain that most of the first, third, and fourth categories of elites would be included within the sample. At the same time, a relatively large number of the members of the department head category as well as city council members would also be included.

The relative importance of different types of elite members led to the use of a stratified design. The 'top-down' character of this design, along with the diversity in the size of local elites, required that where a particular category was exhausted without filling the quota for that category, then the residual slots would be allocated to the last category, i.e., council members, for which a sample would be constructed.

Where particular characteristics within a group were deemed significant, selection was geared toward providing a sample that was representative of the distribution of these characteristics. Such a principle was used in three of the categories. First, within the group of leading executive/administrative elites, a rank ordering was made. Priority for inclusion was based on this ordering with the selection procedure working in a fashion to exhaust the first category and then moving on through the next categories until the designated number (4) of individuals was selected from the overall group (or, where less than four were available, including all of these individuals and adding the residual slot(s) to the council member sample contingent).

The second application of this principle is in the selection of administrative department heads. It was decided that the heads of only fifteen different types of city government administrative departments would be considered for selection within the sample. As the section on the characteristics of the different city administrative structures will describe, there is a bewildering variety of administrative functional units across the cities in these two regions (cf., Norton, 1994). Only a sub-set of these was selected because of their greater significance and importance to the operation of local governments. The procedure here was to categorize heads of departments from these fifteen different functions into six broad categories and, where possible, to randomly select one individual from each grouping. Where there was no individual present within a broader category, an individual was selected at random from one of the other broad categories. Where the list was exhausted, the residual slots were allocated to the council sample contingent.

The third area where this principle was applied was in the selection of city council members. Here important consideration was given to the distribution of seats held by the different parties within the council. The aim of the selection procedure was to insure that the partisan characteristics of the sample drawn (through the direct application of the selection algorithm for normal council members as well as the consequences that arose from including council members because of other roles that they play in local politics) was one that accorded as closely as possible with the actual distribution of party membership within the council.

Finally, to assure that no bias crept into the selection from within any category or subcategory, a random selection procedure was always employed.

Overview of the Sample

Table A.5 provides an overview of the samples of potential respondents that arose through the application of the selection principles described above. Before describing the major groupings, it should be pointed out that the samples have slightly smaller proportions of females than do the sample frames. This arises mainly from the fact that most of the females in the frames are city council members and the shares of council members in the samples are smaller than the shares within the frames. On the other hand, those individuals with more than one local office have an extraordinarily good chance of showing up in the samples. For example, 44 of the 46 officials with three or more offices in the West are in the sample all of those with three offices in the East also came into the sample.

Slightly less than half of the council members made it into the sample and about one-third of the administrative department heads were selected for inclusion. Party chairpersons and council caucus chairpersons almost universally were brought into the sample. In the West, only 12 of 188 party chairpersons in the frame fail to show up in the sample while all of the caucus chairpersons are present. 171 of the 181 caucus chairpersons and 182 of the 197 party chairpersons in the East sample frame were selected for the sample of potential respondents.

Table A.5 Overview of samples by potential respondents' positions

	RMG	FrakV	PV	OBM	BM	SD	Dez	BeiG	Sonst	AL
Germany										
Total	1,449	336	358	46	97	15	135	58	24	445
Sample per cent	62.7	14.6	15.5	2.0	4.2	0.6	5.8	2.5	1.0	19.3
Town average	18.8	4.4	4.6	0.6	1.3	0.2	1.8	0.8	0.3	5.8
West Germany										
Total	782	165	176	27	63	15	55	10	18	234
Sample per cent	65.2	13.8	14.7	2.2	5.2	1.2	4.6	0.8	1.5	19.5
Town average	19.6	4.1	4.4	0.7	1.6	0.4	1.4	0.3	0.5	5.9
East Germany										
Total	666	171	182	19	34	0	80	48	6	211
Sample per cent	60.0	15.4	16.4	1.7	3.1	–	7.2	4.3	0.5	19.1
Town average	18.0	4.6	4.9	0.5	0.9	–	2.2	1.3	0.2	5.7

Key to positions: RMG = Ratsmitglied; FrakV = Fraktionsvorsitzender; PV = Parteivorsitzender; OBM = Oberbürgermeister; BM = Bürgermeister; SD = Stadtdirektor; Dez = Dezernent; BeiG = Beigeordneter; Sonst = Sonstige; AL = Amtsleiter.

* The total number of individuals in the sample of potential respondents came to 2,310, of which 1,200 were in West Germany and 1,100 were in East Germany. Of these there were 477 females in total, 215 located in the West and 262 in the East. Most of the individuals holding more than one office made it into the sample of potential respondents. In the West, this included 253 who held two offices, 40 held three offices, and the four who held four offices. In the East, 249 held two offices and all 29 who held three offices.

The picture is more mixed with respect to the leading executive/administrative grouping. Of course, this follows from the rank-ordering procedure used and the great diversity across cities in the numbers within the sample frame for this grouping. At the highest level, *Oberbürgermeister* and *Stadtdirektor*, there are no individuals within the frames who fail to make it into the sample. Nearly all of the *Bügermeister* enter as well (97 out of 103). Amongst the *Beigeordnete*, 10 of 16 in the West and a much large proportion, 48 out of 57, in the East come into the samples. Slightly more than half of the *Dezernenten* in the West make it into the sample and an even larger share of those in the East, 80 out of 98, have been selected. A much smaller percentage of those in the miscellaneous category, 24 out of 62, are included in the samples.

Leading Political/Administrative Officials

Leading political/administrative officials constitute over 12 per cent of the samples in both regions. Table A.6 provides an overview of the characteristics of these individuals. Here one sees that, relative to the other parts of the samples, much smaller proportions of these groups are women. In addition, these groups clearly are very active in local political-administrative affairs. About 32 per cent in the East and nearly 48 per cent in the West have more than one official function. A limited number of these also head up administrative departments. In the West, in particular, a very large percentage (34.2) of these officials are also members of the city council, while in the East a much smaller percentage (12.8) carries out such a function. While a small number of these officials are heads of council party caucuses, a significant fraction, in both East (5.7) and West (4.1), also hold positions as chairs of local party organizations. It is interesting to note that a large percentage of both the East and West groups are not members of political parties. In the East, 48.2 per cent are non-partisan while 42.5 of the Western officials do not belong to parties. Where individuals in this general category do have partisan affiliations, they overwhelmingly tend to be with either the CDU/CSU or the SPD.

Department Heads

Before describing the samples of department heads drawn for this study, it is useful to provide some background information on the administrative units within the cities of the two sample frames of this study. Figure A.2 shows that there is a tremendous range in the number of distinct functional activities carried out by city governments in both East and West.[2] The average number of functions varies slightly across regions, with slightly more (close to 40) in the West than in the East (about 36 on average).[3]

---

2 Note that the data described here are based on 74 and not 77 communities.
3 Here the unit of analysis is function and not amt or department. Often a department has a number of distinct and different functions for which it is responsible. In the counts provided here, the frequencies refer to these functions.

Appendix: The German Local Elite and Citizen Surveys

Table A.6 Characteristics of higher political/administrative officials in samples

	Germany		East Germany		West Germany	
	Frequency	Per cent	Frequency	Per cent	Frequency	Per cent
Total	287	100.0	141	100.0	146	100.0
Of which:						
– Female	27	9.4	15	10.6	12	8.2
– CDU/CSU	74	25.8	33	23.4	41	28.1
– SPD	66	23.0	32	22.7	34	23.3
– Other parties	17	5.9	8	5.7	9	6.2
– Non-partisan	130	45.3	68	48.2	62	42.5
– Chief mayor (Oberbürgermeister)	46	16.0	19	13.5	27	18.5
– Mayor (Bürgermeister)	97	33.8	34	24.1	63	43.2
– City director (Stadtdirektor)	15	5.2	0	0.0	15	10.3
– Deputy mayor (Beigeordneter)	58	20.2	48	34.0	10	6.8
– Major administrative chief (Dezernent)	135	47.0	80	56.7	55	37.7
– Other major function (Sonstige)	24	8.4	6	4.3	18	12.3
– Department head (Amtsleiter)	8	2.8	6	4.3	2	1.4
– Council member (Ratsmitglied)	68	23.7	18	12.8	50	34.2
– Council party caucus chair (Fraktionsvorsitz)	5	1.7	1	0.7	4	2.7
– Party chair (Parteivorsitz)	14	4.9	8	5.7	6	4.1
– With more than one function	115	40.1	45	31.9	70	47.9

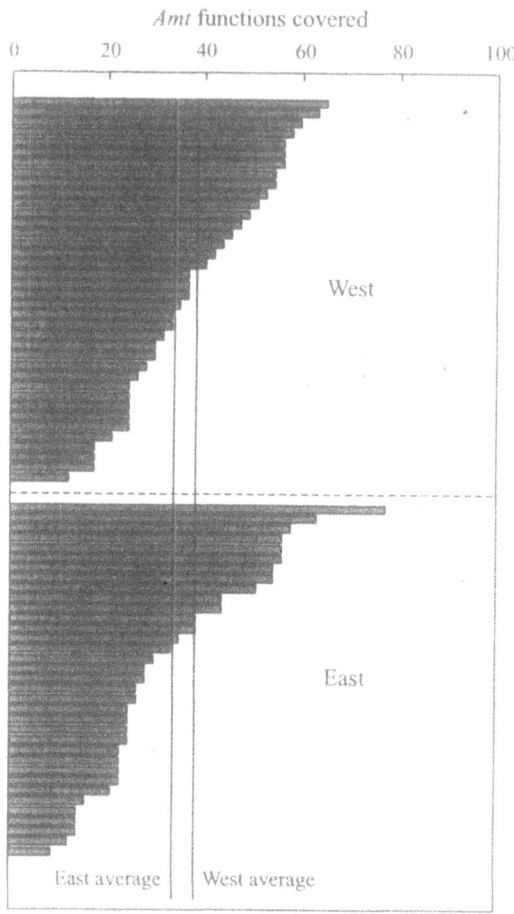

Figure A.2 Coverage of *Amt* functions in West and East Germany (number)

In some towns, less than ten functions are covered while in others more than 60 are carried out. As Figure A.3 suggests, the scope of functional coverage is linked to the size of a city with a fairly rapid increase at lower levels and then a tapering off as the size of the city approaches levels closer to the maximum used in the samples.

Figure A.4 provides an overview of the relative frequencies with which the different functions are covered within the cities of the two samples. It was found that there were 57 different classifiable functional activities for these administrative departments. However, many of these functions are carried out in only a few cities. There are, nevertheless, some that appear to be nearly universal: amongst these are such things as public order *(öffentliche Ordnung)*, main administration *(Hauptverwaltung)* and social welfare *(Soziales)*. There are few major differences between East and West

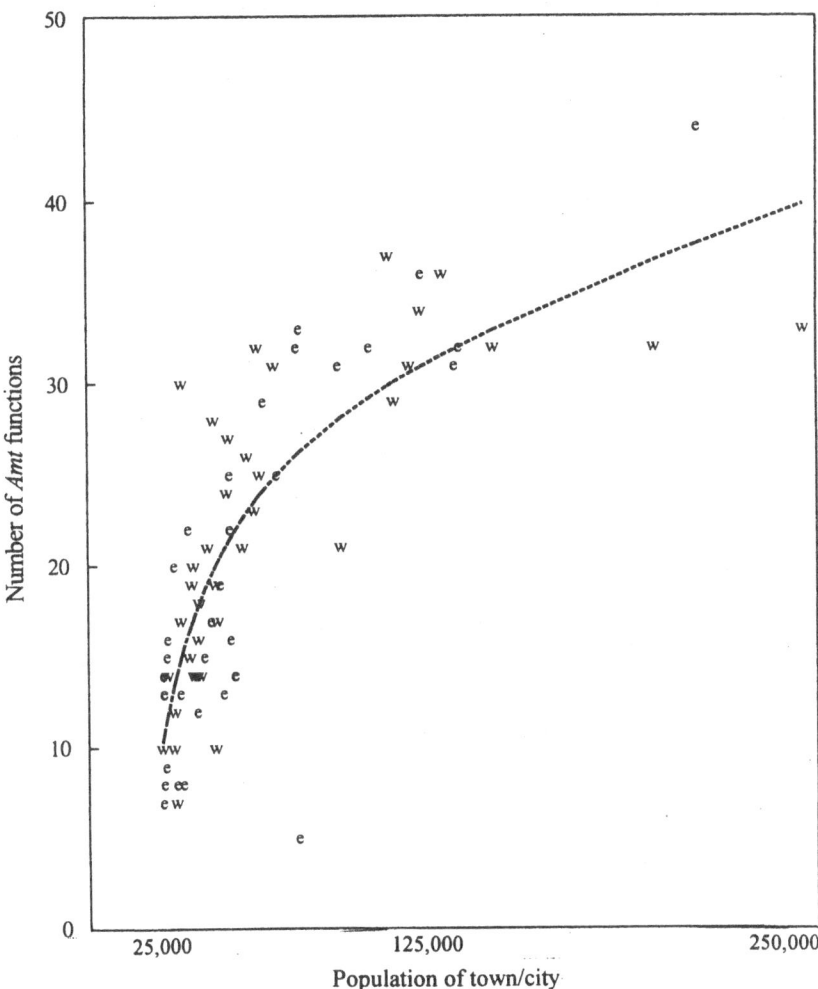

Figure A.3 Number of *Amt* functions and population size

in terms of the kinds of functions that are more widespread than others. One major exception here would be economic promotion *(Wirtschaftsförderung)* that is found in over 70 per cent of the cities in the East and in less than 40 per cent of the cities in the West. Given the massive economic restructuring going on in the new federal states, such emphasis on this function is to be expected.

The relative importance of the functions as well as the interests of a project collaborator in the restructuring of local government public administration in the new federal states led to the decision that the sample of administrative department heads would concentrate on only 15 of these functions. These fifteen have been allocated to six relatively homogeneous groups and include the following:

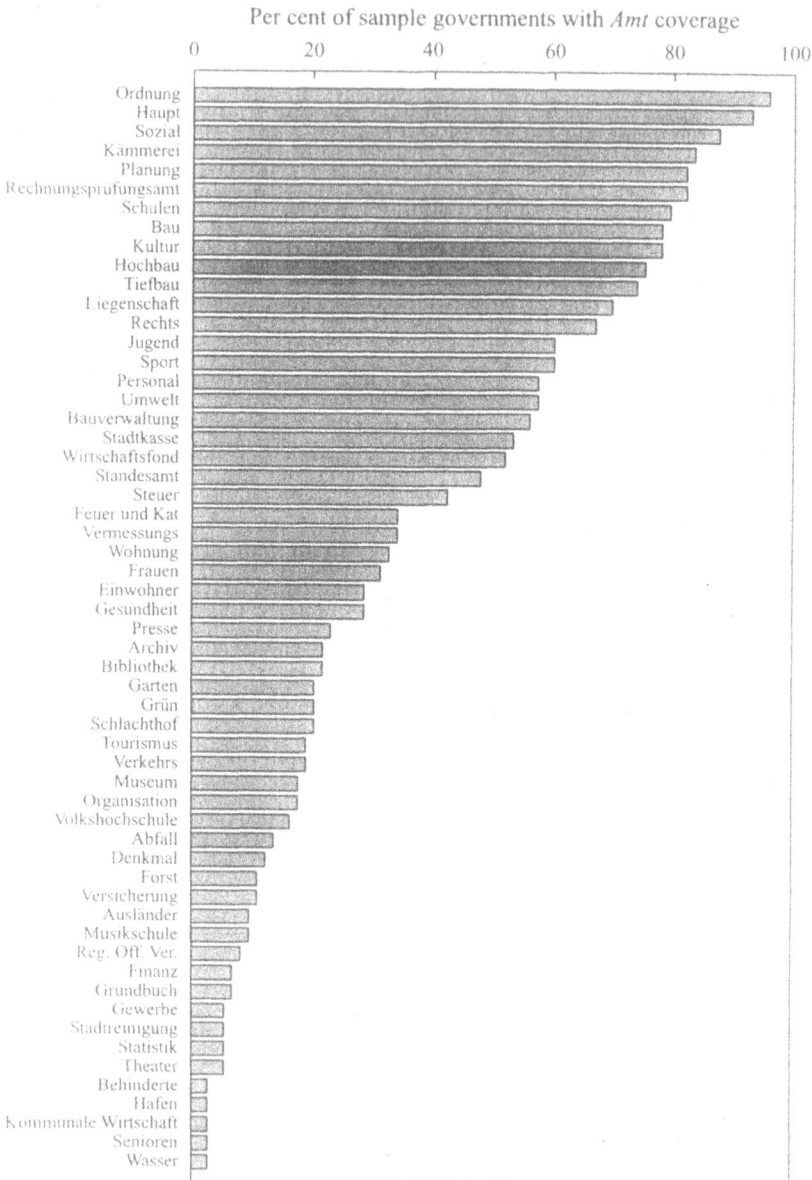

Figure A.4 Relative coverage of *Amt* functions (per cent)

– Group I: *Law and Order* [1. Order *(öffentliche Ordnung)*, 2. Justice *(Justiz)*, 3. Building Reguation *(Bauordnung)*, plus departments that combine two or more of these functions];

- Group II: *Social I* [4. Culture *(Kultur)*, 5. Sport *(Sport)*, 6. Education *(Schulen)*, plus departments that combine two or more of these functions];
- Group III: *Administrative* [7. Central Administration *(Hauptverwaltung)*, 8. Personnel *(Personal)*, plus departments that combine these two functions];
- Group IV: *Economic* [9. City Planning *(Planung)*, 10. Environment *(Umwelt)*, 11. Economic Promotion *(Wirtschaftsförderung)*, plus departments that combine two or more of these functions];
- Group V: *Public Finance* [12. Treasury *(Kämmerei)*, 13. Auditing *(Rechnungsprüfung)*, plus departments that combine these two functions]; and
- Group VI: *Social II* [14. Youth *(Jugend)*, 15. Social Welfare *(Soziales)*, plus departments that combine these two functions].

In addition, departments that combined two or more functions from across the six broader groups have been included in a miscellaneous general group.

The results of the sample selection for department heads are presented in Table A.7. In the East 211 such individuals have been selected while in the West a slightly higher number, 234, could be drawn into the sample. Across the major groups, there are relatively equal numbers of individuals in both samples. However, some specific categories appear more or less frequently than others. A good example of this is to be found in the second group where education (as the sole function of the department) is rarely represented – indeed there are no cases for this unitary function in the East. However, department heads who deal with education are present in the mixed category for the larger group (Social II); indeed, the mixed category in this group is the largest of all the mixed categories.

Party Chairpersons, Caucus Chairpersons and Council Members

As noted previously, the relatively large sample sizes being used for the party and caucus chairpersons, when taken in conjunction with the size of these groups in the sample frames, assures that most individuals within these categories were selected for the two regional samples. Nevertheless, it is still useful to give some information on the partisan distributions that exist in both the frames and samples. As both Tables A.8 and A.9 show, the match-ups between frames and samples are nearly perfect – an unsurprising result. Interesting, though, are the relatively uniform distributions of representation here. Aside from the Republikaner in both regions and the PDS in the West, each of the party groupings constitutes at least 9 per cent of the frames and samples for the two regions. Even the largest parties do not take up as much as 25 per cent of the frames and samples. Assuming no bias in response rates for these two groups, one can expect to acquire a fairly broad range of opinions given the diversity built into the samples.

With far smaller sampling rates for city council members one might expect that the lumpiness that can arise when fitting distributions with a large number of categories might produce some significant distortions in the partisan compositions of the

Table A.7 Frequencies of different types of department heads in samples

Breakdowns by departments	East	West	Total
I Total Law and Order	35	39	74
Of which:			
Order (Ordnung)	15	18	33
Justice (Recht)	8	7	15
Building regulation (Baubehörde)	9	12	21
Mixed	3	2	5
II Total Social I	34	34	68
Of which:			
Culture (Kultur)	11	11	22
Sport (Sport)	9	7	16
Education (Schulen)	0	4	4
Mixed	14	12	26
III Total Administrative	33	38	71
Of which:			
Central administration (Hauptverwaltung)	22	19	41
Personnel (Personal)	9	11	20
Mixed	2	8	10
IV Total Economic	35	36	71
Of which:			
City planning (Planung)	21	15	36
Environment (Umwelt)	6	10	16
Economic promotion (Wirtschaftsförderung)	6	3	9
Mixed	2	8	10
V Total Public Finance	37	43	80
Of which:			
Treasury (Kämmerei)	24	25	49
Auditing (Rechnungsprüfung)	13	18	31
Mixed	0	0	0
VI Total Social II	30	33	63
Of which:			
Youth (Jugend)	4	7	11
Social welfare (Soziales)	22	22	44
Mixed	4	4	8
Mixed	6	11	17
Total	211	234	445

Table A.8 Sample frames and samples for party chairpersons (per cent)

	Greens	CDU/CSU	FDP	PDS	Rep	SPD	Other
Germany							
Sample frame	15.3	20.0	13.8	9.6	3.1	19.7	18.4
Sample	15.6	20.4	14.0	9.2	3.1	19.8	17.9
West Germany							
Sample frame	18.6	20.8	14.4	–	5.9	20.7	19.7
Sample	18.8	21.6	14.8	–	5.7	20.4	18.8
East Germany							
Sample frame	12.2	19.3	13.2	18.8	0.5	18.8	17.3
Sample	12.6	19.2	13.2	18.1	0.6	19.2	17.3

Table A.9 Sample frames and samples for council party caucus chairpersons (per cent)

	Greens	CDU/CSU	FDP	PDS	Rep	SPD	Other
Germany							
Sample frame	14.7	21.9	9.9	10.4	1.4	22.3	19.4
Sample	14.9	22.3	9.8	9.8	1.5	22.3	19.3
West Germany							
Sample frame	18.2	24.2	9.1	–	3.0	24.2	21.2
Sample	18.2	24.2	9.1	–	3.0	24.2	21.2
East Germany							
Sample frame	11.6	19.9	10.5	19.9	–	20.4	17.7
Sample	11.7	20.4	10.5	19.3	–	20.5	17.5

samples. This rarely occurred. One way to measure this distortion is to sum across all party categories the absolute value of the difference between the actual percentage of each party in the council and that in the sample. By this conservative measure, the average distortion rate was only 9 per cent across all the cities in the two samples – a very low rate of built-in bias. Because of the need to assure anonymity, no tables with

Table A.10 Local council members' sample frames and sample distribution by party affiliation (per cent)

	Greens	CDU/CSU	FDP	PDS	Rep	SPD	No party	Other
Germany								
Sample frame	7.8	33.4	4.2	10.2	0.9	32.1	1.1	10.3
Sample	7.9	32.9	4.4	10.3	0.8	32.1	1.2	10.5
West Germany								
Sample frame	9.4	38.3	3.5	–	1.5	35.4	0.5	11.4
Sample	9.3	38.2	3.7	–	1.4	35.5	0.3	11.5
East Germany								
Sample frame	5.8	27.4	5.1	22.8	0.1	28.4	1.9	8.9
Sample	6.3	26.8	5.0	21.8	0.1	28.4	2.2	9.4

individual city council comparisons can be presented. Regional and national comparisons can be shown and they are provided in Table A.10. As one sees there, the fits between frames and samples on the partisan distributions of council members are extremely close. Again, in the absence of biased return rates, the results promise to be reflective of the opinions in the councils of the samples of cities included in this study.

Conduct of the Survey

Three actions were involved in contacting the members of the sample. First, a letter announcing the project (along with a statement to the effect that we hoped the sample members would participate in the study) was sent to all members of the sample. As announced in this letter, the questionnaire, along with another letter, materials documenting the privacy law procedures and guarantees, as well as an envelope (where the Wissenschaftszentrum Berlin für Sozialforschung's address and the postal mark indicating that the project would cover the mailing costs of returning the questionnaire) were sent to the sample members nine days later. Eighteen days after the questionnaire mailing, a follow-up letter was sent to those members of the sample who had not responded to the questionnaire by that time (and had not also communicated that they could not or would not participate in the survey). Forty days after the questionnaire mailing, over 50 per cent of the sample had completed and returned the questionnaires. In the succeeding 20 days, a few more were returned. The final overall number of valid responses reached 1,231 (out of the 2,310 sample members), a response rate of 53.3 per cent.[4]

Of course, during this period some problems arose. A number of unanswered questionnaires were returned or communications (mail or phone) were received from some sample members in which the individuals expressed their unwillingness to participate. Of this number, 19, many indicated that excessive work schedules, illness, or absence would prevent them from completing the questionnaire. In one case, a completed questionnaire was returned which had been filled out by the assistant to the respondent. This questionnaire had to be declared invalid and the data were not entered.

One significant problem arose. Despite the Project's explicit and strong commitment to assuring the privacy of the respondents, nearly 200 of the 1,231 respondents sent the completed questionnaire back after first having removed the cover page with the questionnaire identification number. In more than a quarter of these cases, however, the respondents either placed their names and addresses on the return envelop or on a letter they sent accompanying the returned questionnaire. Of the remaining problem cases, it was possible to at least identify which of the sample cities the respondent was from in more than half of the instances. Some of the information that is provided below on the sample respondents then is based on an incomplete picture of who is involved. For the purposes of the project, however, this has not proven to be a major problem.

The length of the questionnaire (20 pages) certainly was not a strong inducement for the potential respondents. The target sample is composed of individuals with significant responsibilities and tight time schedules, both of which diminish the likelihood of a response. In addition, the natural hesitation of politicians and administrators to answer such a wide range of questions must be taken into account. All of these factors clearly should have worked to lower the number of responses one might expect (Heberlein and Baumgartner, 1978). Despite all of this, however, a final response rate of 53 per cent indicates that by conventional standards of mail surveys, this one met with a relatively positive reception.

An Overview of the Response Patterns

In what follows, major patterns in the responses from the targeted samples are described. Because of the difficulty of identifying some of the respondents, not all of the response rates reported below are based on the 1,231 cases, but rather on those responses that were either full or partially identifiable.

---

4   It should be noted that the Deutscher Städtetag affirmed its support for the survey and this was mentioned in the letter to the potential respondents. This support certainly helped assure the high response rate.

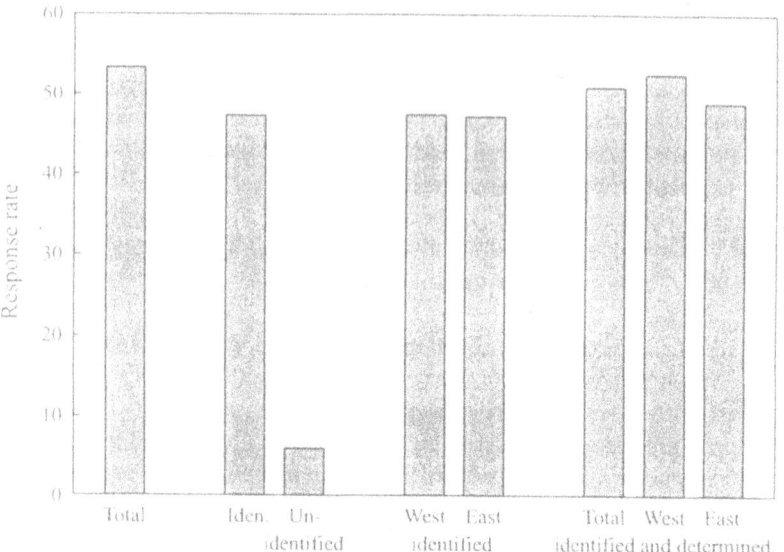

Figure A.5 An overview of response rates

Figure A.5 provides an overview of the response rates across the two parts of Germany, the new and the old federal states. For those groups of respondents that were completely identifiable, the response rates relative to the total samples were 47.2 per cent in the new federal states and 47.4 per cent in the old federal states. Taking into account as well those responses where the identification had been removed from the completed questionnaire but where the city of origin could be determined, the overall response rate rises to 50.9, with 49.1 per cent in the new federal states and 52.6 per cent in the old federal states.

Recall that the target minimum of responses in this study is ten per city. There was indeed wide variation in the numbers of responses per city, but in only two cases was this target not realized, with both of these being cities in the new federal states. The distributions across both regions can be seen in Figure A.6. The values there are based on those responses where, at a minimum, it was possible to identify the city from which the questionnaire was returned. In the new federal states the range in the number of responses per city goes from a low of seven to a high of 20. 36 of the 37 cities had a least ten respondents and 19 had 15 or more respondents. In the old federal states, the lowest number of responses was ten from one city and the highest was a city with 22. 26 cities in this region had 15 more respondents.

It might be noted that the size of the city played different roles across the two regions in terms of response rates. When both regions are combined, it would appear that there was a slightly greater chance of a response if the sample member were in a larger city, i.e., a city with of population of 50,000 or more. In this category of cities,

Appendix: The German Local Elite and Citizen Surveys 221

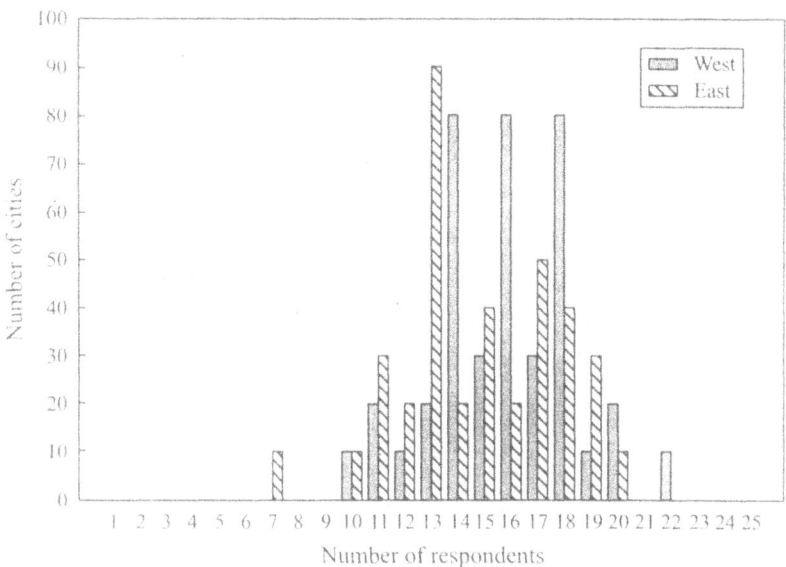

Figure A.6 **Number of respondents: frequency distribution for cities and towns in East and West Germany**

the average response rate was 53.1 per cent. In the other category of cities, i.e., smaller ones with population between 25,000 and 50,000 people, the response rate average was 49.7 per cent. However, this difference due to size was concentrated in the region of the new federal states. Here response rates in larger cities averaged 54.1 per cent and only 46.4 per cent in smaller cities. In the old federal states, there was barely any difference in city size category response rates – indeed, there, the average response rate was 52.9 per cent for smaller cities, slightly higher than it was in the larger cities, viz., 52.2 per cent.

In terms of the functions of the respondents, or the offices they hold, there was variation in the response rates. Figure A.7a provides an overview of these response rates for both regions combined, while A.7b and A.7c provide information on these rates for the new and old federal states, respectively. In addition, information on the response rates for females and males is also provided. Note that this response rate information is based only on those responses that are completely identifiable.

On the legislative side, 48.9 per cent of all members of city councils within both samples responded. A higher response rate was found for those council members who are also council party caucus chairpersons, with 52.4 per cent responding. Local party chairpersons responded at a lower rate, 43.3 per cent.

At the higher levels of political and administrative responsibility, the range in response rates was quite large. The lowest came from the two top positions, chief mayors (32.6 per cent) and city directors (40 per cent). Mayoral response rates were

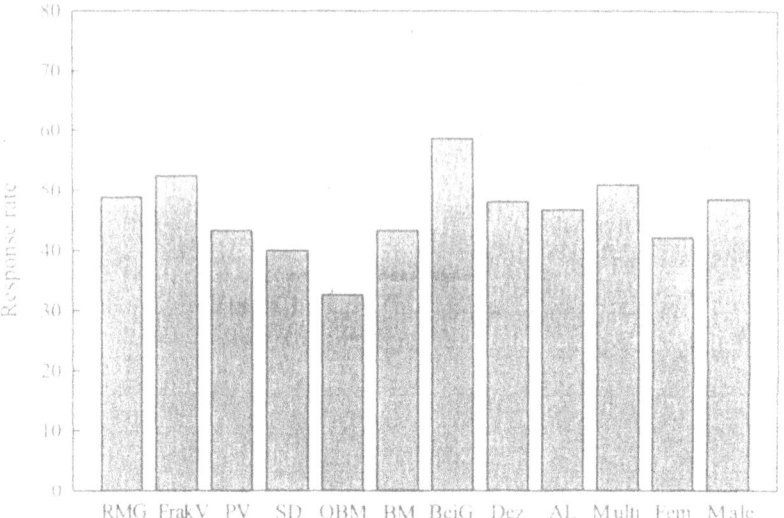

Figure A.7a   Response rates by various categories, East and West Germany combined

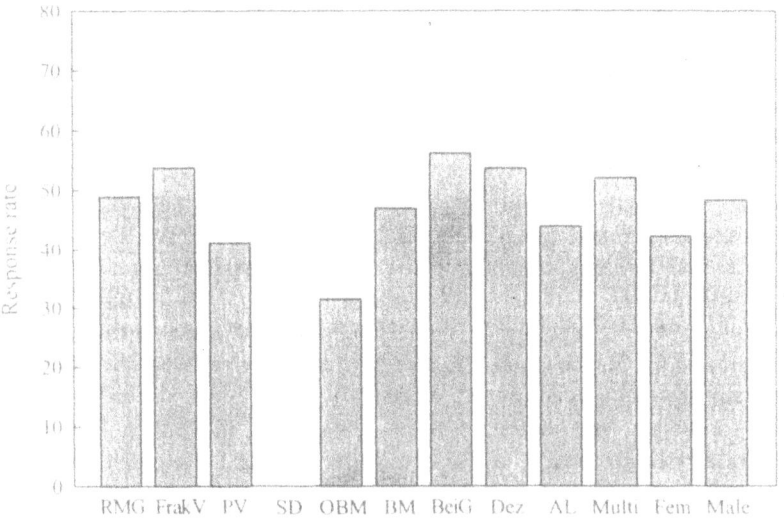

Figure A.7b   Response rates by various categories, East Germany

higher (43.3 per cent). Deputies, such as *Beigeordnete* and *Dezernenten*, had even higher response rates, 58.6 and 48.2 per cent, respectively.

One other functional or office category remains. This is that of the department heads. Here the response rate was 46.7 per cent.

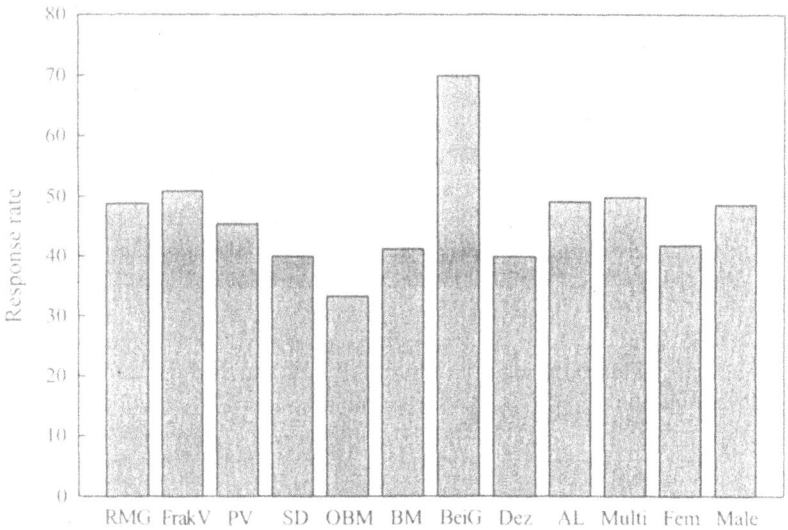

Figure A.7c Response rates by various categories, West Germany

It should also be pointed out that there is a not insignificant difference between the response rate of males and that of females. Males tended to be more likely to respond than females; the former had a response rate of 48.6 per cent while the latter had one of only 42.1 per cent.

Between the two regions, there were some major differences in the response patterns for these groupings. The response rate for local party chairpersons was four per cent lower in the new federal states. In addition, mayors and *Dezernenten* had a noticeably higher response rate in the new federal states. In two other categories, there were noticeably higher rates in the old federal states; these were for department heads and *Beigeordnete*.

Are the respondents among the city council members a biased group in the sense that the party membership pattern among the respondents is markedly different from that within the target sample (which has been shown above to faithfully represent the actual distribution of party membership in the councils)? Figures A.8a, A.8b and A.8c provide information useful for answering this question. The first figures combine data from both regions and matches the relative sizes of a parties' respondents against the relative sizes of the parties' memberships within the sample. Figures A.8b and A.8c break these comparisons down by region. In general, while there are some differences between the relative sizes of the responses and the target samples, they do not appear to be so large as to warrant the conclusion that response rates (based on party affiliation) are biased. Nevertheless, the specifics are as follows. CDU/CSU members responded at a slightly lower rate than would be expected. For the CDU/CSU, this meant that while Union's membership constituted 33 per cent of the combined samples, its

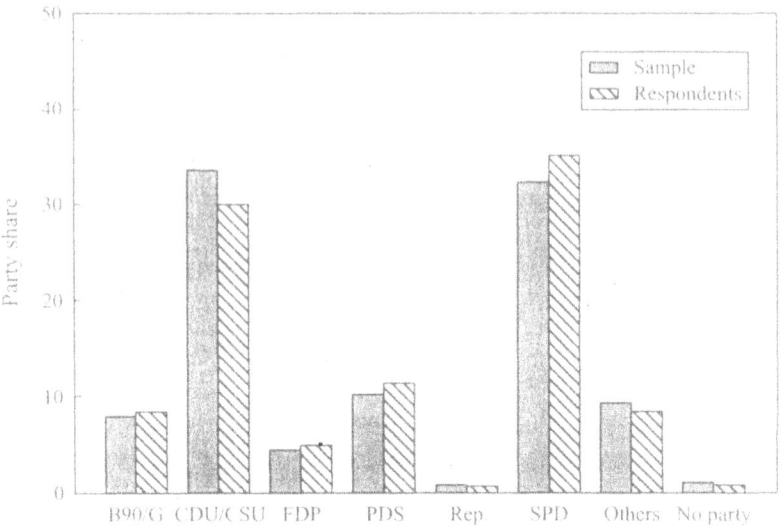

Figure A.8a Council member party affiliation: sample and respondents, East and West Germany combined

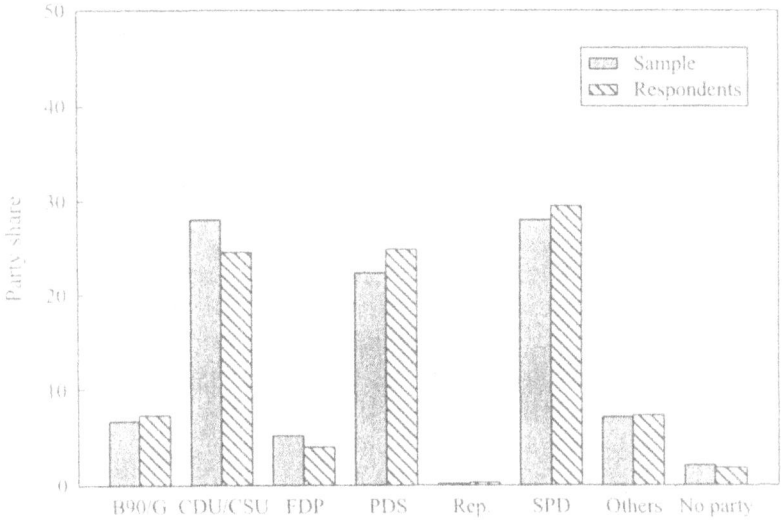

Figure A.8b Council member party affiliation: sample and respondents, East Germany

members represented only 30 per cent of the respondents. The PDS and the Bündnis 90/Die Grünen both had slightly higher response rates than would be expected. The

Appendix: The German Local Elite and Citizen Surveys 225

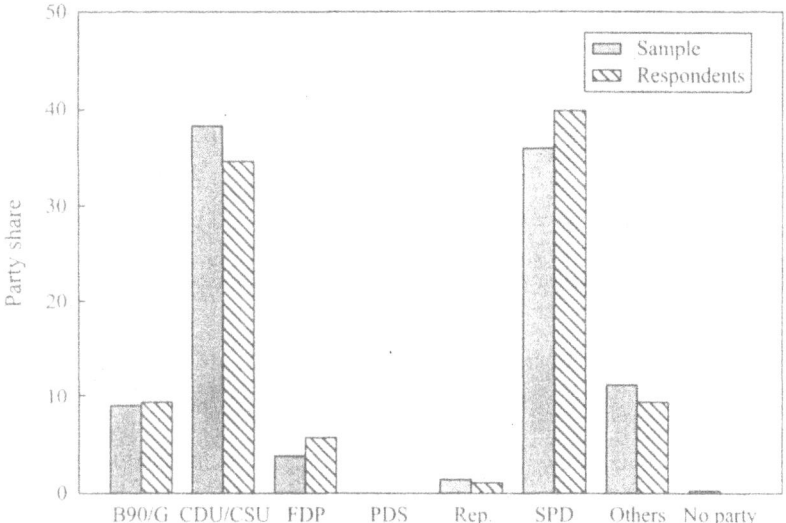

Figure A.8c Council member party affiliation: sample and respondents, West Germany

SPD's response rate was about ten per cent greater than one would have been expected given the average response rate across regions. Generally the differences observed in party response rates is consistent across regions with only the FDP and Republikaner members responding differently in the East than in the West.

Information Related to International Comparisons

In some of the chapters, comparisons are made between the German local elites and local elites of other countries. Data on these other elites are drawn from different national studies conducted in conjunction with the International Project on Democracy and Local Governance. Four of these countries are located in Central Europe and have all been undergoing a transition process during the 1990s. These data from these four countries have been included here for purposes of comparison with the data on the East German elites. The other six countries are long established democracies in Western Europe and North America and the data from these countries have been included for purposes of comparison with the data on the West German elites. Information on the samples for all ten countries is provided in Table A.11.

Table A.11 Comparative information on the German and other surveys from the International Project on Democracy and Local Governance used in this study

	Year of survey	Realized sample size	Number of towns/ cities	Composition of sample (per cent)*	
Germany	1995	1,231	77	Political:	70.3
				Administrative:	17.9
				Other:	11.8
				No information:	2.5
East Germany	1995	545	37	Political:	67.2
				Administrative:	15.8
				Other:	13.4
				No information:	3.7
West Germany	1995	631	40	Political:	69.6
				Administrative:	18.9
				Other:	10.1
				No information:	1.4
Czech Republic	1995	250	22	Elected:	34.8
				Administrative:	35.6
				Party functionary:	29.6
Hungary	1996	394	30	Not available	
Poland	1995	448	30	Political:	73.7
				Administrative:	33.8
Slovakia	1995	214	20	Elected:	37.4
				Appointed:	34.1
				Party functionary:	28.0
				Other:	0.5
Austria	1992	378	31	Political:	82.5
				Administrative:	18.5
				Other:	5.6
Netherlands	1997	423	Not available	Political:	51.3
				Administrative:	48.0
				Other:	0.7

Appendix: The German Local Elite and Citizen Surveys 227

Table A.11 (continued)

	Year of survey	Realized sample size	Number of towns/ cities	Composition of sample (per cent)*	
Spain	1996	444	30	Political:	64.9
				Administrative:	5.4
				Other:	29.1
Sweden	1991	440	20	Political:	72.5
				Administrative:	27.5
Switzerland	1993	819	61	Political:	48.0
				Administrative:	51.3
				Other:	2.7
United States	1991	271	30	Council:	30.6
				Mayor:	2.6
				City manager:	3.7
				Dept. head:	49.8
				Party leader:	7.0
				Other politician:	4.4
				Judge:	1.8

* Because of multiple office-holding, the sum of the percentages across the categories is sometimes grater than 100.

Citizen Survey

Restricted budgetary resources dictated the manner in which the citizen survey could be conducted. Thus, the scale of the survey needed to be limited in both the scope of the questions as well as the sample size. It was possible to use a sub-sample of 15 cities in the new federal states and a sub-sample of the same size in the old federal states. Within each of the communities, the target sample size was 80 respondents (n = 30 cities x 80 respondents per city = 2,400 respondents). The most feasible way to carry out the survey was by conducting a telephone survey. This work was contracted out to a private survey research firm. The survey was successfully carried out during December of 1995.

The sample selection of cities was keyed to variations in the two principal independent variables of this study. Selection of the cities was based on variations in (1) levels of trust amongst elites as reported in the elite survey and (2) location. The first dimension allows one to vary the selection so as to include municipalities with putatively different levels of social capital while the second permits one to include municipalities with different local government institutional forms.[5] Initially, two categories of cities were constructed, (1) those with above average levels of social trust among elites and (2) those with below average levels of social trust. Then within each category a random selection was made with an effort to assure significant variation in the state location of the selected towns, thereby guaranteeing variation in institutional features of the local governments selected.

Based on telephone interviews, the survey focused primarily on citizens' evaluation of local governmental institutions, facets of social capital and political values. The sample size in each municipality averaged 80 persons. In the West, the target sample plus or minus two was met in 13 towns. One fell below this range (68) and one above (85). In the East the target fulfillment success rate was similar. Eleven towns had 80 plus or minus two respondents. Two fell below the target, one with 71 and the other with 77. Two were above, one with 83 and the other with 84. Within each community, sample selection was random and based on the so-called 'last birthday' method. The response rate in the East was 58.1 per cent while that in the West was 53.7. This means that slightly more than 2,000 calls had to be made in each region in order to achieve the 1,200 successfully completed interviews in each. The main reasons for non-response were either refusal to take part in the survey or that the target respondent was not at home. Very few potential respondents broke off the interviews.

Are the demographic, social and economic characteristics of the respondents reasonably representative of the population? A limited number of comparisons are possible to make here and these comparisons suggest that the sample does not appear to be skewed in any significant way.

Information taken from the 1997 Mikrozensus provides only a breakdown for all of the German population by gender. For the population 20 or above, which is close to the sampling criteria used in our survey, the breakdown is as follows: 52.1 per cent female and 47.9 per cent male.[6] This is slightly more balanced than our sample: for both regions: 54.9 per cent female, 45.1 per cent male. Note that in the East the breakdown was 56.9 per cent female and 43.1 per cent male, while in the west it was 52.8 per cent female and 47.2 per cent male.

Table A.12 presents information of the age structures of the actual German population in the two regions and the corresponding age structures found in the samples. Overall, it would appear that the samples in both regions are slightly younger than those to be seen in the results from the Mikrozensus. In terms of position in the labor market, it is difficult to make comparisons with the results from the Mikrozensus

---

5   These two characteristics are at the core of the theoretical and empirical analysis in Chapter 5. In addition, the second trait, location, obviously enhances the representativeness of the citizen sample surveys.

6   This is based on the 1997 Mikrozensus. The figures are drawn from Statistisches Bundesamt (1998b, pp. 86–7).

Appendix: The German Local Elite and Citizen Surveys   229

Table A.12   Percentage breakdowns of age distribution for the regional samples of citizen surveys (population figures in parentheses are from the 1997 Mikrozensus*)

Age category	East Germany	West Germany
18–24	4.7 (3.6)	8.1 (4.0)
25–34	18.7 (16.2)	20.6 (18.3)
35–44	20.6 (19.5)	19.8 (18.2)
45–54	18.5 (15.7)	16.4 (16.1)
55–64	17.1 (19.8)	15.8 (18.2)
65+	20.3 (25.2)	19.2 (25.2)

* Mikrozensus figures are drawn from Statistisches Bundesamt (1998b, p. 29).

Table A.13   Percentage breakdowns by positions in the labor markets for the regional samples of citizen surveys (population figures in parentheses are from the 1997 Mikrozensus*)

Position	East Germany	West Germany
Employed	52.7 (50.8)	54.3 (57.2)
Unemployed	10.0 (10.1)	3.3 (4.2)
Pensioner	31.9 (35.8)	24.8 (32.8)

* Mikrozensus figures are drawn from Statistisches Bundesamt (1998b, p. 29).

Table A.14 Percentage distribution by net household monthly income for the regional samples of citizen surveys (population figures in parentheses are from the 1997 Mikrozensus*)

Income (DM)	East Germany	West Germany
0–2,499	40.8	27.4
	(46.6)	(36.4)
2,500–7,499	57.7	65.8
	(51.5)	(57.4)
7,500+	1.5	6.7
	(1.8)	(6.2)

* Mikrozensus figures are drawn from Statistisches Bundesamt (1998b, p. 29).

because the latter focuses exclusively on the 'head of the household'. Nevertheless, as seen in Table A.13, the characteristics of our samples fit reasonably close to those reported in the Mikrozensus. Income comparisons are also somewhat difficult because the Mikrozensus figures deal with the entire population while our survey relates to small and medium-sized towns and cities.

Table A.14 provides breakdowns for each region within three categories of net household monthly income. In sum, the socio-economic characteristics of the members of the sample appear to be quite comparable to the population of both regions. Inferences drawn from the data based on the sample then are not likely to be biased.

Bibliography

Aberbach, Joel D., Putnam, Robert D. and Rockman, Bert A. (1981), *Bureaucrats and Politicians in Western Democracies*, Harvard University Press, Cambridge.

Aberbach, Joel D., Derlien, Hans-Ulrich et al. (1990), 'American and German Federal Executives – Technocratic and Political Attitudes', *International Social Science Journal*, 2 (3), pp. 3–18.

Alesina, Alberto and La Ferrara, Eliana (2001), *Preferences for Redistribution in the Land of Opportunities*, NBER Working Paper Series No. 8267, Cambridge.

ALLBUS (1992), *Die allgemeine Bevölkerungsumfrage der Sozialwissenschaften, 1992*, Zentralarchiv für Empirische Sozialforschung der Universität zu Köln, ZA Nr. 2140, Köln.

ALLBUS (1994), *Die allgemeine Bevölkerungsumfrage der Sozialwissenschaften, 1994*, Zentralarchiv für Empirische Sozialforschung der Universität zu Köln, ZA Nr. 2400, Köln.

Arzberger, Klaus (1980), *Bürger und Eliten in der Kommunalpolitik*, Kohlhammer/Deutscher Gemeindeverlag, Stuttgart.

Bachrach, Peter (1967), *The Theory of Democratic Elitism*, Little Brown, Boston.

Baldersheim, Harald, Blaas, Gezja, Horvath, Tamas M., Illner, Michal and Swianiewic, Pawel (1996), 'New Institutions of Local Government: A Comparison', in H. Baldersheim, M. Illner, A. Offerdal, L. Rose and P. Swianiewicz (eds), *Local Democracy and the Process of Transformation in East-Central Europe*, Westview Press, Boulder, pp. 23–42.

Baldersheim, Harald, Bodnarova, Beba, Horvath, Tamas and Vajdov, Zdenka (1996), 'Functioning of the Executive: Power, Leadership and Management', in H. Baldersheim, M. Illner, A. Offerdal, L. Rose and P. Swianiewicz (eds), *Local Democracy and the Process of Transformation in East-Central Europe*, Westview Press, Boulder, pp. 197–224.

Baldersheim, Harald and Illner, Michal (1996a), 'Local Democracy: The Challenges of Institution-Building', in H. Baldersheim, M. Illner, A. Offerdal, L. Rose and P. Swianiewicz (eds), *Local Democracy and the Process of Transformation in East-Central Europe*, Westview Press, Boulder, pp. 1–22.

Baldersheim, Harald and Illner, Michal (1996b), 'Virtuous Circles: Local Democracy in a Post-Communist Environment', in H. Baldersheim, M. Illner, A. Offerdal, L. Rose and P. Swianiewicz (eds), *Local Democracy and the Process of Transformation in East-Central Europe*, Westview Press, Boulder, pp. 225–41.

Banner, Gerhard (1982), 'Zur politisch-administrative Steuerung in der Kommune', *Archiv für Kommunalwissenschaft*, 21, pp. 26–47.

Banner, Gerhard (1983), 'Haushaltssteuerung in der Krise', *Städte- und Gemeindebund*, 5, pp. 163 6.

Banner, Gerhard (1984), 'Kommunale Steuerung zwischen Gemeideordnung und Parteipolitik', *Die Öffentliche Verwaltung*, 9, pp. 364–72.

Banner, Gerhard (1989), 'Kommunalverfassungen und Selbstverwaltung', in D. Shimanke (ed.), *Stadtdirektor oder Bürgermeister: Beiträge zu einer aktuellen Kontroverse*, Birkhäuser, Basel, pp. 37–61.

Barnes, Samuel H. (1994), 'Politics and Culture', in F.D. Weil and M. Gautier (eds), *Research on Democracy and Society – Political Culture and Political Structure: Theoretical and Empirical Studies*, JAI Press, Greenwich, pp. 45–64.

Barro, Robert J. and Lee, Jong-Wha (2000a), *International Educational Attainment Updates and Implications*, NBER Working Paper No. 7911, Cambridge.

Barro, Robert J. and Lee, Jong-Wha (2000b), *International Educational Attainment Updates and Implications*. Data set available at <http://www.cid.harvard.edu/ciddata/ciddata.html>.

Bauer-Kaase, Petra and Kaase, Max (1996), 'Five Years of Unification: The Germans on the Path to Inner Unity?', *German Politics*, 15 (1), pp. 267–99.

Baylis, Thomas A. (1989), *Governing By Committee: Collegial Leadership in Advanced Societies*, State University of New York Press, Albany.

Baylis, Thomas A. (1998), 'Elites, Institutions and Political Changes in East Central Europe: Germany, the Czech Republic and Slovakia', in J. Higley, J. Pakulski and W. Wesolowski (eds), *Postcommunist Elites in Democracy in Eastern Europe*, Macmillan Press, London, pp. 107–30.

Berg, Frank, Nagelschmidt, Martin and Wollmann, Helmut (1996), *Kommunaler Institutionenwandel*, Leske + Budrich, Opladen.

Berking, Helmuth and Neckel, Sighard (1991), 'Außenseiter als Politiker: Rekrutierung und Identitäten neuer lokaler Eliten in einer ostdeutschen Gemeinde', *Soziale Welt*, 42 (3), pp. 283–300.

Bernet, Wolfgang (1993), 'Gemeinden und Gemeinderecht in Regimewandel. Von der DDR zu den neuen Bundesländern', *Aus Politik und Zeitgeschichte*, B36, pp. 27–38.

BfLR (1995), *Laufende Raumbeobachtung 1995*, Bundesforschungsanstalt für Landeskunde und Raumordnung, Bonn.

BMA (2001), *Lebenslagen in Deutschland, Daten und Fakten: Der ersten Armuts- und Reichtumsbericht der Bundesregierung*, Berlin, Bundesministerium für Arbeit. <http://www.bma.de>.Boeri, Tito, Börsch-Supan, Axel and Tabellini, Guido (2001), 'Would You Like to Shrink the Welfare State? A Survey of Citizens', *Economic Policy*, 32, pp. 8–50.

Borchert, Jens and Golsch, Lutz (1999), 'Deutschland: Von der "Honoratiorenzunft" zur politischen Klasse', in J. Borchert and J. Zeiß (eds), *Politik als Beruf: Die politische Klasse in westlichen Demokratien*, Leske + Budrich, Opladen, pp. 114–40.

Brennen, Geoffrey and Hamlin, Alan (1994), 'A Revisionist View of the Separation of Powers', *Journal of Theoretical Politics*, 6 (3), pp. 345–68.

Bretschneider, Michael (1994), *Aktuelle Probleme der Stadtentwicklung und der Kommunalpolitik: Umfrageergebnisse 1994*, Deutsches Institut für Urbanistik, Bericht 7/94, Berlin.

Brinkmann, Christoph (1995), 'Labor Market Policy in East Germany', *European Employment Observatory*, No. 16/17.

Bürklin, Wolfgang (1997a), 'Die Potsdamer Elitestudie von 1995: Problemstellungen und wissenschaftliches Programm', in W. Bürklin and H. Rebenstorf (eds), *Eliten in Deutschland: Rekrutierung und Integration*, Leske + Budrich, Opladen, pp. 11–34.

Bürklin, Wolfgang (1997b), 'Demokratische Einstellung im Wandel: Von der repräsentativen zur plebiszitären Demokratie?', in W. Bürklin and H. Rebenstorf (eds), *Eliten in Deutschland: Rekrutierung und Integration*, Leske + Budrich, Opladen, pp. 391–420.

Card, David (1999), 'The Causal Effect of Education on Earnings', in O. Ashenfelter and D. Card (eds), *Handbook of Labor Economics, Vol. 3*, Elsevier, Amsterdam, pp. 1801–63.

Corneo, Giacomo (2000), *Inequality and the State: Comparing U.S. and German Preferences*, CESifo Working Paper No. 398, Center for Economic Studies and Ifo Institute for Economic Research, München.

Corneo, Giacomo and Grüner, Hans Peter (2001), *Individual Preferences for Political Redistribution*, CEPR Discussion Paper No. 2694, Centre for Economic Policy Research, London.

Cusack, Thomas R. (1997), *On the Road to Weimar? The Political Economy of Popular Satisfaction with Government and Regime Performance in Germany*, Discussion Paper of the Research Unit on Economic Change and Employment, Wissenschaftszentrum Berlin für Sozialforschung, Berlin.

Cusack, Thomas R. (1999), 'The Shaping of Popular Satisfaction with Government and Regime Performance in Germany', *British Journal of Political Science*, 29, pp. 641–72.

Dahl, Robert A. and Tufte, Edward R. (1973), *Size and Democracy*, Stanford University Press, Stanford.

Dalton, Russell (1994), 'Communists and Democrats: Democratic Attitudes in the Two Germanies', *British Journal of Political Science*, 24, pp. 469–93.

Deno, Kevin T. and Mehay, Stephen L. (1987), 'Municipal Management Structure and Fiscal Performance: Do City Managers Make a Difference?', *Southern Economic Journal*, 53 (3), pp. 627–42.

Derlien, Hans-Ulrich (1993), 'German Unification and Bureaucratic Transformation', *International Political Science Review*, 14, pp. 319–34.

Derlien, Hans-Ulrich (1994), 'Kommunalverfassungen zwischen Reform und Revolution', in O.W. Gabriel and R. Voigt (eds), *Kommunalwissenschaftliche Analysen*, Universitätsverlag Dr. N. Brockmeyer, Bochum, pp. 47–78.

Derlien, Hans-Ulrich (1995), 'Über Beurteilungskritierien der Gestaltung von Kommunalverfassungen', *Der Landkreis*, 5, pp. 232–4.

Derlien, Hans-Ulrich (1998), 'Elitezirkulation in Ostdeutschland 1989–1995', *Aus Politik und Zeitgeschichte*, B5, pp. 3–17.

Derlien, Hans-Ulrich, Gürtler, Christoph, Holler, Wolfgang and Schreiner, Hermann Josef (1976), *Kommunalverfassung und kommunales Entscheidungssystem: Eine vergleichende Untersuchung in vier Gemeinden*, Meisenheim am Glan.

Derlien, Hans-Ulrich and Lock, Stefan (1994), 'Eine neue politische Elite? Rekrutierung und Karrieren der Abgeordneten in den fünf neuen Landtagen', *Zeitschrift für Parlamentsfragen*, 25 (1), pp. 61–94.

Deutscher Städtetag (1976), *Statistisches Jahrbuch Deutscher Gemeinden*, J.P. Bachem, Köln.
Deutscher Städtetag (1992), *Statistisches Jahrbuch Deutscher Gemeinden*, J.P. Bachem, Köln.
Deutscher Städtetag (1994), *Statistisches Jahrbuch Deutscher Gemeinden*, J.P. Bachem, Köln.
Deutscher Städtetag (1996), *Statistisches Jahrbuch Deutscher Gemeinden*, J.P. Bachem, Köln.

Edinger, Lewis J. (1960), 'Post-Totalitarian Leadership: Elites in the German Federal Republic', *American Political Science Review*, 54 (1), pp. 58–82.

Edinger, Lewis J. (1961), 'Continuity and Change in the Background of German Decision-Makers', *The Western Political Quarterly*, 14 (1), pp. 17–36.

Edinger, Lewis J. and Searing, D. (1967), 'Social Background in Elite Analysis: A Methodological Analysis', *American Political Science Review*, 61, pp. 428–45.

Eisen, Andreas and Wollmann, Helmut (eds) (1996), *Institutionenbildung in Ostdeutschland*, Leske + Budrich, Opladen.

Eldersveld, Samuel J. (1989), *Political Elites in Modern Societies: Empirical Research and Democratic Theory*, University of Michigan Press, Ann Arbor.

Eldersveld, Samuel J., Strömberg, Lars and Derksen, Wim (1995), *Local Elites in Western Democracies: A Comparative Analysis of Urban Political Leadership in the U.S., Sweden, and The Netherlands*, Westview Press, Boulder.

Enelow, James M. and Hinich, Melvin J. (1984), *The Spatial Theory of Voting: An Introduction*, Cambridge University Press, Cambridge.

Esping-Andersen, Gosta (1999), *Social Foundations of Postindustrial Society*, Oxford University Press, Oxford.

Esping-Andersen, Gosta, Assimakopoulou, Zina and van Kersbergen, Kees (1993), 'Trends in Contemporary Class Structration: A Six-nation Comparison', in G. Esping-Andersen (ed.), *Changing Classes: Stratification and Mobility in Post-Industrial Societies*, Sage, London, pp. 32–57.

Evans, Geoffrey and Heath, Anthony (1995), 'The Measurement of Left-Right and Libertarian-Authoritarian Values: Comparing Balanced and Unbalanced Scales', *Quality and Quantity*, 29, pp. 191–206.

Evans, Geoffrey, Heath, Anthony and Lalljee, Mansur (1996), 'Measuring Left-Right and Libertarian-Authoritarian Values in the British Electorate', *British Journal of Sociology*, 47 (1), pp. 93–112.

Fiorina, Morris P. and Shepsle, Kenneth A. (1989), 'Formal Theories of Leadership: Agents, Agenda Setters and Entrepreneurs', in B.D. Jones (ed.), *Leadership and Politics: New Perspectives in Political Science*, University of Kansas Press, Lawrence, pp. 18–40.

Fox, John (1991), *Regression Diagnostics*, Sage, London.

Frey, Rainer (1989), 'Das institutionelle Feld der politischen Entscheidungen auf der Kommunalebene', in D. Shimanke (ed.), *Stadtdirektor oder Bürgermeister: Beiträge zu einer aktuellen Kontroverse*, Birkhäuser, Basel, pp. 121–35.

Fuchs, Dieter (1999), 'The Democratic Culture of Unified Germany', in P. Norris (ed.), *Critical Citizens: Global Support for Democratic Governance*, Oxford University Press, Oxford, pp. 123–45.

Fuchs, Dieter, Roller, Edeltraud and Weßels, Bernhard (1997), 'Die Akzeptanz der Demokratie des vereinigten Deutschland', *Aus Politik und Zeitgeschichte*, B51, pp. 3–12.

Fukyama, Francis (1995), *Trust*, Free Press, New York.

Gabriel, Oscar (ed.) (1989), *Kommunale Demokratie zwischen Politik und Verwaltung*, Minerva, München.

Gau, Doris (1983), *Politische Führungsgruppen auf kommunaler Ebene. Eine empirische Untersuchung zum Sozialprofil und den politischen Karrieren der Mitglieder des Rates der Stadt Köln*, Minerva, München.

Gibson, James, Duch, Raymond and Tedin, Kent (1992), 'Democratic Values and the Transformation of the Soviet Union', *Journal of Politics*, 54, pp. 329–71.

Glaeßner, Gert-Joachim (1996), 'Regime Change and Public Administration in East Germany – Some Findings from a Research Project in Brandenburg and Saxony', *German Politics*, 5 (2), pp. 185–200.

Goldberg, Ellis (1996), 'Thinking About How Democracy Works', *Politics and Society*, 24 (1), pp. 7–18.

Grunrow, Dieter (1992), 'Constitutional Reform in Local Government in Germany: The Case of North Rhine-Westphalia (NRW)', *Local Government Studies*, 18 (1), pp. 44–57.
Gunlicks, Arthur B. (1969), 'Representative Role Perceptions Among Local Councilors in Western Germany', *Journal of Politics*, 31, pp. 443–64.
Gunlicks, Arthur B. (1977), 'Restructuring Service Delivery Systems in West Germany', in V. Ostrom and F. Pennell Bish (eds), *Comparing Urban Service Delivery Systems: Structure and Performance*, Sage, London, pp. 173–97.
Gunlicks, Arthur B. (1986), *Local Government in the German Federal System*, Duke University Press, Durham.
Hayes, Kathy and Chang, Semoon (1990), 'The Relative Efficiency of City Manager and Mayor-Council Forms of Government', *Southern Journal of Economics*, 57 (1), pp. 167–77.
Heath, Anthony, Evans, Geoffrey and Martin, J. (1993), 'The Measurement of Core Beliefs and Values: The Development of Balanced Socialist/Laissez Faire and Libertarian/Authoritarian Scales', *British Journal of Political Science*, 24, pp. 115–32.
Heberlein, Thomas A. and Baumgartner, Robert (1978), 'Factors Affecting Response Rates to Mailed Questionnaires: A Quantitative Analysis of the Published Literature', *American Sociological Review*, 43, pp. 447–62.
Hocker, Beate (1996), 'Politische Partizipation von Frauen im vereinigten Deutschland', *Aus Politik und Zeitgeschichte*, B21–22, pp. 23–33.
Hoffmann-Lange, Ursula (1991), 'West German Elites: Cartel of Anxiety, Power Elite or Responsive Representatives?', in U. Hoffmann-Lange (ed.), *Social and Political Structures in West Germany*, Westview Press, Boulder, pp. 81–104.
Hoffmann-Lange, Ursula (1992), *Eliten, Macht und Konflikt in der Bundesrepublik*, Leske + Budrich, Opladen.
Hoffmann-Lange, Ursula (1998), 'Elites Transformation and Democratic Consolidation in Germany after 1945 and 1989', in J. Higley, J. Pakulski and W. Wesolowski (eds), *Postcommunist Elites in Democracy in Eastern Europe*, Macmillan Press, London, pp. 141–62.
Hoffmann-Lange, Ursula and Bürklin, Wilhelm P. (1998), *Elite Change in (West) Germany Since the 1960s*, Paper presented at Annual Meeting of the American Political Science Association, Boston.
Holtmann, Everhard (1990), 'Kommunalpolitik im politischen System der Bundesrepublik', *Aus Politik und Zeitgeschichte*, B25, pp. 3–14.
Holtmann, Everhard (1992), 'Politisierung der Kommunalpolitik und Wandlungen im lokalen Parteiensystem', *Aus Politik und Zeitgeschichte*, B22–23, pp. 13–22.
Horowitz, Donald L. (1990), 'Presidents vs. Parliaments: Comparing Democratic Systems', *Journal of Democracy*, 1 (4), pp. 73–9.
Inglehart, Ronald (1988), 'The Renaissance of Political Culture', *American Political Science Review*, 82 (4), pp. 1203–30.
International Parliamentary Union (1999), *Women in National Parliaments*. <www.ipu.org/wmn-e/classif.htm>
International Social Survey Project (1990), *Role of Government II*, ZA Study 1950, Zentralarchiv für Empirische Sozialforschung der Universität zu Köln, Köln.
International Social Survey Project (1992), *Social Inequality II*, ZA Study 2310, Zentralarchiv für Empirische Sozialforschung der Universität zu Köln, Köln.
International Social Survey Project (1996), *Role of Government III*, ZA Study 2900, Zentralarchiv für Empirische Sozialforschung der Universität zu Köln, Köln.

Iversen, Torben (1994), 'Political Leadership and Representation', *American Journal of Political Science*, 38 (1), pp. 45–74.
Jackman, Robert W. and Miller, Ross A. (1998), 'Social Capital and Politics', in N.W. Polsby (ed.), *Annual Review of Political Science*, Annual Reviews No. 1, Palo Alto, pp. 47–73.
Jacob, Betty, Ostrowski, Krzysztof and Teune, Henry (eds) (1993), *Democracy and Local Governance: Ten Empirical Studies*, Matsunaga Institute for Peace, Honolulu.
Jacob, Philip et al. (1971), *Values and the Active Community: A Cross-National Study of the Influence of Local Leadership*, Free Press, New York.
Kaase, Max (1995), 'Demokratie im Spannungsfeld von politischer Kultur und politischer Struktur', in W. Link, E. Schütt-Wetschky and G. Schwan (eds), *Jahrbuch für Politik*, Nomos, Baden-Baden, pp. 199–220.
Kaina, Viktoria (1997), 'Wertorientierungen im Eliten-Bevölkerungsvergleich: Vertikale Distanzen, geteilte Loyalitäten und das Erbe der Trennung', in W. Bürklin and H. Rebenstorf (eds), *Eliten in Deutschland: Rekrutierung und Integration*, Leske + Budrich, Opladen, pp. 351–90.
King, Gary, Tomz, Michael and Wittenberg, Jason (2000), 'Making the Most of Statistical Analyses: Improving Interpretation and Presentation', *American Journal of Political Science*, 44 (2), pp. 341–55.
Kitschelt, Herbert and Hellemans, Staf (1990), 'The Left-Right Semantics and the New Politics Cleavage', *Comparative Political Studies*, 23 (2), pp. 210–38.
Kitschelt, Herbert (1993), *The Transformation of European Social Democracy*, Cambridge University Press, Cambridge.
Kitschelt, Herbert with Anthony J. McGann (1997), *The Radical Right in Western Europe: A Comparative Analysis*, University of Michigan Press, Ann Arbor.
Kluegel, James R., Maxon, David S. and Wagner, Bernd (1999), 'The Legitimation of Capitalism in the Postcommunist Transition: Public Opinion about Market Justice 1991–1996', *European Sociological Review*, 15 (3), pp. 251–83.
Knack, Stephen and Keefer, Philip (1997), 'Does Social Capital Have an Economic Payoff? A Cross-Country Investigation', *Quarterly Journal of Economics*, 112, pp. 1251–88.
Knutson, Oddbjorn (1997), 'The Partisan and the Value-based Components of Left-Right Self-Placement: A Comparative Study', *International Political Science Review*, 18, pp. 191–225.
Koch, Rainer (1989), 'Effizienz kommunaler Verwaltungsführungen. Zur Bedeutung von Struktur- und Situationsgrößen als Effizienzdeterminanten', in D. Shimanke (ed.), *Stadtdirektor oder Bürgermeister: Beiträge zu einer aktuellen Kontroverse*, Birkhäuser, Basel, pp. 190–205.
Köser, Helmut (1991), 'Der Gemeinderat in Baden-Württemberg: Sozialprofil, Rekrutierung', in T. Pfizer and H.-G. Wehling (eds), *Politikverständnis. Kommunalpolitik in Baden-Württemberg*, Kohlhammer, Stuttgart, pp. 141–61.Köser, Helmut and Caspers-Merk, Marion (1989), 'Einfluß und Steuerungspotential kommunaler Mandatsträger in Baden-Württemberg', in D. Shimanke (ed.), *Stadtdirektor oder Bürgermeister: Beiträge zu einer aktuellen Kontroverse*, Birkhäuser, Basel, pp. 97–120.
Krehbiel, Keith (1996), 'Institutional and Partisan Sources of Gridlock: A Theory of Divided and Unified Government', *Journal of Theoretical Politics*, 8 (1), pp. 7–40.
Kuhlberg, Judith S. and Zimmerman, William (1999), 'Liberal Elites, Socialist Masses and Problems of Russian Democracy', *World Politics*, 51, pp. 323–58.

Kunz, Volker and Zapf-Schramm, Thomas (1989), 'Ergebnisse der Haushaltsentscheidungsprozesse in den kreisfreien Städten der Bundesrepublik', in D. Shimanke (ed.), *Stadtdirektor oder Bürgermeister: Beiträge zu einer aktuellen Kontroverse*, Birkhäuser, Basel, pp. 161–89.
Laitin, David D. (1995), 'The Civic Culture at 30', *American Political Science Review*, 89 (1), pp. 168–73.
La Palombara, Joseph (1993), 'Review of Making Democracy Work', *Political Science Quarterly*, 108 (3), pp. 549–50.
Leif, Thomas, Legrand, Hans-Josef and Klein, Ansgar (eds) (1992), *Die politische Klasse in Deutschland*, Bouvier, Bonn.
Leonardi, Robert (1995), 'Regional Development in Italy: Social Capital and the Mezzogiorno', *Oxford Review of Economic Policy*, 11 (2), pp. 165–79.
Levi, Margaret (1996), 'Social and Unsocial Capital', *Politics and Society*, 24 (1), pp. 45–56.
Liebig, Stefan and Verwiebe, Roland (2000), 'Einstellungen zur sozialen Ungleichheit in Ostdeutschland: Plädoyer für eine doppelte Vergleichsweise', *Zeitschrift für Soziologie*, 29, pp. 3–26.
Lijphart, Arend (1984), *Democracies: Patterns of Majoritarian and Consensus Government in Twenty-One Countries*, Yale University Press, New Haven.
Lijphart, Arend (1989), 'Democratic Political Systems: Types, Cases, Causes and Consequences', *Journal of Theoretical Politics*, 1 (1), pp. 33–48.
Lijphart, Arend (1991), 'Constitutional Choices for New Democracies', *Journal of Democracy*, 2 (1), pp. 72–84.
Linder, Wolf (1994), *Swiss Democracy: Possible Solutions to Conflict in Multicultural Societies*, St. Martin's Press, New York.
Linder, Wolf and Nabholz, Ruth (1994), *Local Governance and New Democracy: The Swiss Project*, Technical Report, University of Bern, Bern.
Linz, Juan J. (1990), 'Presidents vs. Parliaments: The Virtues of Parliamentarism', *Journal of Democracy*, 1 (4), pp. 84–91.
Lipset, Seymour M. (1990), 'Presidents vs. Parliaments: The Centrality of Political Culture', *Journal of Democracy*, 1 (4), pp. 80–3.
Lorenz, Sabine and Wegrich, Kai (1998), 'Lokale Ebene im Umbruch: Aufbau und Modernisierung der Kommunalverwaltung in Ostdeutschland', *Aus Politik und Zeitgeschichte*, B5, pp. 29–38.
Machatzke, Jörg (1997), 'Die Potsdamer Elitestudie – Positionsauswahl und Ausschöpfung', in W. Bürklin and H. Rebenstorf (eds), *Eliten in Deutschland: Rekrutierung und Integration*, Leske + Budrich, Opladen, pp. 35–68.
Machatzke, Jörg (1997), 'Einstellungen zum Umfang staatlicher Verantwortung – Zum Staatsverständis der Eliten im vereinten Deutschland', in W. Bürklin and H. Rebenstorf (eds), *Eliten in Deutschland: Rekrutierung und Integration*, Leske + Budrich, Opladen, pp. 321–50.
McFalls, Laurence (1999), 'Eastern Germany Transformed: From Postcommunist to Late Capitalist Poltical Culture', *German Politics and Society*, 17 (2), pp. 1–24.
McIntosh, Mary, MacIver, Martha A., Abele, Daniel G. and Smeltz, Dina (1994), 'Publics Meet Market Democracy in Central and East Europe, 1991–1993', *Slavic Review*, 53, pp. 483–512.
Melbeck, Christian (1990), 'Die Machtstruktur deutscher und amerikanischer Städte in Abhängigkeit von institutionellen Rahmenbedingungen', *Aus Politik und Zeitgeschichte*, B25, pp. 37–45.

Meltzer, Alan H. and Richard, Scott F. (1978), 'Why Government Grows (and Grows) in a Democracy', *Public Interest*, 52, pp. 111-18.
Meltzer, Alan H. and Richard, Scott F. (1981), 'A Rational Theory of Government Size', *Journal of Political Economy*, 89, pp. 914-27.
Meltzer, Alan H. and Richard, Scott F. (1983), 'Tests of a Rational Theory of Government Size', *Public Choice*, 41, pp. 403-18.
Miller, Arthur H., Hesli, Vicki L. and Reisinger, William M. (1995), 'Comparing Citizen and Elite Belief Systems in Post-Soviet Russia and Ukraine', *Public Opinion Quarterly*, 59, pp. 1-40.
Miller, Arthur H., Hesli, Vicki L. and Reisinger, William M. (1997), 'Conceptions of Democracy Among Mass and Elite in Post-Soviet Societies', *British Journal of Political Science*, 27, pp. 157-90.
Morgan, David R. (1997), 'Structural Arrangements in Local Government: Organizing for Effective Management', in J.J. Gargan (ed.), *Handbook of Local Government Administration*, Marcel Decker, Inc., New York, pp. 129-57.
Morgan, David R. and Pelissero, John P. (1980), 'Urban Policy: Does Political Structure Matter?', *American Political Science Review*, 74, pp. 999-1006.
Morgan, David R. and Watson, Sheilah S. (1995), 'The Effects of Mayoral Power on Urban Fiscal Policy', *Policy Studies Journal*, 22 (2), pp. 231-43.
Mouritzen, Poul Erik (1989), 'City Size and Citizens' Satisfaction: Two Competing Theories Revisited', *European Journal of Political Research*, 17, pp. 661-88.
Naßmacher, Karl-Heinz (1978), 'Analysen und Reformvorstellungen zur kommunalen Verfassungsstruktur', in P. Kevenhörster and H. Wollmann (eds), *Kommunalpolitische Praxis und lokale Politikforschung*, Deutsches Institut für Urbanistik, Berlin, pp. 289-323.
Naßmacher, Hiltrud (1989), 'Kommunale Entscheidungsstrukturen', in D. Shimanke (ed.), *Stadtdirektor oder Bürgermeister: Beiträge zu einer aktuellen Kontroverse*, Birkhäuser, Basel, pp. 62-83.
Newton, Ken (1974), 'Role Orientations and Their Sources Among Elected Representatives in English Local Politics', *Journal of Politics*, 36, pp. 615-36.
Newton, Ken (1982), 'Is Small Really so Beautiful? Is Big Really so Ugly? Size, Effectiveness and Democracy in Local Government', *Political Studies*, 30, pp. 190-206.
Nielsen, Hans Jorgen (1981), 'Size and Evaluation of Government: Danish Attitudes towards Politics at Multiple Levels of Government', *European Journal of Political Research*, 9, pp. 47-61.
Noelle-Neumann, Elisabeth and Köcher, Renate (1997), *Allensbacher Jahrbuch der Demoskopie 1993-1997*, Bd. 10, K.G. Sauer, München.
North, Douglass C. (1990), *Institutions, Institutional Change and Economic Performance*, Cambridge University Press, Cambridge.
Norton, Alan (1994), *International Handbook of Local and Regional Government: A Comparative Analysis of Advanced Democracies*, Edward Elgar, Aldershot.
Nurmi, Hannu (1993), 'Problems in the Theory of Institutional Design: An Overview', *Journal of Theoretical Politics*, 5 (4), pp. 523-40.
Offerdal, Adjun, Hansprach, Dan, Kowalczyk, Andrezj and Patocka, Jiri (1996), 'Elites and Parties – The New Elites', in H. Baldersheim, M. Illner, A. Offerdal, L. Rose and P. Swianiewicz (eds), *Local Democracy and the Process of Transformation in East-Central Europe*, Westview Press, Boulder, pp. 105-40.
OECD (1997), *OECD Economic Surveys: Germany, 1997*, OECD, Paris.

Osterland, Martin (1994), 'Coping with Democracy: The Re-Institution of Local Self-Government in Eastern Germany', *European Urban and Regional Studies*, 1 (1), pp. 5–18.

Osterland, Martin (1996), 'Kommunale Demokratie in den neuen Bundesländern', *Aus Politik und Zeitgeschichte*, B50, pp. 41–6.

Page, Edward C. and Goldsmith, Michael J. (1987), 'Centre and Locality: Explaining Cross-National Variation', in E.C. Page and M.J. Goldsmith (eds), *Central and Local Government Relations: A Comparative Analysis of West European Unitary States*, Sage, London, pp. 256–68.

Parry, Gerraint (1969), *Political Elites*, George Allen and Unwin, London.

Parry, Gerraint, Moyser, George and Day, Neil (1992), *Political Participation and Democracy in Britain*, Cambridge University Press, Cambridge.

Pfizer, Theodor (1991), 'Rat und Bürgermeister im Zusammenspiel', in T. Pfizer and H.-G. Wehling (eds), *Kommunalpolitik in Baden-Württemberg*, Stuttgart, pp. 177–86.

Priller, Eckhard (1996), 'Veränderungen in der politischen und sozialen Beteiligung in Ostdeutschland', in W. Zapf and R. Habich (eds), *Wohlfahrtsentwicklung im vereinten Deutschland*, edition sigma, Berlin, pp. 283–305.

Psacharopoulos, George (1985), 'Returns to Education: A Further International Update and Implications', *The Journal of Human Resources*, 20 (4), pp. 583–604.

Putnam, Robert D. (1973), *The Beliefs of Politicians: Ideology, Conflict and Democracy in Britain and Italy*, Yale University Press, New Haven.

Putnam, Robert D. (1976), *The Comparative Study of Political Elites*, Prentice-Hall, Englewood Cliffs.

Putnam, Robert D. (1977), 'Elite Transformation in Advanced Industrial Societies: An Empirical Assessment of the Theory of Technocracy', *Comparative Political Studies*, 10 (3), pp. 383–412.

Putnam, Robert D. (1993), *Making Democracy Work*, Princeton University Press, Princeton.

Putnam, Robert D., Leonardi, Robert, Nanetti, Raffaella Y. and Pavoncello, Franco (1983), 'Explaining Institutional Success: The Case of Italian Regional Government', *American Political Science Review*, 77, pp. 55–74.

Putnam, Robert D. (1995), 'Bowling Alone: America's Declining Social Capital', *Journal of Democracy*, 6 (1), pp. 65-78.

Putnam, Robert D. (1995), 'Tuning in, Tuning Out: The Strange Disappearance of Social Capital in America', *P.S. Political Science and Politics* (December), pp. 664–83.

Püttner, Günter, ed. (1982), *Handbuch der kommunalen Wissenschaft und Praxis*, Bd. 2: Kommunalverfassung, Springer, Berlin.

Range, Volker (1994), 'Der Zeitaspekt ehrenamtlichen Engagements in der Kommunalpolitik', *Zeitschrift für Parlamentsfragen*, 25 (2), pp. 267–82.

Rebenstorf, Hilke (1997), 'Integration und Segmentation der Führungsschicht – Stratifikationstheoretische Determinanten', in W. Bürklin and H. Rebenstorf (eds), *Eliten in Deutschland: Rekrutierung und Integration*, Leske + Budrich, Opladen, pp. 123–56.

Rebenstorf, Hilke (1997), 'Karrieren und Integration – Werdegänge und Common Language', in W. Burklin and H. Rebenstorf (eds), *Eliten in Deutschland: Rekrutierung und Integration*, Leske + Budrich, Opladen, pp. 157–200.

Redlingshöfer, Bernd and Hoffmann-Lange, Ursula (1998), 'Die Transformation der kommunalen politischen Elite in den neuen Bundesländern am Beispiel der Gemeidevertretung der Stadt Jena', in H. Bertram, W. Kreher and I. Müller-Hartmann (eds), *Systemwechsel zwischen Projekt und Prozeß: Analysen zu den Umbrüchen in Ostdeutschland*, Leske + Budrich, Opladen, pp. 697–725.

Reisinger, William M. (1995), 'The Renaissance of a Rubric: Political Culture as a Concept and Theory', *International Journal of Public Opinion Research*, 7 (4), pp. 328–52.

Reisinger, William M., Miller, Arthur H., Hesli, Vicki L. and Maher, Kristen (1994), 'Political Values in Russia, Ukraine and Lithuania: Sources and Implications for Democracy', *British Journal of Political Science*, 4, pp. 183–223.

Richter, Bodo (1989), 'Institutionelle Überanstrengung und Wiederherstellung der Verantwortlichkeit', in D. Shimanke (ed.), *Stadtdirektor oder Bürgermeister: Beiträge zu einer aktuellen Kontroverse*, Birkhäuser, Basel, 136–42.

Röber, Manfred (1996), 'Germany', in D. Farnham, S. Horton, J. Barlow and A. Hondeghem (eds), *New Public Managers in Europe: Public Servants in Europe*, Macmillan Press, London, pp. 169–93.

Rohrschneider, Robert (1994), 'Report from the Laboratory: The Influence of Institutions on Political Elites's Democratic Values in Germany', *American Political Science Review*, 88 (4), pp. 927–41.

Rohrschneider, Robert (1996a), 'Pluralism, Conflict and Legislative Elites in the United Germany', *Comparative Politics*, 29, pp. 43–67.

Rohrschneider, Robert (1996b), 'Institutional Learning versus Value Diffusion: The Evolution of Democratic Values Among Parliamentarians in Eastern and Western Germany', *Journal of Politics*, 58 (2), pp. 442–66.

Rohrschneider, Robert (1996c), 'Cultural Transmission Versus Perceptions of the Economy: The Sources of Political Elites' Economic Values in United Germany', *Comparative Political Studies*, 29 (1), pp. 78–104.

Rohrschneider, Robert (1999), *Learning Democracy: Democratic and Economic Values in Unified Germany*, Oxford University Press, Oxford.

Roller, Edeltraud (1994), 'Ideological Basis of the Market Economy: Attitudes Toward Distribution Principles and the Role of Government in Western and Eastern Germany', *European Sociological Review*, 10 (2), pp. 105–7.

Roller, Edeltraud (1999), 'Staatsbezug und Individualismus: Dimensionen des soziokulturellen Wertewandels', *PVS*, 30 (Sonderheft), pp. 229–46.

Ronge, Volker (1994), 'Der Zeitaspekt ehrenamtlichen Engagements in der Kommunalpolitik', *Zeitschrift für Parlamentsfragen*, 2, pp. 267–82.

Rose, Lawrence, Buchta, Stanislav, Gajduschek, György, Grochowski, Miroslav and Hubacek, Ondrej (1996), 'Political Culture and Citizen Involvement', in H. Baldersheim, M. Illner, A. Offerdal, L. Rose and P. Swianiewicz (eds), *Local Democracy and the Process of Transformation in East-Central Europe*, Westview Press, Boulder, pp. 43–104.

Rose, Richard, Mishler, William and Haerpfer, Christan (1998), *Democracy and Its Alternatives: Understanding Post-Communist Societies*, Johns Hopkins University Press, Baltimore.

Roubini, Nouriel and Sachs, Jeffrey (1989), 'Political and Economic Determinants of Budget Deficits in the Industrial Democracies', *European Economic Review*, 8, pp. 903–33.

Rürup, Bert (2000), *The German Pension System: Status Quo and Reform Options*, Paper presented at the NBER-Kiel Institute Conference 'Coping with the Pension Crisis – Where Does Europe Stand?', Berlin.

Sabetti, Filippo (1996), 'Some Lessons From Italy About Interpreting Social Experiments', *Politics and Society*, 24 (1), pp. 19–44.

Sauer, Martina and Schnapp, Kai-Uwe (1997), 'Elitenintegration durch Kommunikation? Eine Analyse der Kontaktmuster der Positionseliten', in W. Bürklin and H. Rebenstorf (eds), *Eliten in Deutschland: Rekrutierung und Integration*, Leske + Budrich, Opladen, pp. 239–84.

Scharpf, Fritz W. (1988), 'The Joint Decision Trap: Lessons from German Federalism and European Integration', *Public Administration*, 66, pp. 239–78.

Schefold, Dian and Neumann, Maja (eds) (1996), *Entwicklungstendenzen der Kommunalverfassungen in Deutschland: Demokratisierung und Dezentralisierung?*, Birkhäuser, Basel.

Schleth, Uwe (1971), 'Once Again: Does It Pay to Study Social Background in Elite Analysis?', in R. Wildenmann (ed.), *Sozialwissenschaftliches Jahrbuch für Politik*, Olzog, München, pp. 99–118.

Schmidt, Manfred (1995), *Demokratietheorien*, Leske + Budrich, Opladen.

Schmidt-Eichstaedt, Gerd (1985), 'Die Machtverteilung zwischen der Gemeindevertretung und dem Hauptverwaltungsbeamten im Vergleich der deutschen Kommunalverfassungssysteme', *Archiv für Kommunalwissenschaft*, 24, pp. 20–37.

Schmidt-Eichstaedt, Gerd (1991a), 'Das Deutsche Institut für Urbanistik: Forschungseinrichtung der Städte und Seismograph der Stadtforschung', in T. et al. (eds), *Jahrbuch zur Staats- und Verwaltungswissenschaft*, Bd. 5, Nomos, Baden-Baden, pp. 191–208.

Schmidt-Eichstaedt, Gerd (1991b), 'Kommunalrecht und Kommunalverfassung in Deutschland. Kommunalpolitik in Stadt und Land', in F. Braschos and R. Voigt (eds), *Beiträge zu Theorie und Praxis der Kommunalpolitik*, Deutscher Kommunal-Verlag, Erfurt.

Schmidt-Eichstaedt, Gerd (1993), 'Kommunale Gebietsreform in den neuen Bundesländern', *Aus Politik und Zeitgeschichte*, B36, pp. 3–17.

Schmitt-Eichstaedt, Gerd (1994), *Die Gemeindeordnungen in der Bundesrepublik Deutschland* (Loseblatt-Ausgabe), Kohlhammer, Stuttgart.

Schmidt-Jortzig, Edzard (1987), 'Gemeindeverfassungstypen in der Bundesrepublik Deutschland', *Die Öffentliche Verwaltung*, 7, pp. 281–85.

Schnapp, Kai-Uwe (1997a), 'Soziale Zusammensetzung von Elite und Bevölkerung – Verteilung von Aufstiegschancen in die Elite im Zeitvergleich', in W. Bürklin and H. Rebenstorf (eds), *Eliten in Deutschland: Rekrutierung und Integration*, Leske + Budrich, Opladen, pp. 69–100.

Schnapp, Kai-Uwe (1997b), 'Soziodemographische Merkmale der bundesdeutschen Eliten', in W. Bürklin and H. Rebenstorf (eds), *Eliten in Deutschland: Rekrutierung und Integration*, Leske + Budrich, Opladen, pp. 101–22.

Schneider, Herbert (1993), 'Der Aufbau der Kommunalverwaltung und der kommunalen Selbstverwaltung in den neuen Bundesländern', *Aus Politik und Zeitgeschichte*, B36, pp. 18–26.

Schönfelder, Hermann (1979), *Rat und Verwaltung im kommunalen Spannungsfeld. Praktische Vorschläge für eine Verbesserung der Zusammenarbeit*, Deutscher Gemeindeverlag, Köln.

Seidendorf, Heinrich (1980), 'West Germany: A Survey', in D.C. Rowat (ed.), *International Handbook of Local Government Reorganization*, Aldwych Press, London, pp. 85–92.

Shepsle, Kenneth A. (1989), 'Studying Institutions: Some Lessons from the Rational Choice Approach', *Journal of Theoretical Politics*, 1 (2), pp. 131–47.

Shepsle, Kenneth A. and Weingast, Barry R. (1981), 'Structure-Induced Equilibrium and Legislative Choice', *Public Choice*, 37, pp. 503–19.

Shimanke, Dieter (1989), 'Institutionelle Spannungslagen in der kommunalen Verwaltungsführung', in D. Shimanke (ed.), *Stadtdirektor oder Bürgermeister: Beiträge zu einer aktuellen Kontroverse*, Birkhäuser, Basel, pp. 7–14.

Shimanke, Dieter and Stanke, M. (1989), 'Kommunale Führungsorganisation als politische Institution', in D. Shimanke (ed.), *Stadtdirektor oder Bürgermeister: Beiträge zu einer aktuellen Kontroverse*, Birkhäuser, pp. 218–32.

Shugart, Matthew Soberrg and Carey, John M. (1992), *Presidents and Assemblies: Constitutional Design and Electoral Dynamics*, Cambridge University Press, Cambridge.

Statistisches Bundesamt (1998a), *Gemeindeverzeichnis GV 100-P2*, Berichtsstand 30.9.1994, Statistisches Bundesamt, Wiesbaden.

Statistisches Bundesamt (1998b), *Bevölkerung und Erwerbstätigkeit*, Fachserie 1, Reihe 3: Haushalte und Familien, 1997 (Ergebnisse des Mikrozensus), Statistisches Bundesamt, Wiesbaden.

Statistisches Bundesamt (1999), *Tabellensammlung zur wirtschaftlichen und sozialen Lage in den neuen Bundesländern*, Ausgabe 2/99, Statistisches Bundesamt, Wiesbaden.

Statistisches Bundesamt (2000), *Statistisches Jahrbuch 2000*, Statistisches Bundesamt, Wiesbaden.

Stoker, Gerry and Wolman, Harold (1992), 'Drawing Lessons from US Experience: An Elected Mayor for British Local Government', *Public Administration*, 70, pp. 24–67.

Svara, James H. (1990), *Official Leadership in the City: Patterns of Conflict and Cooperation*, Oxford University Press, Oxford.

Swianiewicz, Pawel (1992), 'The Polish Experience of Local Democracy: Is Progress Being Made?', *Policy and Politics*, 20 (2), pp. 87–98.

Swianiewicz, Pawel and Clark, Terry N. (1996), 'Elites and Parties: The New Local Parties', in H. Baldersheim, M. Illner, A. Offerdal, L. Rose and P. Swianiewicz (eds), *Local Democracy and the Process of Transformation in East-Central Europe*, Westview Press, Boulder, pp. 141-160.

Tarrow, Sidney (1996), 'Making Social Science Work Across Space and Time: A Critical Reflection on Robert Putnam's Making Democracy Work', *American Political Science Review*, 90 (2), pp. 389–97.

Teune, Henry (ed.) (1995), *Local Governance*, special issue No. 540, The Annals of the American Academy of Political and Social Sciences.

Thränhardt, Dietrich (1989a), 'Kommunalverfassung in einer Welt des Wandels', in D. Shimanke (ed.), *Stadtdirektor oder Bürgermeister: Beiträge zu einer aktuellen Kontroverse*, Birkhäuser, Basel, pp. 15–36.

Thränhardt, Dietrich (1989b), 'Partizipation und kommunale Institutionen: Die innere Gliederung der Stadt', in D. Shimanke (ed.), *Stadtdirektor oder Bürgermeister: Beiträge zu einer aktuellen Kontroverse*, Birkhäuser, Basel, pp. 206–17.

Thränhardt, Dietrich and Uppendahl, Herbert (1981), *Alternativen lokaler Demokratie. Kommunalverfassung als politisches Problem*, Hein, Königstein.

Tomz, Michael, Wittenberg, Jason and King, Gary (1999), *Clarify: Software for Interpreting and Presenting Statistical Results*. <http://GKing.Harvard.Edu/stats.shtml>

Tsebelis, George (1995), 'Decision Making in Political Systems: Veto Players in Presidentialism, Parliamentarism, Multicameralism and Multipartyism', *British Journal of Political Science*, 25, pp. 289–325.

Vetterlein, Thomas (1979), 'Parlamentarische Willensbildung auf Kommunalebene: Krise und Reform eines Verfassungsorgans', *Zeitschrift für Parlamentsfragen*, 7, pp. 531–48.

Voigt, Rüdiger (1992), 'Kommunalpolitik zwischen exekutiver Führerschaft und legislatorischer Programmsteuerung', *Aus Politik und Zeitgeschichte*, B22–23, pp. 3–12.
Voigt, Rüdiger (1994), 'Lokale Politiksteuerung zwischen exekutiver Führerschaft und City Management', in O.W. Gabriel and R. Voigt (eds), *Kommunalwissenschaftliche Analysen*, Universitätsverlag Dr. N. Brockmeyer, Bochum, pp. 3–24.
von Beyme, Klaus (1996), 'The Concept of Political Class: A New Dimension of Research on Elites?', *West European Politics*, 19 (1), pp. 68–87.
Weaver, R. Kent and Rockman, Bert A. (eds) (1993), *Do Institutions Matter? Government Capabilities in the United States and Abroad*, Brookings, Washington, DC.
Wehling, Hans-Georg (1984), 'Der Bürgermeister und "sein" Rat: Kommunalpolitik in der Bundesrepublik im Vergleich', *Politische Studien*, 273, pp. 27–36.
Wehling, Hans-Georg (1989), 'Auswirkung der Kommunalverfassung auf das lokale politische-administrative Handeln: Erfahrungen mit dem baden-württembergischen Modell', in D. Shimanke (ed.), *Stadtdirektor oder Bürgermeister: Beiträge zu einer aktuellen Kontroverse*, Birkhäuser, Basel, pp. 84–96.
Wehling, Hans-Georg (1991), 'Der Bürgermeister: Rechtsstellung, Sozialprofil, Funktionen', in T. Pfizer and H.-G. Wehling (eds), *Kommunalpolitik in Baden-Württemberg*, Stuttgart, pp. 162–77.
Welch, Roy (1980), 'Regression Sensitivity Analysis and Bounded-Influence Estimation', in J. Kmenta and J. Ramsey (eds), *Evaluation of Econometric Models*, Academic Press, New York, pp. 153–67.
Welsh, Helga (1996), 'Parliamentary Elites in Times of Political Transition: The Case of Eastern Germany', *Western European Politics*, 19 (3), pp. 507–24.
Welzel, Christian (1997a), 'Rekrutierung und Sozialisation der ostdeutschen Elite – Eine Analyse der Kontaktmuster der Positionseliten', in W. Bürklin and H. Rebenstorf (eds), *Eliten in Deutschland: Rekrutierung und Integration*, Leske + Budrich, Opladen, pp. 201–38.
Welzel, Christian (1997b), *Demokratischer Elitenwandel. Der Erneuerung der ostdeutschen Elite aus demokratie-soziologischer Sicht*, Leske + Budrich, Opladen.
Welzel, Christian (1998), *Vom Konsens zum Dissens? Politische Ordnungspräferenzen von Eliten und Bürgern im ost-westdeutschen Vergleich*, Wissenschaftszentrum Berlin für Sozialforschung, Berlin.
Weßels, Bernhard (1998), 'Social Alliances and Coalitions: The Organizational Underpinnings of Democracy in West Germany', in D. Rueschemeyer et al. (eds), *Participation and Democracy: An East West Comparison*, M.E. Sharpe, Armonk, pp. 202–32.
Wiesenthal, Helmut (1995), 'East Germany as a Unique Case of Societal Transformation: Main Characteristics and Emergent Misconceptions', *German Politics*, 4 (3), pp. 49–74.
Winkler-Haupt, Uwe (1988), *Gemeindeordnung und Politikfolgen. Eine vergleichende Untersuchung in vier Mittelstädten*, Minerva, München.
Winkler-Haupt, Uwe (1989), 'Die Auswirkungen unterschiedlicher kommunaler Führungsorganisationstypen auf den Policy-Output. Ergebnisse einer empirischen Untersuchung zum kommunalen Willensbildungs- und Haushaltsentscheidungsprozeß in zwei Bundesländern', in D. Shimanke (ed.), *Stadtdirektor oder Bürgermeister: Beiträge zu einer aktuellen Kontroverse*, Birkhäuser, Basel, pp. 84–97.
Wollmann, Hellmut (1994), *The Transformation of Political and Administrative Institutions in East-Germany: Between External Determinants and "Endogenous" Factors*, Paper presented at 16th World Congress of the International Political Science Association, Berlin.

Wollmann, Hellmut (1995), 'Regelung kommunaler Institutionen in Ostdeutschland zwischen "exogener Pfadabhängigkeit" und endogenen Entscheidungsfaktoren', *Berliner Journal für Soziologie*, 4, pp. 497–514.

Wollmann, Hellmut (1996), 'Institutionenbildung in Ostdeutschland: Rezeption, Eigenentwicklung oder Innovation', in A. Eisen and H. Wollmann (eds), *Institutionenbildung in Ostdeutschland: Zwischen exogener Steuerung und Eigendynamik*, Leske + Budrich, Opladen, pp. 79–112.

Wollmann, Hellmut (1998), 'Um- und Neubau der politischen und administrativen Landesstrukturen in Ostdeutschland', *Aus Politik und Zeitgeschichte*, B5, pp. 18–28.

Wolman, Harold (1995), 'Local Governance Institutions and Democratic Governance', in D. Judge, G. Stoker and H. Wolman (eds), *Theories of Urban Politics*, Sage, London, pp. 135–59.

Wolman, Harold, Page, Edward and Reavley, Martha (1990), 'Mayors and Mayoral Careers', *Urban Affairs Quarterly*, 25 (3), pp. 500–14.

Wolman, Harold, Strate, John and Melchior, Alan (1996), 'Does Changing Mayors Matter?', *Journal of Politics*, 58 (1), pp. 201–23.

Wolter, Werner (1990), 'Wissenschaftlich-technische Bildung und personelles Forschungspotential in der DDR', in H. Meyer (ed.), *Intelligenz, Wissenschaft und Forschung in der DDR*, Walter de Gruyter, Berlin, pp. 85–96.

Yoder, Jennifer (1997), *From GDR Citizens to FRG Politicians? Developments in Post-Communist Elite-Building in Eastern Germany*, Department of Government, Colby College, Waterville, ME.

Yoder, Jennifer (1999), *From East Germans to Germans? The New Postcommunist Elites*, Duke University Press, Durham.

Zapf, Wolfgang (1966), *Wandlungen der deutschen Elite: Ein Zirkulationsmodell deutscher Führungsgruppen 1919–1961*, Piper, München.

Zelle, Carsten (1999), 'Socialist Heritage or Current Unemployment: Why Do the Evaluation of Democracy and Socialism Differ Between East and West Germans?', *German Politics*, 8 (1), pp. 1–20.

Index

administrator 7, 20, 32, 37, 41, 43, 54
age 2, 12, 18, 24, 50, 58, 93, 95–7, 102–4
associational member(ship) 7, 8, 32, 35–7, 53, 58
    correspondence between elite and citizen involvement 35–7
    cultural, environmental, sports, religious, welfare 32–3, 35
Austria 5, 24, 55, 71, 118, 122, 127
authoritarianism-libertarianism 3, 82–3, 87, 109, 185

background of elites 5–8, 57–8
    age 12
    class origins 5–6, 20–23, 25
    education 6, 23–5, 27
    female 13–16
    geographic origins 8–11
    length of involvement in politics and administration 16–20
    occupation 28–9, 31–2
    parents in politics 5–6, 20
    party membership 17
    residence in community 11–12, 18
    'transplants' 10, 12
    'Wende' 16–20
'Balkanization' 160
'Banner thesis' 158, 160

capitalism 3, 69, 71, 73, 83, 93, 96, 102, 108, 186
caucus leader(s) 2, 9–11, 15, 17, 22–3, 28–9, 32, 41–2, 46, 50, 54–6
    in sample frame, sample and response rate 199, 207, 208, 210, 215, 221
CDU/CSU (*see also* Union) 11, 16, 19, 29, 58, 83, 85, 185
Central Europe 5, 9, 12, 14, 16, 18, 24, 55, 58, 71, 82, 112, 126–7, 185

chairperson 2, 41, 155
chief executive 146, 155–6, 158, 160–162, 172, 181, 188–9
citizen participation 67, 69
city/town administration 155–6
city/town council 9, 11, 14, 17, 31, 55, 60, 145–6, 154–6, 158, 160, 162, 173
    partisan composition 204, 206, 208, 215, 218, 223–5
city manager 9, 2, 155, 173, 188
class origin 2, 20–23, 25, 184
colonization (of East by West) 6, 12, 58, 185
conflicts 3, 4, 43, 69, 104, 109, 111, 130–132, 134, 137, 140, 147, 153, 175–7, 185–7
control of local government administration 114–115, 119, 125–6, 132, 140, 154, 160
costs of local government administration 114, 117, 123, 126, 140, 183, 187
council member(s) 2, 9, 10, 14, 17–18, 23, 28–9, 31–2, 41–2, 46–7, 50, 54, 56, 60
    in sample frame, sample and response rate 192, 199, 204, 206–210, 215, 217–218, 221, 223
culture 151–3, 179–81
Czech Republic 5, 14, 118, 122, 127, 140

Democracy and Local Governance Project (DLG) 1–2, 67, 73, 77, 102, 108, 191, 226
democratic government performance 1, 149–51, 153, 173–4, 176, 181, 189
department function 210, 212–215
department head(s) 2, 9, 10–12, 16–17, 23, 28–9, 32, 39, 41–2, 46, 50, 53–5
    in sample frame, sample and response rate 199, 204, 206–208, 210,

215–216, 223
decision-making 150, 155–6, 158–9, 160–161, 171
Deutscher Städtetag 219
development 111–112, 114–115, 117, 123, 126–7, 130–132, 137, 140, 147
direct democracy 60, 67

East-West differences and similarities 1, 3–4, 183, 185–6, 189–190
  between elites and citizens 5–7, 12, 20–5,32, 35–7, 82–6, 97, 109, 111, 115, 117, 123, 143, 185, 187
  citizens' assessments of the effects of redistribution 103–107
  citizens' political assessments 143–8, 174–5, 179–81, 187
  citizens' values 82–7, 91–3, 97, 99, 101–3, 185–6
  elites' assessments of policy effectiveness 137, 140, 186–7
  elites' background, ties and roles 9–12, 14–25, 27–9, 31–3, 35–7, 39, 41–2, 46–7, 53–8
  elites' perceptions of conflict 130–32, 134, 137
  elites' perceptions of problems 111–112, 114–115, 117, 118, 122–3, 186–7
  elites' satisfaction with working of democracy 143
  elites' values 71, 73, 82–7, 185
  elites' views on meaning of democracy 59–60, 67
  elites' views on power and responsibilities 123, 125–7, 186–7
  response rates 221–2, 228
  sample coverage 199–202
economic development 54, 69, 71, 73, 77, 114–115, 117, 122–3, 126–7, 140, 186–7
economic equality 69, 71, 73
economic growth 132, 134, 137
economic system 5, 69, 91, 97, 183
education 6, 21, 23–5, 27, 31, 54, 57–8, 93, 95–7, 99, 101, 103, 115, 117, 134, 184

education and training 6, 50, 53
effectiveness of local government 137, 140, 158
efficiency of local government administration 154, 174
electoral groups 11, 16, 19, 20, 23, 31, 33, 35, 37, 47, 50, 53–4
elites' backgrounds 1, 5–9, 17, 20, 22–3, 25, 27–9, 32, 49, 50, 53–4, 57–8, 184–5
elites' roles 2, 5, 7–8, 15, 37, 41, 43, 46–7, 49, 52–4, 56, 58
elites' ties to community 2, 5, 7–8, 185
  organizational involvement 32–3, 35–37, 50, 53, 58
  patterns of reliance 37, 39
environment 114, 126–7, 132, 134, 137, 140, 151, 187
established democracies 5, 7, 71, 86, 108, 112, 185
external influence 154

FDP 11, 16, 19, 23, 35, 56, 58, 73, 83–5, 185
Federal Republic of Germany 87, 97, 107, 151, 154, 175, 181, 183
females 53, 95, 97, 103, 208
  lower response rate in elite survey 221, 223
  number in elite positions 204, 208
  overrepresentation in citizen survey 228
  progress in entering political elite 13–16
  social position and political values 95, 97
financial capacity of local government 112, 114–15, 117, 119, 122–3, 126–7, 140, 187

gender 2, 12, 50, 53, 95, 97, 103
German Democratic Republic (GDR) 3, 6, 10–12, 27, 58, 67, 87, 91, 107, 183, 185
government performance 149–150, 152, 153, 158–9, 161, 173, 177, 184, 187–9

Index

Greens 11–12, 16–19, 22–3, 27, 31, 33, 35–6, 39, 42, 47, 52, 56, 73, 83–4

higher official 9–10, 12, 14–16, 20–3, 28–9, 32, 39–43, 49, 54–5, 193
   in sample frame, sample and response rate 199, 206–207, 210, 221–23
'homo oeconomicus effect' 92
honesty 69, 71, 73, 77
housing 54, 114, 117, 123, 126, 187
Hungary 5, 14, 118, 122, 127, 140

ideological values 1–3, 59, 67–8, 71, 73, 77, 82–3, 86, 108, 119, 126, 146
improvements in public infrastructure 54, 114, 117, 126
incentives and preferences 94–7, 101–109
income 93, 95–6, 101, 103–108
institutional engineering 152, 154, 158, 180–181, 188
institutions 1, 4, 6, 37, 67, 93, 111, 150–51, 153, 175, 179–81, 183, 187–190, 228
interest in politics 144, 186
international comparisons
   elites' assessments of policy effectiveness 140
   elites' backgrounds 9–10, 12–14, 16–18, 20, 24
   elites' perception of problems 118, 119, 122–3
   elites' perceptions of conflicts 131, 137
   elite samples 225
   elites' values 71, 77, 82, 108
   elites' views on power and responsibilities 126–7
   elites' views on their influence 55
ISSP (International Social Survey Project) 97, 102, 104, 106

labor market 108, 114, 186
Lasswell's 'agglutination' model 5
law and social science background of Western elites 25, 27
'law of increasing disproportion' 57, 158
(local) political and administrative elites 1, 5–9, 11–13, 15–20, 23–4, 32, 35, 37, 41, 47, 53, 55–5, 67, 108, 111–112, 117–118, 122–3, 126–7, 130–132, 134, 137, 140, 143–4, 146–7, 184–7
localism 69, 71, 73

Magistrat form 154–6, 158, 162, 188
mayor(s) 2, 9, 15, 39, 154–6, 158, 162, 172–3, 188
   in sample frame, sample and response rate 194, 194, 221, 224
meaning of democracy 2, 59–60, 67
meritocratic 6, 8, 25
minority rights 69, 71, 73

Netherlands 5, 118
new federal states 10, 14, 41, 53, 57–8, 127, 134, 140, 151, 154, 158, 162, 172, 176–7, 184, 187, 191, 193, 199, 204, 206, 213, 220–221, 223, 225
non-partisan 11, 18, 48–50, 53, 56, 58, 154
North German Council form 154, 156, 158, 162

occupation 8, 15, 21, 25, 27–9, 31–2, 41, 49, 154–5
old federal states 8, 127, 140, 151, 158, 172, 176–7, 180, 187, 191, 193, 199, 220, 221, 223, 225
origins 2, 5–9, 20–23, 25, 57

parents in politics 6, 20–21, 28–9, 49, 58, 184
party leader(s) 9, 10, 15–16, 22–3, 28–9, 32, 42, 46, 50, 54, 56
   in sample frame, sample and response rate 199, 207, 208, 215, 221, 223
party member(ship) 15, 19, 33, 35, 49, 58, 185
PDS 11, 16, 18 20, 23, 31, 35, 37, 39, 42, 47, 52, 54, 56, 58, 73, 83, 185
performance 7, 56–7, 111, 143–9, 150–153, 158–61, 173–7, 179, 181, 184, 187–190
pessimism 91, 108, 109, 186, 190

Poland 5, 14, 77, 118, 122, 127, 131, 140
policy influence 54–57
    German elites report greater influence 55
    influence and satisfaction with workings of democracy 56–7
political culture 1–3, 59, 67, 103, 108, 109, 149–51, 153, 181, 187–9
political equality 69, 71, 73
political party(ies) 19, 35, 37, 47, 49, 56, 59, 71, 86, 145, 173
political system 59, 91, 111, 132, 145, 152, 161, 173–5, 183
political values 1, 60, 91, 185
politician 6, 7, 20–21 32, 37, 39, 43, 46–7, 49–50, 53, 108
Politbarometer (Forschungsgruppe Wahlen) 144, 151
power and autonomy of local government 3, 123, 125–7, 130–131, 140, 147, 186–7
privileged backgrounds 5–6, 20–25, 57
problems facing local government 3, 32, 43, 49, 111–112, 114–115, 117, 119, 122–3, 127, 130–132, 137, 147, 153, 175, 184, 186–8
problem-solving 130–132, 134, 137
public infrastructure 54, 114, 117, 126, 140
public safety 114–115, 117, 123, 140, 187

redistribution 69, 104–107
region 1–3, 5–6, 9, 11–12, 15–20, 235, 29, 32, 35–7, 39, 42, 46–7, 50, 54–6, 59, 60, 67, 71, 77, 82–3, 85, 87, 91, 93, 95–7, 99, 101–109, 111, 114–115, 117–118, 123, 126, 130–134, 137, 140, 143–7, 149–51, 153–4, 174–5, 177, 179, 185–7, 191–3, 200, 202–208, 210, 215, 218–225, 228, 230
relations between Germans and foreigners 115, 119
reliance 7, 37, 39
    differences between administrative officials and politicians 39
representativeness of local elites 6. 58

residence in community 8, 11–12, 58
response rate 2, 191–2, 207, 216, 219, 220–5, 228
    and size of community 220–221
    effect of endorsement 219
    female response rate 221, 223
    minimum target 192, 220–221
responsibility of local government 9, 54, 69, 114, 123, 125–7, 183–4, 186–7
role 1, 2, 4, 156, 160–161, 187
    in intermediate zone 41–42
role orientation 43, 47, 49, 58
    administrative 50,53
    non-partisan 48, 53
    partisan politician 43, 54

(sub-)sample 2, 8–9, 10–12, 21–3, 25, 27, 31–2, 36, 60, 67, 77, 102, 111, 115, 117, 161, 175, 179
    sample frame 177, 191–3, 199, 200, 202, 204, 206–208, 210, 215, 218
    sample guidelines 192–3
    sample of cities in Germany 193, 199–202
    sample of citizens in Germany 227–8
    sample of elites in Germany 219–225
    sampling algorithm 206–208
satisfaction with democracy 143, 174
satisfaction with performance 2, 146–7, 149, 150, 153, 161, 173–4, 176, 179, 181, 184, 187, 189
self-interest 3, 91–3, 95–7, 101, 103, 108–109, 186
size (of community) 14, 174–5, 177, 192, 199–200, 212
Slovakia 5, 14, 82, 118, 122, 127, 140
social capital 1–2, 4, 7, 149–53, 173, 175–7, 179, 180–181, 188–9, 227–22
social equality 60, 67, 108
social services 54, 95, 114, 127
socialism 3, 91, 95, 102–103, 108, 186
socialism-capitalism 77, 82–3, 85, 87, 91, 93, 95, 97, 99, 101–104, 109, 185–6
socialization 3, 91, 93, 108–109, 186
South German Council form 58, 154, 156, 158, 162, 172, 188

Spain 5, 24, 119, 140
SPD 11, 18, 23, 33, 35, 39, 73, 83–4
state legislature 188
strong mayor (chief executive) 155, 160–62, 172
strong mayor form 156, 162, 188
success of local government 111, 130, 137, 140, 147, 149, 151–2, 176, 186–7
Sweden 5, 13, 16, 24, 71, 119, 127, 185
Switzerland 5, 82, 119, 122, 127, 131

technical training background of Eastern elites 25, 27
time
  at job 12, 39, 41
  in party 16–17, 19
  in politics/administration 8, 16, 18, 39, 41, 58, 185
  in residence 11–12, 185
traditional leading classes 6, 20, 58, 184

traffic and parking problems 114–115, 123, 132, 187
transitional democracy 5, 9, 16, 18, 24, 55, 97, 103, 185
trust 57, 144, 150–152, 176–7, 179–180, 189

unemployment 12, 114–115, 117, 122–3, 126, 140, 177, 183, 186–7
Union 11, 18, 23, 31, 33, 35, 37, 39, 47, 50, 56, 73 (*see also* CDU/CSU)
union membership 32–3, 35, 95, 97, 102–103
United States 5, 11, 14, 24, 82, 119, 131, 140, 149, 151, 154–5, 183, 188

veto player 150, 159–61, 188
voter(s) 36–7, 83–5, 155–61

weak mayor 155, 188
'Wende' 9–12, 16–17, 19